for all Competitive Exams

Synonyms AND Antonyms

for all Competitive Exams

Synonyms AND Antonyms

Essential ~ Intermediate
Advanced ~ Super Nuts

Roshan Tolani

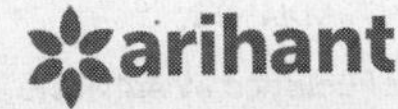

Arihant Publications (India) Limited

Arihant Publications (India) Ltd.

Administrative & Production Offices

Regd. Office
'Ramchhaya' 4577/15, Agarwal Road, Darya Ganj, New Delhi -110002
Tele: 011- 47630600, 43518550; Fax: 011- 23280316

Head Office
Kalindi, TP Nagar, Meerut (UP) - 250002
Tele: 0121-2401479, 2512970, 4004199; Fax: 0121-2401648

Sales & Support Offices
Agra, Ahmedabad, Bengaluru, Bhubaneswar, Bareilly, Chennai, Delhi, Guwahati, Hyderabad, Jaipur, Jhansi, Kolkata, Lucknow, Meerut, Nagpur & Pune

ISBN : 978-93-13160-18-2

Price : ₹ 175.00

PO No. : TXT-59-T070769-5-26

PUBLISHED BY ARIHANT PUBLICATIONS (INDIA) LTD.

For further information about books Published by Arihant log on to www.arihantbooks.com or email to info@arihantbooks.com

PREFACE

Nobody else has described the utility of language in our life as pertinently as Austrian Philosopher Ludwig Wittgenstein, who said: The limits of my language mean the limits of my world, And what lends power to language, and its users, words are one of the tools.

There is nothing wrong in the belief that dictionary and thesaurus containing synonyms and antonyms are two of the most powerful tools that a communicator can possess. It was true when typewriter was a luxury product as well as today when laptops and hand-held mobiles are treasure troves of all knowledge and creativity.

Though primarily written for students appearing in competitive and entrance exams, this book Synonyms and Antonyms can be used by its readers to support their learning process, expand their word power and improve their verbal skills.

In view of the different needs of the students preparing for examinations of varying difficulty levels, the content of the book has been divided into four parts: **Essential, Intermediate, Advanced** and **Super Nuts.** The students can either move from one difficulty level to another or refer the contents as per the need of their target examination.

The book contains numerous exercises to help the students consolidate their learning. Moreover, the section Previous Years' Questions, contains actual questions asked in different examinations to help them understand the recent trends.

If this book contributes, in any small way, to your success in examination of your choice and progress in life, it will have served its purpose.

Roshan Tolani

CONTENTS

PART I

ESSENTIAL

abandon
syn. desert, leave, quit, forgo, renounce, surrender
ant. continue, keep, pursue

abolish
syn. cancel, nullify, annul, invalidate, negate, set aside
ant. establish, set up, found

abrupt
syn. hurried, sudden, blunt, curt, brief, brusque
ant. smooth, gradual, courteous

accomplish
syn. achieve, attain, gain, reach, realise, fulfil
ant. fail, forsake, give up

abstract
syn. hypothetical, theoretic, academic, speculative, ideal, abstruse
ant. concrete, definite, factual

absurd
syn. foolish, idiotic, silly, insane, nonsensical, moronic
ant. logical, reasonable, rational

abundant
syn. ample, generous, heavy, bountiful, plentiful, substantial
ant. rare, tight, scarce

accelerate
syn. hasten, hurry, quicken, hustle, expedite, speed up
ant. decelerate, retard, slow down

accumulate
syn. aggregate, amass, collect, garner, gather, pile up
ant. disperse, scatter, dissipate

accuracy
syn. correctness, exactness, truth, veracity, precision, rightness
ant. inaccuracy, error, anomaly

accuse
syn. arraign, charge, indict, denounce, incriminate, allege
ant. absolve, defend, exonerate

acquire
syn. gain, get, procure, obtain, secure, win
ant. forfeit, forgo, relinquish

acute
syn. critical, crucial, piercing, sharp, incisive, shrill
ant. dim, dull, obtuse

adequate
syn. enough, satisfactory, sufficient, comfortable, average, decent
ant. deficient, wanting, insufficient

admire
syn. appreciate, praise, value, respect, like, regard
ant. blame, condemn, disapprove

adopt
syn. affirm, approve, confirm, sanction, pass, ratify
ant. disclaim, disown, spurn

adventurous
syn. bold, daredevil, daring, enterprising, dangerous, risky
ant. cautious, safe, timid

adversity
syn. misfortune, unluckiness, haplessness, affliction, hardship, bother
ant. prosperity, fortune, happiness

affection
syn. attachment, liking, love, fondness, loyalty, sentiment
ant. enmity, hatred, dislike

aggregate
syn. amount, sum, total, totality, entirety, gross
ant. single, individual, separate

aggressive
syn. hostile, militant, combative, contentious, belligerent, attacking
ant. complaisant, laid back, easy-going

agree
syn. accept, consent, nod, accede, tally, concur
ant. disagree, differ, contradict

alert
syn. observant, vigilant, wary, watchful, keen, witted
ant. asleep, drowsy, inattentive

alliance
syn. coalition, league, union, association, group, confederation
ant. antagonism, discord, hostility

alone
syn. lonely, single, solitary, detached, isolated, apart
ant. together, accompanied, escorted

amazing
syn. astonishing, fantastic, fabulous, incredible, marvellous, wonderful
ant. ordinary, commonplace, average

ambitious
syn. aspiring, desirous, emulous, eager, longing, ardent
ant. content, unassuming, satisfied

amend
syn. improve, correct, rectify, redress, revamp, ameliorate
ant. blemish, impair, worsen

amplify
syn. boost, enlarge, expand, increase, magnify, develop
ant. lessen, compress, summarise

amuse
syn. entertain, recreate, regale, divert, delight, please
ant. bore, annoy, fatigue

ancient
syn. old, archaic, timeworn, primal, obsolete, outdated
ant. modern, new, young

anonymous
syn. nameless, unnamed, unsigned, unidentified, mysterious, shadowy
ant. identified, known, named

anxiety
syn. distress, nervousness, unease, concern, worry, angst
ant. composure, assurance, quietude

appealing
syn. tempting, interesting, alluring, fascinating, charming, engaging
ant. disagreeable, unappealing, off-putting

appreciate
syn. value, welcome, admire, cherish, escalate, recognise
ant. disregard, condemn, disapprove

apprentice
syn. learner, beginner, novice, student, intern, trainee
ant. mentor, teacher, experienced

approve
syn. accept, like, support, ratify, recognise, endorse
ant. censure, deplore, disallow

arrogance
: ***syn.*** haughtiness, insolence, egotism, pride, superciliousness, conceit
: ***ant.*** humility, meekness, servility

artificial
: ***syn.*** synthetic, sham, fake, deceptive, unnatural, false
: ***ant.*** genuine, real, natural

ascend
: ***syn.*** rise, mount, spring, climb, soar, increase
: ***ant.*** decline, descend, lower

assist
: ***syn.*** help, support, aid, abet, relieve, back
: ***ant.*** hinder, oppose, thwart

assurance
: ***syn.*** guarantee, promise, certainty, belief, pledge, warrant
: ***ant.*** uncertainty, doubt, hesitancy

astonishing
: ***syn.*** surprising, astounding, amazing, fabulous, incredible, marvellous
: ***ant.*** dull, unimpressive, boring

attain
: ***syn.*** achieve, accomplish, reach, gain, get, realise
: ***ant.*** desert, forfeit, surrender

attentive
: ***syn.*** intent, heedful, regardful, considerate, responsive, conscientious
: ***ant.*** heedless, inattentive, neglectful

attract
: ***syn.*** appeal, draw, entice, allure, magnetise, fascinate
: ***ant.*** repel, repulse, deter

auspicious
: ***syn.*** opportune, propitious, favourable, timely, benign, fortunate
: ***ant.*** hopeless, unlucky, ill-fated

authentic
: ***syn.*** credible, genuine, trustworthy, valid, real, original
: ***ant.*** counterfeit, fake, unreal

autonomous
: ***syn.*** free, independent, sovereign, self-governing, separate, unrestrained
: ***ant.*** dependent, bound, subject

average
: ***syn.*** common, acceptable, moderate, usual, typical, ordinary
: ***ant.*** exceptional, outstanding, unusual

avoid

syn. escape, shun, evade, elude, duck, dodge
ant. face, seek, want

awake

syn. conscious, aware, alert, stirring, roused, wakeful
ant. asleep, unconscious, lull

aware

syn. alive, awake, cognizant, mindful, attentive, responsive
ant. ignorant, unaware, insensitive

awful

syn. dreadful, shocking, horrible, terrible, ghastly, appalling
ant. pleasing, charming, beautiful

awkward

syn. clumsy, graceless, inept, cumbersome, inelegant
ant. dexterous, adept, skilful

Exercise

Choose the word which is CLOSEST in meaning to the given word.

1. Astute
   (a) bastion (b) copious (c) clever (d) abject
2. Ambivalent
   (a) demure (b) misogynist (c) materialist (d) uncertain
3. Apprentice
   (a) mentor (b) average (c) trainee (d) outstanding
4. Awful
   (a) shocking (b) plain (c) symphony (d) reticent

Choose the word which is MOST SIMILAR in meaning to the underlined word in the given sentence.

5. He found himself in an awkward situation.
   (a) pioneer (b) clumsy (c) enigmatic (d) approving
6. Noopur was acquitted of all the charges levelled against her.
   (a) convicted (b) denied
   (c) arrested (d) cleared
7. Shobhit amassed a lot of property in his life.
   (a) gathered (b) donated
   (c) designed (d) demolished

Choose the word which is OPPOSITE in meaning to the given word.

8. Acclaim
(a) criticism (b) praise
(c) protest (d) feedback

9. Altruism
(a) selflessness (b) selfishness
(c) aggressiveness (d) forgiveness

10. Accrue
(a) divulge (b) hate
(c) gather (d) spend

11. Autonomous
(a) free (b) separate
(c) bound (d) altruism

Choose the word which is MOST OPPOSITE in meaning to the underlined word in the given sentence.

12. One can <u>attain</u> success only by hardwork.
(a) gather (b) peculiar
(c) surmount (d) surrender

13. The car halted <u>abruptly</u>.
(a) gradually (b) suddenly
(c) closely (d) briefly

14. The uprising was suppressed with <u>abominable</u> cruelty.
(a) delightful (b) detestful
(c) great (d) moderate

B

baffle
syn. amaze, confuse, puzzle, rattle, stun, astound
ant. enlighten, explain, clarify

ban
syn. boycott, prohibition, restriction, censorship, embargo, suppression
ant. allowance, permission, approval

bankrupt
syn. insolvent, penniless, ruined, destitute, broke, impoverished,
ant. solvent, prosperous, wealthy

barbarous
syn. brutal, cruel, ferocious, monstrous, ruthless, uncivilized
ant. polite, refined, sophisticated

beat
syn. bang, bash, batter, cane, castigate, drub
ant. aid, assist, help

beneath
syn. below, underneath, under, down, unworthy, covered
ant. up, overhead, above

benevolent
syn. benign, caring, chivalrous, considerate, humane, generous
ant. malevolent, mean, spiteful

beneficent
syn. charitable, kind, helpful, generous, compassionate, philanthropic
ant. malicious, misanthropic, uncharitable

betray
syn. deceive, delude, forsake, abandon, break faith, cross
ant. defend, protect, support

bewilder
syn. baffle, confuse, daze, muddle, mystify, perplex
ant. enlighten, illuminate, explain

biased
syn. discriminating, favouring, partial, prejudiced, unfair, unjust
ant. fair, impartial, judicious

bind
syn. attach, affix, annex, rivet, secure, append
ant. detach, break, free

bland
syn. boring, dull, flat, insipid, unexciting, monotonous
ant. delicious, distinctive, sharp

blend
syn. combine, mix, brew, concoct, fuse, instil, mingle
ant. separate, disintegrate, dissociate

block
syn. bar, impede, obstruct, choke, clog, congest
ant. open, clear, release

bloom
syn. blossom, flower, flourish, grow, succeed, thrive
ant. shrink, fail, wither

blunt
syn. dull, abrupt, curt, gruff, short, brusque
ant. pointed, sharp, polite

boast
syn. brag, praise, crow, exult, vaunt, prate
ant. deprecate, be modest, be quiet

bothersome
syn. annoying, irksome, troubling, irritating, vexatious, provoking
ant. convenient, helpful, smooth

boundless
syn. endless, limitless, unlimited, infinite, immeasurable, plenty
ant. limited, restricted, less

brisk
syn. agile, quick, dynamic, energetic, lively, vigorous
ant. slow, sluggish, dull

bombastic
syn. flowery, showy, overblown, rhetorical, grandiloquent, sonorous
ant. humble, restrained, reserved

broadminded
syn. liberal, progressive, open, tolerant, flexible, radical
ant. orthodox, conservative, narrow-minded

bulky
syn. massive, big, oversized, heavy, hefty, huge
ant. small, thin, tiny

bully
syn. intimidate, menace, threaten, browbeat, bludgeon
ant. support, ease, assuage

Exercise

Choose the word which is CLOSEST in meaning to the given word.

1. Barbarous
   (a) kind (b) heavy (c) energetic (d) ferocious
2. Brisk
   (a) severe (b) sluggish (c) dynamic (d) activity
3. Bloom
   (a) impede (b) pester (c) flourish (d) flounder

Choose the word which is MOST SIMILAR in meaning to the underlined word in the given sentence.

4. The piano is a <u>bulky</u> object.
   (a) hefty (b) tolerant
   (c) tall (d) flexible
5. He was <u>bullied</u> by his friends in school.
   (a) pampered (b) threatened
   (c) confused (d) loved

Choose the word which is OPPOSITE in meaning to the given word.

6. Boundless
   (a) infinite (b) energetic (c) restricted (d) terrible
7. Blend
   (a) concoct (b) disintegrate (c) fabricate (d) unexciting
8. Benevolent
   (a) refined (b) mean (c) deficient (d) bankrupt

Choose the word which is MOST OPPOSITE in meaning to the underlined word in the given sentence.

9. The custard made by my sister tasted <u>bland</u>.
   (a) insipid (b) detached
   (c) delicious (d) mixed
10. Sonam was <u>bewildered</u> on seeing so many clothes in the store.
   (a) perplexed (b) dazed
   (c) enlightened (d) muddled

C

calm

syn. peaceful, quiet, serene, placed, detached, nonchalant
ant. turbulent, violent, wild

casual

syn. accidental, informal, natural, spontaneous, relaxed, unrestrained
ant. planned, premeditated, deliberate

caustic

syn. acerbic, biting, scathing, sharp, pungent, slashing
ant. calm, mild, soothing

cautious

syn. careful, prudent, wary, chary, circumspect, gingerly
ant. rash, hasty, imprudent, unguarded, heedless, careless

cease

syn. check, discontinue, halt, stall, arrest, belay
ant. commence, continue, initiate

certainty

syn. assurance, confidence, conviction, sureness, surety, credence
ant. ambiguity, doubt, uncertainty

charming

syn. delightful, enchanting, heavenly, attractive, appealing, lovely
ant. offensive, repellent, terrifying

chaos

syn. clutter, confusion, disarray, jumble, muddle, disorder
ant. calm, harmony, order

cheater

syn. defrauder, swindler, trickster, crook, scammer, deceiver
ant. honest, truthful, simple

check

syn. arrest, stop, quit, stall, bridle, constrain
ant. allow, assist, permit

clumsy

syn. awkward, graceless, unskilled, inept, unwieldy, unmanageable
ant. expert, dexterous, adroit

coarse

syn. crude, rough, uncivilized, uncouth, obscene, filthy
ant. smooth, refined, sophisticated

collision
syn. conspiracy, connivance, intrigue, collaboration, scheme, complicity
ant. discord, separation, estrangement

commence
syn. begin, embark, inaugurate, initiate, launch, undertake
ant. cease, finish, end

compact
syn. dense, close, crowded, packed, tight, heavy
ant. loose, slack, uncondensed

compel
syn. coerce, oblige, pressure, force, obligate, make
ant. impede, obstruct, hinder

competent
syn. capable, skilled, proficient, efficient, decent, sufficient
ant. inefficient, incapable, inept

compile
syn. assemble, gather, garner, collate, congregate, consolidate
ant. disperse, disassemble, scatter

complain
syn. grouch, grump, whine, fret, fuss, grieve
ant. applaud, commend, praise

complex
syn. complicated, intricate, elaborate, knotty, tangled, convoluted
ant. evident, obvious, plain

conceal
syn. block, hide, obscure, clock, shroud, mask
ant. disclose, divulge, expose

concise
syn. brief, compendious, laconic, succinct, terse, summary
ant. expansive, elaborate, lengthy

conflict
syn. confrontation, hostility, strife, discord, dissent, variance
ant. agreement, concord, peace

conquer
syn. defeat, overcome, subdue, rout, surmount, vanquish
ant. retreat, succumb, yield

consensus
syn. unanimity, accord, agreement, unison, harmony, consent
ant. disagreement, discord, dissonance

consistent
syn. accordant, congruous, consonant, correspondent, harmonious, unchanging
ant. incongruous, varying, erratic

contradictory
syn. contrary, converse, diametric, opposite, polar, reverse
ant. consistent, reconciled, agreeing

convincing
syn. cogent, persuasive, satisfactory, authentic, credible, valid
ant. dubious, implausible, incredible

courteous
syn. attentive, considerate, polite, solicitous, genteel, mannerly
ant. rude, impolite, uncivilized

curtail
syn. abbreviate, abridge, condense, reduce, shorten, cut
ant. extend, lengthen, prolong

Exercise

Choose the word which is CLOSEST in meaning to the given word.

1. Chaos
(a) disarray (b) credence
(c) scheme (d) order

2. Concise
(a) laconic (b) expansive
(c) polar (d) congruous

3. Compel
(a) coerce (b) fret
(c) shroud (d) whine

4. Curtail
(a) extend (b) scatter (c) reduce (d) jovial

Choose the word which is MOST SIMILAR in meaning to the underlined word in the given sentence.

5. The man behaved in a <u>courteous</u> way.
(a) polite (b) bizzare (c) envious (d) pious

6. The first computers were bulky and <u>clumsy</u> to use.
(a) dexterous (b) adroit
(c) repellent (d) unwieldly

7. Nandita was dressed <u>casually</u> for the outing.
(a) nicely (b) heavily (c) informally (d) formally

Choose the word which is OPPOSITE in meaning to the given word.

8. Convincing
(a) credible (b) valid
(c) authentic (d) implausible

9. Compile
(a) grouch (b) commend
(c) espouse (d) scatter

10. Conceal
(a) subdue (b) divulge
(c) rout (d) obstruct

11. Contradictory
(a) condition (b) agreeing
(c) signify (d) succumb

Choose the word which is MOST OPPOSITE in meaning to the underlined word in the given sentence.

12. Ashoka <u>conquered</u> many regions during his reign.
(a) surmounted (b) defeated
(c) soothed (d) yielded

13. Can we reach a <u>consensus</u> on this matter?
(a) connivance (b) grump
(c) accord (d) discord

14. India beat Australia in the rain-<u>curtailed</u> match.
(a) reduced (b) extended
(c) dispersed (d) cancelled

D

deadly
syn. fatal, lethal, mortal, ghastly, malignant, baneful
ant. nonfatal, harmless, lively

decline
syn. refuse, reject, dismiss, fall, deteriorate, descend
ant. increase, rise, accept

deficient
syn. defective, incomplete, lacking, wanting, inadequate, scarce
ant. flawless, adequate, sufficient

dejected
syn. depressed, down, gloomy, desolate, melancholic, sad
ant. cheerful, happy, joyous

delicate
syn. elegant, exquisite, fine, feeble, fragile, sensitive
ant. coarse, harsh, robust

delight
syn. pleasure, joy, cheer, exult, rejoice, gladden, gratify
ant. trouble, sadden, dismay

demolish
syn. destroy, destruct, raze, shatter, wreck, smash
ant. build, repair, restore

deny
syn. contradict, negate, disallow, reject, refuse, repudiate
ant. admit, allow, confess

depart
syn. exit, leave, retire, drop, demise, deviate
ant. arrive, come, enter

depressed
syn. dejected, desolate, gloomy, sad, melancholic, deprived
ant. elated, exalted, happy

deprive
syn. dispossess, divest, rob, strip, disinherit, bereave
ant. bestow, endow, confer

despair
syn. anguish, dejection, melancholy, misery, sorrow, despondency
ant. joy, cheerfulness, happiness

detached
syn. isolated, solitary, indifferent, apathetic, nonchalant, unruffled
ant. attached, combined, involved

detain
syn. delay, retard, hold, lag, confine, imprison
ant. liberate, release, free

deteriorate
syn. decline, worsen, languish, degenerate, putrefy, spoil
ant. improve, strengthen, better

devastate
syn. ravage, waste, plunder, smash, pillage, raze
ant. build, construct, enrich

diligent
syn. assiduous, industrious, studious, earnest, attentive, conscientious
ant. languid, lazy, lethargic

diminish
syn. abate, decrease, dwindle, lessen, rebate, reduce
ant. expand, prolong, extend

din
syn. clamour, hubbub, noise, pandemonium, tumult, uproar
ant. calm, peace, quiet

diplomatic
syn. discreet, sensitive, tactful, politic, astute, adept
ant. artless, tactless, boorish

discard
syn. dispose, jettison, abdicate, eliminate, expel, banish
ant. embrace, retain, keep

disclose
syn. bare, show, unveil, convey, transmit, impart
ant. conceal, hide, withhold

disgusting
syn. horrid, repulsive, repellent, abhorrent, repugnant, shabby
ant. pleasant, delightful, inviting

disperse
syn. dissipate, scatter, diffuse, disseminate, spread, strew
ant. assemble, collect, garner

disrupt
syn. disturb, unsettle, upset, disarray, disorganise, derange
ant. arrange, organise, reassure

distant
syn. far, faraway, remote, offish, reticent, solitary
ant. adjacent, close, neighbouring

distinct
syn. clear, sharp, pronounced, visible, manifest, unambiguous
ant. fuzzy, hazy, vague

distinguished
syn. eminent, famed, noted, prominent, celebrated, renowned
ant. obscure, unimportant, inferior

distract
syn. disturb, flurry, fluster, perturb, ruffle, unsettle
ant. appease, reassure, pacify

docile
syn. gentle, meek, amenable, compliant, submissive, mild
ant. inflexible, obstinate, stubborn

doldrums
syn. dejection, depression, blues, gloom, melancholy, mournfulness
ant. elation, glee, joy

dominant
syn. commanding, governing, ruling, authoritative, prevailing, masterful
ant. humble, modest, reserved

downfall
syn. descent, collapse, fall, bane, ruination, undoing
ant. ascent, rise, success

drastic
syn. dire, radical, strong, forceful, harsh, exorbitant
ant. cal, easy, superficial

dreadful
syn. appalling, direful, fearful, frightful, horrendous, ghastly
ant. pleasant, wonderful, inoffensive

drubbing
syn. beating, defeat, thrashing, rout, vanquishment, whipping
ant. aid, assistance, protection

drowsy
syn. dozy, sleepy, slumberous, somnolent, soporific, nodding
ant. alert, awake, lively

dubious
syn. doubtful, skeptical, uncertain, ambiguous, chancy, questionable
ant. certain, reliable, trustworthy

dumb

syn. inarticulate, mute, silent, stupid, dimwitted
ant. articulate, vocal, smart

dupe

syn. deceive, beguile, misguide, cross, fool, trick
ant. guide, lead, advise

Exercise

Choose the word which is CLOSEST in meaning to the given word.

1. Disrupting
(a) imparting (b) dissipate (c) swaying (d) innovative

2. Doldrums
(a) boom (b) depression (c) swoon (d) interpret

3. Denial
(a) negation (b) approval (c) connival (d) survival

Choose the word which is MOST SIMILAR in meaning to the underlined word in the given sentence.

4. Rickets has been associated with vitamin-D <u>deficiency</u>.
(a) surrogacy (b) shortage (c) sufficiency (d) portability

5. I was rather <u>dubious</u> about the whole idea.
(a) inarticulate (b) sceptical (c) inflexible (d) horrendous

Choose the word which is OPPOSITE in meaning to the given word.

6. Drowsy
(a) alert (b) soporific (c) belligerent (d) healthy

7. Deprive
(a) attach (b) bestow (c) liberate (d) strengthen

8. Disperse
(a) arrange (b) assemble (c) organise (d) retain

Choose the word which is MOST OPPOSITE in meaning to the underlined word in the given sentence.

9. Rekha is a very <u>docile</u> girl.
(a) compliant (b) submissive
(c) obstinate (d) yielding

10. The rapidly <u>diminishing</u> water reserves are a cause of concern for everyone.
(a) decreasing (b) increasing
(c) stagnant (d) abysmal

E

ebb
syn. abatement, letup, wane, dwindling, drop, slackening
ant. incline, increase, rise

efficacy
syn. effect, potency, competence, influence, strength, power
ant. inefficiency, unproductiveness, uselessness

elegant
syn. graceful, exquisite, delicate, fine, stylist, pleasing
ant. crude, unrefined, rough

elongate
syn. extend, lengthen, prolong, stretch, spin, increase
ant. construct, contract, shorten

eminent
syn. celebrated, established, illustrious, notable, famed, prominent
ant. unremarkable, lowly, unknown

emit
syn. release, vent, let out, let off, project, radiate
ant. contain, repress, withhold

enhance
syn. aggravate, heighten, intensify, boost, plug, embellish
ant. lower, minimise, reduce

enormous
syn. giant, herculean, immense, mammoth, massive, stupendous
ant. insignificant, minute, tiny

erase
syn. delete, efface, expunge, obliterate, abolish, extinguish
ant. add, insert, create

erratic
syn. devious, inconsistent, spotty, capricious, temperamental, volatile
ant. regular, steady, consistent

essential
syn. basic, fundamental, vital, integral, elementary, requisite
ant. auxiliary, subsidiary, secondary

eternal
syn. everlasting, infinite, incessant, perpetual, relentless, immortal
ant. brief, ephemeral, transient

evident
syn. apparent, obvious, pronounced, visible, manifest, noticeable
ant. obscure, vague, uncertain

exaggerate
syn. inflate, magnify, overstate, hyperbolise, boast, emphasise
ant. play down, understate, depreciate

excel
syn. outshine, surpass, outdo, exceed, transcend, better
ant. fail, lose, fall behind

excessive
syn. exorbitant, boundless, extreme, immoderate, extravagant, profligate
ant. moderate, reasonable, insufficient

exclude
syn. debar, eliminate, bar, except, rule out, omit
ant. accept, include, allow

excuse
syn. condone, remit, absolve, spare, relieve, discharge
ant. blame, condemn, incriminate

execute
syn. do, perform, exercise, implement, effectuate, administer
ant. fore go, mismanage, neglect

exemplary
syn. admirable, commendable, meritorious, worthy, praiseworthy
ant. contemptible, repugnant, loathsome

exhaustive
syn. intensive, thorough, complete, extensive, profound, radical
ant. exclusive, incomplete, deficient

expel
syn. banish, deport, exile, ostracise, dismiss, eject
ant. allow, keep, welcome

expensive
syn. costly, dear, high, exorbitant, over-priced, lavish
ant. cheap, inexpensive, moderate

exile
syn. banishment, deportation, expatriation, extradition, ostracism, transportation
ant. import, arrival, entrance

extend
syn. expand, outstretch, prolong, unfold, protract, broaden
ant. contract, curtail, shorten

extensive
syn. large-scale, spacious, considerable, sweeping, far-reaching, expansive
ant. narrow, restricted, limited

extinct
syn. dead, defunct, lifeless, departed, vanished, lost
ant. alive, extant, existing

extinguish
syn. douse, quench, annihilate, abolish, quash, obliterate
ant. light, enact, establish

extravagant
syn. lavish, prodigal, exorbitant, spendthrift, opulent, profuse
ant. stingy, thrifty, economical

extrovert
syn. gregarious, outgoing, communicative, unreserved, boisterous, loud
ant. introvert, reserved, quiet

Exercise

Choose the word which is CLOSEST in meaning to the given word.

1. Elegant
(a) chic (b) potent
(c) crude (d) sombre

2. Extrovert
(a) spendthrift (b) gregarious
(c) prodigal (d) soothing

3. Exemplary
(a) perpetual (b) pluralistic
(c) worthy (d) exorbitant

4. Extravagant
(a) purile (b) champion
(c) economical (d) spend thrift

Choose the word which is MOST SIMILAR in meaning to the underlined word in the given sentence.

5. The office has put a fire extinguisher.
(a) burner (b) brighter
(c) blow up (d) defunctor

6. The world is full of modest people brimming with esoteric knowledge.
(a) familiar (b) cocky
(c) obscure (d) fragmented

7. A number of people were exiled from Siberia.
(a) banished (b) acquitted
(c) admitted (d) annexed

Choose the word which is OPPOSITE in meaning to the given word.

8. Extend

(a) expatriate (b) ostracise

(c) curtail (d) prolong

9. Extinct

(a) endangered (b) restricted

(c) existing (d) dangerous

10. Evident

(a) obvious (b) obscure

(c) provident (d) portent

11. Extensive

(a) limited (b) expansive

(c) arrival (d) lavish

Choose the word which is MOST OPPOSITE in meaning to the underlined word in the given sentence.

12. The house looks <u>elegant</u>.

(a) inflate (b) magnify

(c) crude (d) rotten

13. The cameraman's treatment of the subject is very <u>exhaustive</u>.

(a) deficient (b) pompous

(c) ridiculous (d) thorough

14. <u>Excessive</u> indulgence in any particular thing is bad.

(a) moderate (b) liberal

(c) extreme (d) lowly

F

fabricate
syn. devise, formulate, concoct, assemble, mold, fake
ant. destroy, ruin, wreck

fabulous
syn. amazing, astounding, phenomenal, legendary, splendid, terrific
ant. ordinary, simple, common

facilitate
syn. ease, expedite, aid, promote, further, speed up
ant. block, detain, hinder

fair
syn. attractive, gorgeous, pretty, auspicious, benign, unbiased
ant. partial, unjust, ugly

faithful
syn. allegiant, loyal, trustworthy, credible, rigorous, precise
ant. dishonest, unreliable, treacherous

fake
syn. bogus, counterfeit, fraudulent, phony, spurious, sham
ant. genuine, original, true

familiar
syn. versed, acquainted, conversant, friendly, rude, brash
ant. foreign, strange, unremarkable

fascinate
syn. beguile, bewitch, captivate, charm, enchant, enthrall
ant. bore, disenchant, repel

fatal
syn. deadly, lethal, mortal, vital, disastrous, critical
ant. nourishing, helpful, harmless

ferocious
syn. barbarous, cruel, fierce, savage, vicious, truculent
ant. gentle, mild, tender

fictitious
syn. fanciful, invented, made-up, artificial, assumed, fabricated
ant. actual, factual, genuine

filthy
syn. dirty, soiled, foul, abhorrent, detestable, rotten
ant. clean, pure, sterile

finite
syn. definite, limited, precise, restricted, specific, exact
ant. endless, infinite, unlimited

flatter
syn. adulate, enhance, praise, blandish, butter up, slaver
ant. belittle, castigate, condemn

flaw
syn. blemish, defect, bug, imperfection, shortcoming, fault
ant. perfection, strength, fine point

flexible
syn. ductile, malleable, pliable, resilient, adaptable, supple
ant. rigid, stiff, unyielding

flourish
syn. bloom, thrive, prosper, flower, shine, brandish
ant. languish, stunt, hinder

fluctuate
syn. alter, oscillate, swing, waver, shift, veer
ant. persist, hold, stay

fluent
syn. easy, effortless, flowing, fluid, graceful, smooth
ant. uneven, intermittent, irregular

foe
syn. hostile, enemy, nemesis, adversary, antagonist, rival
ant. friend, ally, protagonist

foul
syn. atrocious, disgusting, horrid, fetid, filthy, ribald
ant. flagrant, pure, pleasing

frank
syn. candid, forthright, ingenuous, straightforward, open, plainspoken
ant. secretive, evasive, divisive

fraud
syn. cheat, swindle, charlatan, impostor, phony, fake
ant. honest, ethical, forthright

fundamental
syn. basic, elementary, essential, rudiment, root, axiom
ant. extra, trivial, unimportant

futile
syn. barren, useless, vain, fruitless, unsuccessful, unprofitable
ant. useful, productive, fertile

Exercise

Choose the word which is CLOSEST in meaning to the given word.

1. Fabulous
(a) marvellous (b) surprising (c) credible (d) rigorous

2. Flaw
(a) adulation (b) bug (c) deviation (d) strength

3. Fake
(a) ugly (b) acquainted (c) foreign (d) phony

Choose the word which is MOST SIMILAR in meaning to the underlined word in the given sentence.

4. Why are you wearing this <u>filthy</u> jacket?
(a) ragged (b) delicate
(c) mucky (d) chic

5. The two countries were involved in a <u>ferocious</u> battle.
(a) disastrous (b) fanciful
(c) arduous (d) savage

Choose the word which is OPPOSITE in meaning to the given word.

6. Fraud
(a) impostor (b) swindle (c) forthright (d) miscreant

7. Foe
(a) nemesis (b) phony (c) ally (d) blemish

8. Flatter
(a) bewitch (b) castigate (c) resent (d) devastate

Choose the word which is MOST OPPOSITE in meaning to the underlined word in the given sentence.

9. Their business <u>flourished</u> once they introduced new products.
(a) increased (b) survived
(c) famished (d) languished

10. His <u>futile</u> efforts in reviving the company went in vain.
(a) useless (b) productive
(c) trivial (d) fetid

G - H

gain
syn. acquire, procure, secure, accomplish, attain, realise
ant. forfeit, lose, waste

gala
syn. festive, joyous, merry, jovial, convivial, festal
ant. gloomy, sombre, depressed

gallant
syn. audacious, dauntless, heroic, plucky, valiant, mettlesome
ant. cowardly, timid, afraid

generous
syn. lavish, liberal, magnanimous, bountiful, copious, substantial
ant. mean, miserly, stingy

genius
syn. brilliance, aptitude, flair, knack, talent, bent
ant. inability, incapacity, weakness

gentle
syn. mild, tender, delicate, faint, moderate, slight
ant. crude, rough, violent

genuine
syn. authentic, real, unquestionable, sincere, unfeigned, hearty
ant. counterfeit, illegitimate, sham

gigantic
syn. behemoth, colossal, enormous, immense, massive, mighty
ant. miniature, miniscule, tiny

gloomy
syn. cheerless, bleak, dismal, morose, sullen, melancholic
ant. cheerful, sunny, bright

glorify
syn. exalt, acclaim, eulogise, laud, praise, extol
ant. castigate, condemn, criticise

gorgeous
syn. ravishing, stunning, glorious, magnificent, splendid, attractive
ant. homely, ugly, ordinary

gracious
syn. affable, hospitable, courtly, amiable, compassionate, cordial
ant. nasty, mean, rude

grant
syn. accord, award, concede, give, vouchsafe, confer
ant. forfeit, lose, refuse

grateful
syn. appreciative, thankful, congenial, agreeable, gratifying, welcome
ant. thankless, heedless, critical

grief
syn. sorrow, anguish, despair, heartbreak, distress, gloom
ant. delight, exhilaration, ecstasy

guilty
syn. culpable, blameworthy, censured, damned, condemned, doomed
ant. blameless, innocent, truthful

haphazard
syn. indiscriminate, unplanned, random, arbitrary, casual, incidental
ant. systematic, organised, planned

harass
syn. beset, hound, annoy, plague, pester, torment
ant. aid, facilitate, support

hardship
syn. asperity, difficulty, adversity, affliction, catastrophe, distress
ant. benefit, assistance, ease

harmony
syn. accord, agreement, conformity, congruence, rapport, symmetry
ant. disagreement, discord, clash

harsh
syn. coarse, jagged, rugged, hoarse, jarring, acerbic
ant. mild, pleasing, soft

hateful
syn. malicious, malevolent, malignant, nasty, spiteful, vicious
ant. amiable, harmless, loving

hazardous
syn. dangerous, jeopardous, perilous, treacherous, chancy, risky
ant. guarded, safe, secure

hoax
syn. con, deceit, fake, fraud, gimmick, prank
ant. frankness, openness, uprightness

homely
syn. plain, unattractive, uncomely, simple, ordinary, comfortable
ant. attractive, modern, charming

homogeneous
syn. akin, alike, analogous, identical, uniform, similar
ant. heterogeneous, varied, discrete

horrific
syn. horrible, horrid, terrible, awful, dreadful, beastly
ant. comforting, reassuring, satisfying

hostile
syn. belligerent, combative, contentious, pugnacious,
ant. agreeable, friendly, gentle

humorous
syn. amusing, comic, jocular, witty, facetious, funny
ant. morose, sad, tragic

hurdle
syn. bar, barrier, block, clog, hamper, impediment
ant. furtherance, assistance, help

Exercise

Choose the word which is CLOSEST in meaning to the given word.

1. Grief
(a) knack (b) despair
(c) acclaim (d) exhilaration

2. Hoax
(a) spite (b) deceit
(c) distress (d) congruence

3. Harsh
(a) miniscule (b) heedless
(c) rugged (d) meticulous

4. Gain
(a) acquire (b) resume
(c) support (d) defunct

Choose the word which is MOST SIMILAR in meaning to the underlined word in the given sentence.

5. The plan was executed in a haphazard manner.
(a) planned (b) unplanned
(c) scheduled (d) orderly

6. Many gallant soldiers lost their lives in the battle.
(a) dauntless (b) festal (c) timid (d) gracious

7. Anushka was looking gorgeous in her wedding gown.
(a) congenial (b) compassionate
(c) stunning (d) copious

Choose the word which is OPPOSITE in meaning to the given word.

8. Generous
(a) mean (b) crude
(c) liberal (d) cowardly

9. Glorify
(a) eulogise (b) castigate
(c) forfeit (d) hamper

10. Gracious
(a) witty (b) analogous
(c) cold (d) morose

11. Gala
(a) joyous (b) grateful
(c) gloomy (d) bacon

Choose the word which is MOST OPPOSITE in meaning to the underlined word in the given sentence.

12. There was a homely atmosphere there.
(a) acerbic (b) accord
(c) innocent (d) modern

13. Does he really have a sense of humour?
(a) wit (b) analogy
(c) horrid (d) tragedy

14. Men and nature should live in harmony with each other.
(a) discord (b) congruence
(c) affliction (d) impediment

I - K

ideal

syn. exemplary, model, standard, perfect, supreme, hypothetical

ant. flawed, imperfect, problematic

identical

syn. same, similar, equal, equivalent, tantamount, even

ant. distinct, diverse, dissimilar

ignite

syn. kindle, fire, light, inflame, alight, burn, incense

ant. extinguish, pacify, quench

ignorant

syn. illiterate, uneducated, unaware, oblivious, unacquainted, benighted

ant. aware, knowledgeable, literate

illegitimate

syn. illegal, illicit, outlawed, bastard, spurious, misbegotten

ant. authorised, ethical, moral

illicit

syn. lawless, unlawful, wrongful, felonious, clandestine, adulterous

ant. legitimate, noble, proper

immense

syn. enormous, monumental, vast, titanic, colossal, elephantine

ant. minute, tiny, paltry

impartial

syn. dispassionate, equitable, indifferent, unbiased, nonpartisan, just

ant. prejudiced, partial, discriminating

impromptu

syn. extemporary, improvised, offhand, unrehearsed, ad-lib, unprepared

ant. deliberate, planned, premeditated

inclusive

syn. comprehensive, expansive, extensive, sweeping, widespread, extended

ant. exclusive, narrow, selective

increment

syn. advance, boost, hike, increase, jump, raise

ant. decrease, loss, slump

indifferent

syn. dispassionate, objective, just, apathetic, nonpartisan, square

ant. concerned, caring, sympathetic

industrious

syn. assiduous, diligent, hardworking, studious, sedulous, laborious

ant. indolent, lethargic, slack

inevitable

syn. certain, inescapable, unavoidable, definite, sure, doomed

ant. uncertain, unlikely, unsure

infinite

syn. boundless, eternal, endless, unlimited, countless, innumerable

ant. definite, limited, measurable

initial

syn. inceptive, beginning, introductory, maiden, primary, primordial

ant. closing, final, last

innovative

syn. ingenious, inventive, original, improvised, unprecedented, novel

ant. customary, habitual, traditional

inquisitive

syn. curious, nosy, snoopy, inquiring, questioning, investigative

ant. disinterested, indifferent, incurious

insane

syn. crazy, daft, unsound, maniac, lunatic, dotty

ant. sane, rational, logical

insignificant

syn. trivial, inconsequent, inconsiderable, meager, immaterial, negligible

ant. significant, substantial, valuable

intensify
syn. aggravate, deepen, enhance, heighten, redouble, increase
ant. weaken, soothe, lower

intervene
syn. interfere, intrude, meddle, obtrude, intercede, interpose
ant. ignore, withdraw, avoid

intimate
syn. close, familiar, friendly, interior, confidential, personal
ant. formal, incompatible, cool

invert
syn. reverse, transpose, turn, flip, upturn, backtrack
ant. advance, forward, hold

invincible
syn. impregnable, indomitable, unconquerable, unbeatable, unyielding, insurmountable
ant. beatable, conquerable, breakable

irritate
syn. aggravate, bug, exasperate, fret, peeve, nettle
ant. assuage, please, aid

isolate
syn. seclude, segregate, insulate, separate, detach, remove
ant. integrate, incorporate, mingle

itinerant
syn. nomadic, vagabond, vagrant, migratory, migrant, wanderer
ant. permanent, settled, resident

jade
syn. wear, fatigue, drain, tire, down, enervate
ant. amuse, excite, exhilarate

jarring
syn. rasping, agitating, harsh, raspy, raucous, strident
ant. subdued, soft, quiet

jocular
syn. comedic, facetious, humorous, funny, witty, frolicsome
ant. morose, serious, grave

jolt
syn. bump, collision, smash, shock, crash, blow
ant. luck, fortune, expected

jovial
syn. blithe, jolly, mirthful, jocund, convivial, gleeful
ant. sad, unhappy, serious

jubilant
syn. exultant, happy, triumphant, elated, euphoric, gleeful
ant. depressed, sorrowful, dejected

judicious
syn. prudent, rational, balanced, sensible, sound, reasonable
ant. reckless, thoughtless, irrational

jumble
syn. muddle, scramble, disarray, disrupt, befuddle, confound
ant. order, organise, harmonise

jumbo
syn. behemoth, colossal, stupendous, mighty, mammoth, massy
ant. miniature, tiny, small

junk
syn. discard, dispose of, scrap, dump, jettison, chuck
ant. keep, hold, preserve

just
syn. equitable, fair, square, appropriate, cogent, objective
ant. inequitable, partial, unjust

justify
syn. rationalise, vindicate, corroborate, substantiate, apologise, defend
ant. assail, impugn, protest

keen
syn. alert, ardent, fervent, perceptive, sensitive, sharp
ant. reluctant, uninterested, indifferent

knit
syn. fasten, affix, link, loop, intermingle, weave
ant. detach, severe, break

knock
syn. censure, criticism, condemnation, blame, rap, smash
ant. compliment, praise, endorsement

knotty
syn. complex, complicated, convoluted, daedal, intricate, tangled
ant. unsnarled, systematic, uncoiled

kudos
syn. accolade, distinction, acclaim, applause, eulogy, plaudit
ant. censure, condemnation, vituperation

Exercise

Choose the word which is CLOSEST in meaning to the given word.

1. Intervene
(a) obtrude (b) alight (c) aggravate (d) nettle

2. Jade
(a) segregate (b) exasperate (c) snoopy (d) fatigue

3. Kudos
(a) reprehension (b) acclaim (c) mirth (d) amusement

Choose the word which is MOST SIMILAR in meaning to the underlined word in the given sentence.

4. Heroin is an example of an illicit drug.
(a) approved (b) banned
(c) illuminative (d) oblivious

5. It is quite difficult to give an impromptu speech.
(a) equitable (b) deliberate
(c) unrehearsed (d) impervious

Choose the word which is OPPOSITE in meaning to the given word.

6. Ignite
(a) extinguish (b) pacify (c) oust (d) aggravate

7. Inquisitive
(a) gregarious (b) meagre (c) dotty (d) indifferent

8. Judicious
(a) reckless (b) prudent (c) euphoric (d) triumphant

Choose the word which is MOST OPPOSITE in meaning to the underlined word in the given sentence.

9. Our anxieties can be controlled by isolating thoughts, feelings and emotions.
(a) assuaging (b) insulating (c) mingling (d) transposing

10. The banning of Padmavati is not justified.
(a) illegitimate (b) probate (c) prudent (d) honest

L - M

lavish
syn. luxurious, opulent, extravagant, prodigal, profuse, generous
ant. economical, scanty, scarce

lean
syn. bony, lanky, meagre, slender, succinct, brief
ant. plump, chubby, overweight

legitimate
syn. lawful, legal, licit, justifiable, logical, valid
ant. invalid, illegal, unwarranted

lethal
syn. deadly, fatal, mortal, vital, destructive, ruinous
ant. beneficial, harmless, helpful

lethargic
syn. sluggish, stuporous, torpid, apathetic, detached, indifferent
ant. active, lively, vivacious

liability
syn. obligation, arrears, debt, exposure, vulnerability, indebtedness
ant. irresponsibility, accountability, assets

liberal
syn. progressive, tolerant, broad-minded, modern, generous, munificent
ant. conservative, narrow-minded, orthodox

lively
syn. brisk, sprighty, animated, vivacious, dynamic, vigorous
ant. dispirited, boring, dull

loafer
syn. bum, drone, idler, sluggard, lazybones, wanderer
ant. hard worker, workaholic, overachiever

loyal
syn. faithful, staunch, steadfast, devoted, allegiant, trustworthy
ant. unfaithful, undependable, disloyal

lunatic
syn. crazy, demented, insane, distraught, maniac, unsound
ant. sane, sensible, balanced

luxurious
syn. lavish, palatial, plush, rich, opulent, sumptuous
ant. destitute, tiny, scarce

magnificent
syn. glorious, splendid, grand, noble, outstanding
ant. atrocious, shameful, awful

majestic
syn. august, imposing, grandiose, lordly, stately, sublime
ant. shabby, low, humble

mammoth
syn. colossal, enormous, huge, prodigious, mighty, heroic
ant. little, miniature, tiny

marvel
syn. miracle, phenomenon, prodigy, sensation, wonder
ant. anticipation, normalcy, usualness

masculine
syn. macho, male, manly, manlike, mannish, virile
ant. feminine, ladylike, womanly

meagre
syn. scant, skimpy, sparse, tiny, lanky, slim
ant. plenty, substantial, sufficient

mean
syn. malevolent, spiteful, vicious, ignoble, sordid, niggard
ant. affectionate, gentle, dignified

mediocre
syn. average, common, plain, standard, mean, shabby
ant. exceptional, unusual, extraordinary

mentor
syn. advisor, consultant, counsellor, trainer, coach, guide
ant. adversary, opponent, student

merge
syn. blend, fuse, mingle, amalgamate, stir, mix
ant. divide, separate, part

meticulous
syn. careful, painstaking, scrupulous, fussy, choosy, particular
ant. careless, sloppy, unorganised

midst
syn. centre, median, middle, midpoint, deep, interior
ant. exterior, outside, outer

minute
syn. diminutive, dwarf, minuscule, tiny, pygmy, wee
ant. giant, huge, mighty

miserly
syn. close-fisted, niggard, parsimonious, penurious, stingy, pinching
ant. generous, lavish, prodigal

misfortune
syn. adversity, hopelessness, affliction, casualty, mishap, unluckiness
ant. blessing, fortune, favour

mislead
syn. beguile, betray, deceive, dupe, hoodwink, trick
ant. guide, counsel, lead

mock
syn. deride, gibe, jeer, ridicule, imitate, mimic
ant. flatter, praise, exalt

moderate
syn. modest, reasonable, temperate, conservative, restrained, mild
ant. outrageous, considerable, significant

monopoly
syn. cartel, consortium, holding, syndicate, trust, corner
ant. sharing, distribution, scattering

monstrous
syn. atrocious, heinous, gruesome, scandalous, gigantic, mighty
ant. average, common, cultured

motivate
syn. goad, impel, prod, prick, spur, stimulate
ant. depress, dissuade, impede

muddy
syn. murky, roiled, turbid, cloudy, drab
ant. bright, lucid, explicit

mute
syn. dumb, inarticulate, mum, silent, voiceless, wordless
ant. articulate, communicative, vocal

Exercise

Choose the word which is CLOSEST in meaning to the given word.

1. Lethargic
   (a) torpid (b) ruinous (c) munificent (d) unwarranted
2. Meagre
   (a) sordid (b) shabby (c) substantial (d) sparse
3. Masculine
   (a) prodigy (b) virile (c) skimpy (d) undaunted

Choose the word which is MOST SIMILAR in meaning to the underlined word in the given sentence.

4. Remembering all the words in a dictionary is a <u>mammoth</u> task.
   (a) modest (b) miniature (c) colossal (d) disturbing
5. She endured the <u>monstrous</u> behaviour of her husband.
   (a) cultured (b) spurious (c) niggard (d) gruesome

Choose the word which is OPPOSITE in meaning to the given word.

6. Lunatic
   (a) distraught (b) sane (c) allegiant (d) imprudent
7. Motivate
   (a) impede (b) prod (c) jeer (d) facilitate
8. Lustrous
   (a) dazzling (b) banal (c) dim (d) finicky

Choose the word which is OPPOSITE in meaning to the underlined word in the given sentence.

9. The painting has been painted with <u>meticulous</u> attention to detail.
   (a) fussy (b) stingy (c) temperate (d) sloppy
10. Anything eaten in <u>moderate</u> quantity is good for health.
   (a) restrained (b) outrageous (c) outspoken (d) low

N - O

nab

syn. apprehend, arrest, seize, catch, clutch, grab
ant. release, free, discharge

native

syn. congenial, inherited, inborn, indigenous, aboriginal, raw
ant. alien, foreign, outside

naughty

syn. mischievous, immodest, indecent, unbecoming, unseemly, untoward
ant. modest, proper, behaved

neglect

syn. disregard, ignore, slight, default, fail, omit
ant. honour, respect, regard

negligent

syn. derelict, lax, careless, neglectful, remiss, slack
ant. attentive, careful, mindful

negligible

syn. inconsiderable, paltry, petty, trifling, slender, slight
ant. significant, major, important

nervous

syn. agitated, anxious, concerned, jittery, restive, tense
ant. calm, content, unconcerned

nominal

syn. formal, apparent, stated, purported, ostensible, seeming
ant. actual, real, true

nurture

syn. cultivate, foster, nourish, nurse, discipline, train
ant. deprive, ignore, neglect

obedient

syn. amenable, compliant, conformable, docile, submissive, supple
ant. insolent, mutinous

obese

syn. corpulent, fleshy, gross, portly, overweight, stout
ant. emaciated, underweight, skinny

objective
syn. concrete, substantial, equitable, nonpartisan, realistic, unbiased
ant. prejudiced, partial, subjective

obsolete
syn. outdated, useless, discarded, archaic, antique, superseded
ant. contemporary, current, modern

obstacle
syn. bar, barrier, block, clog, hurdle, hindrance
ant. assistance, clearance, opening

obvious
syn. apparent, clear, distinct, visible, plain, evident
ant. ambiguous, obscure, vague

offensive
syn. atrocious, disgusting, foul, repellent, sickening, vile
ant. agreeable, pleasing, wonderful

omit
syn. drop, eliminate, remove, default, fail, neglect
ant. include, insert, inject

opaque
syn. blurred, dusky, foggy, hazy, misty, sooty
ant. lucid, unclouded, transparent

opulent
syn. lavish, lush, luxuriant, palatial, rich, sumptuous
ant. depressed, destitute, poor

ordeal
syn. trial, crucible, affliction, agony, distress, tribulation
ant. happiness, relief, pleasure

original
syn. fundamental, prime, authentic, genuine, innovative, initial
ant. derivative, latest, newest

orthodox
syn. conventional, recognised, sanctioned, conservative, traditionalist, conformist
ant. heterodox, progressive, radical

oscillate
syn. sway, swing, dangle, flicker, seesaw, vacillate
ant. stay, steady, remain

oust
syn. bump, dismiss, eject, evict, expel, remove
ant. hold, keep, retain

outstanding

syn. noticeable, prominent, remarkable, salient, extraordinary, singular

ant. inferior, ordinary, average

Exercise

Choose the word which is CLOSEST in meaning to the given word.

1. Nab
   (a) discharge (b) eliminate (c) nourish (d) apprehend
2. Obsolete
   (a) outdated (b) contemporary (c) amenable (d) hazardous
3. Negligible
   (a) jittery (b) derelict (c) paltry (d) purported

Choose the word which is MOST SIMILAR in meaning to the underlined word in the given sentence.

4. The CEO had an <u>opulent</u> lifestyle.
   (a) destitute (b) swanky (c) authentic (d) conformist
5. You need to pay your <u>outstanding</u> dues before Tuesday.
   (a) overdraft (b) regular (c) genuine (d) pending

Choose the word which is OPPOSITE in meaning to the given word.

6. Nurture
   (a) deprive (b) discipline (c) clog (d) eliminate
7. Obese
   (a) fleshy (b) submissive (c) nominal (d) emaciated
8. Ordeal
   (a) relief (b) affliction (c) default (d) relevant

Choose the word which is MOST OPPOSITE in meaning to the underlined word in the given sentence.

9. It was <u>obvious</u> that he was not interested in the deal.
   (a) apparent (b) obscure (c) repellent (d) sooty
10. We all know that bats are <u>nocturnal</u>.
   (a) biennial (b) social (c) diurnal (d) ephemeral

P - Q

pacify
syn. appease, assuage, conciliate, mollify, propitiate, soothe,
ant. agitate, incite, upset

palatial
syn. lavish, luxuriant, opulent, plush, rich, sumptuous
ant. cramped, minor, tiny

pardonable
syn. excusable, forgivable, venial, defensible, justifiable, passable
ant. inexpiable, unpardonable, inexcusable

partisan
syn. biased, prejudiced, partial, tendentious, prepossessed, one-sided
ant. impartial, unbiased, fair

pathetic
syn. pitiable, rueful, deplorable, lamentable, distressing, miserable
ant. cheerful, worthwhile, delightful

peerless
syn. matchless, incomparable, singular, unmatched, alone, unequal
ant. inferior, mediocre, subordinate

pessimist
syn. defeatist, cynic, doomsayer, killjoy, downer, worrier
ant. optimist, dreamer, hoper

pinnacle
syn. acme, apex, crest, crown, peak, summit
ant. base, bottom, nadir

potent
syn. mighty, strong, powerful, commanding, dominant, authoritative
ant. fragile, incapable, ineffective

precise
syn. categorical, definite, accurate, specific, genteel, puritanical
ant. ambiguous, inexact, false

prescribe
syn. decree, dictate, fix, impose, lay down, ordain
ant. dismiss, reject, ban

preserve
syn. conserve, save, guard, shield, maintain, sustain
ant. destroy, hurt, ruin

prime
syn. superior, splendid, foremost, paramount, premier, original
ant. inferior, secondary, unimportant

prodigal
syn. extravagant, lavish, spendthrift, profuse, wasteful, luxuriant
ant. thrifty, stingy, reasonable

proficient
syn. adept, crack, masterly, professional, skilled, expert
ant. clumsy, inept, incompetent

profuse
syn. luxuriant, exuberant, profligate, lavish, spendthrift, lush
ant. lacking, sparse, wanting

prohibit
syn. ban, debar, forbid, inhibit, interdict, outlaw
ant. allow, favour, permit

prolific
syn. fecund, fertile, fruitful, productive, proliferous, rich
ant. barren, impotent, unproductive

prolong
syn. elongate, extend, lengthen, protract, stretch, prolongate
ant. abbreviate, shorten, compress

prominent
syn. arresting, marked, outstanding, remarkable, salient, distinguished
ant. inconspicuous, unexceptional, inferior

prompt
syn. foment, goad, impel, instigate, motivate, pique
ant. depress, halt, dissuade

propagate
syn. breed, cultivate, procreate, proliferate, promulgate, spawn
ant. destroy, decline, conceal

proscribe
syn. enjoin, debar, taboo, prohibit, inhibit, ban
ant. allow, favour, permit

prosperous
syn. booming, flourishing, prospering, thriving, auspicious, propitious
ant. languishing, stunted, losing

provisional
syn. interim, temporary, acting, conditional, provisory, tentative
ant. certain, definite, permanent

provoke
syn. enrage, incense, aggravate, annoy, nettle, incite
ant. please, soothe, placate

proximate
syn. adjacent, close, contiguous, near, imminent, momentary
ant. definite, distant, remote

prudent
syn. rational, sage, sapient, sensible, cautious, circumspect
ant. indiscreet, unrealistic, unwise

pungent
syn. piquant, zesty, acerbic, mordant, stinging, scathing
ant. bland, dull, sweet

pushy
syn. audacious, brazen, cheeky, insolent, impertinent, sassy
ant. unassuming, modest, quiet

puzzling
syn. arcane, cabalistic, cryptic, enigmatic, mysterious, occult
ant. comprehensible, intelligible, understandable

quack
syn. charlatan, fake, fraud, humbug, impostor, phony
ant. genuine, original, real

queer
syn. bizarre, cranky, eccentric, freaky, idiosyncratic, odd
ant. regular, typical, usual

quick-witted
syn. alert, clever, intelligent, keen, sharp, smart
ant. slow, stupid, dim

quieten
syn. hush, quiet, shush, shut up, silence, still
ant. agitate, excite, ruffle

Exercise

Choose the word which is CLOSEST in meaning to the given words.

1. Prolific
(a) barren (b) fecund (c) masterly (d) trite
2. Queer
(a) impostor (b) idiosyncratic (c) phony (d) brazen
3. Pinnacle
(a) nadir (b) splendour (c) crest (d) prominence

Choose the word which is MOST SIMILAR in meaning to the underlined word in the given sentence.

4. Educating women is <u>proscribed</u> in some tribal communities.
(a) stunted (b) placate (c) concealed (d) prohibited
5. He is too <u>partisan</u> to become a referee.
(a) venial (b) worthwhile (c) opulent (d) biased

Choose the word which is OPPOSITE in meaning to the given word.

6. Prudent
(a) indiscreet (b) mordant (c) acerbic (d) cryptic
7. Quieten
(a) shush (b) placate (c) ruffle (d) zoom
8. Profuse
(a) scathing (b) cheeky (c) freaky (d) sparse

Choose the word which is MOST OPPOSITE in meaning to the underlined word in the given sentence.

9. There have been rumours that he has been <u>prodigal</u> in spending his father's hard earned money.
(a) stingy (b) profuse (c) inept (d) commanding
10. Tendulkar was at the <u>pinnacle</u> of his career when he retired.
(a) peak (b) nadir (c) acme (d) middle

R

random

syn. desultory, haphazard, indiscriminate, spot, unplanned, chance
ant. definite, specific, systematic

eash

syn. brash, foolhardy, impetuous, impulsive, reckless, temerarious
ant. cautious, planned, thoughtful

rational

syn. analytical, judicious, prudent, sagacious, sapient, logical
ant. ridiculous, unsound, illogical

reasonable

syn. consequent, levelheaded, sage, discreet, restrained, modest
ant. immoderate, irrational, rash

rebuke

syn. admonish, castigate, chastise, chide, reprimand, reprove
ant. applaud, commend, extol

rectify

syn. amend, emend, redress, reform, reconcile, resolve
ant. damage, ruin, worsen

refute

syn. belie, disprove, rebut, abnegate, contravene, counter
ant. endorse, ratify, sanction

regard

syn. contemplation, concern, solicitude, caution, cognizance, observance
ant. neglect, thoughtlessness, indifference

relevant

syn. applicable, pertinent, apropos, cognate, concerning, congruent
ant. inappropriate, inapplicable, unsuitable

reliable

syn. dependable, responsible, trustworthy, impeccable, loyal, decisive
ant. deceptive, undependable, disloyal

relieve

syn. allay, alleviate, assuage, mitigate, lessen, palliate
ant. harm, hurt, incite

reluctant
syn. averse, indisposed, disinclined, loath, unwilling, diffident
ant. anxious, eager, enthusiastic

rely
syn. bank, depend, confide, entrust, commit, reckon
ant. distrust, doubt, disbelieve

remarkable
syn. arresting, marked, salient, preeminent, outstanding, singular
ant. ordinary, insignificant, common

remedy
syn. cure, antidote, nostrum, medicament, countermeasure, medication
ant. disease, injury, pain

renovate
syn. reinstate, rejuvenate, restitute, refurbish, restore, revamp
ant. demolish, destroy, ruin

renowned
syn. celebrated, eminent, distinguished, illustrious, prominent, noted
ant. unknown, inferior, unremarkable

repel
syn. fend, repulse, keep off, ward off, cast aside, drive away
ant. attract, draw, lure

resemblance
syn. affinity, alikeness, similarity, analogy, conformity, correspondence
ant. contrast, diversity, dissimilarity

resist
syn. withstand, buck, challenge, contest, dispute, traverse
ant. conform, comply, harmonise

resolve
syn. conclude, determine, analyse, decipher, unravel, reconcile
ant. encode, scramble, tangle

resourceful
syn. ingenious, inventive, aggressive, talented, venturesome, enterprising
ant. dull, unimaginative, inactive

respect
syn. admiration, appreciation, esteem, repute, prestige, regard
ant. disdain, dishonour, disrespect

restrain
syn. bridle, constrain, curb, hold back, inhibit, rein
ant. free, liberate, release

restrict
syn. circumscribe, confine, limit, constrict, cramp, demarcate
ant. enlarge, extend, expand

retain
syn. hold, recollect, reminisce, revive, engage, hire
ant. release, lose, spend

reveal
syn. betray, divulge, expose, unmask, manifest, evince
ant. conceal, hide, suppress

revengeful
syn. spiteful, vengeful, vindictive, rancorous, implacable, resentful
ant. compassionate, merciful, considerate

revive
syn. restore, rekindle, reinstate, restore, revitalise, renew
ant. destroy, kill, suppress

rewarding
syn. advantageous, lucrative, profitable, remunerative, bountiful, beneficial
ant. ungratifying, inopportune, marginal

riddle
syn. conundrum, enigma, mystery, perplexity, puzzle, maze
ant. solution, understanding, knowledge

ridicule
syn. deride, gibe, jeer, jest, mock, scoff
ant. praise, regard, consider

rigid
syn. inflexible, unyielding, immutable, adamant, incompliant, stubborn
ant. bending, pliant, yielding

rival
syn. competitor, contender, contestant, opponent, combatant, emulous
ant. associate, partner, aide

ruthless
syn. unscrupulous, merciless, unprincipled, fierce, callous, implacable
ant. sympathetic, sparing, merciful

Exercise

Choose the word which is CLOSEST in meaning to the given word.

1. Revive
   (a) reinstate (b) vindicate (c) divulge (d) revoke
2. Refute
   (a) amend (b) reconcile (c) rebut (d) differ
3. Reluctant
   (a) anxious (b) cognate (c) impeccable (d) shy

Choose the word which is MOST SIMILAR in meaning to the underlined word in the given sentence.

4. She was so angry that she could hardly <u>restrain</u> herself.
   (a) liberate (b) hold back (c) reconcile (d) apprehend
5. I was <u>rebuked</u> by my manager for taking too many leaves.
   (a) denied (b) chided (c) extolled (d) ratify

Choose the word which is OPPOSITE in meaning to the given word.

6. Random
   (a) specific (b) desultory (c) impetuous (d) probing
7. Resist
   (a) traverse (b) decipher (c) comply (d) retort
8. Resemblance
   (a) conformity (b) complexity (c) gravity (d) diversity

Choose the word which is MOST OPPOSITE in meaning to the underlined word in the given sentence.

9. The company had <u>rigid</u> rules for its employees.
   (a) immutable (b) pliant (c) callous (d) limpid
10. Some people believe that one needs to be <u>ruthless</u> to manage one's time.
    (a) flexible (b) unscrupulous (c) combatant (d) yielding

S

scatter
syn. dispel, disperse, dissipate, diffuse, disseminate, radiate
ant. hoard, gather, accumulate

sever
syn. carve, cleave, slice, cut, separate, split
ant. combine, join, unite

severe
syn. demanding, stern, bleak, brutal, dour, momentous
ant. amenable, comprising, willing

shabby
syn. decrepit, dilapidated, scruffy, tattered, abominate, loathsome
ant. kempt, tidy, preserved

shatter
syn. fracture, rift, smash, ruin, splinter, wreck
ant. fix, mend, repair

shield
syn. defend, guard, preserve, protect, secure, ward
ant. endanger, uncover, open

shortcoming
syn. deficiency, defect, inadequacy, paucity, scarcity, flaw
ant. advantage, sufficiency, plenty

shrewd
syn. astute, canny, perspicacious, cagey, slick, smart
ant. stupid, inept, silly

significant
syn. eloquent, meaningful, suggestive, considerable, consequential, monumental
ant. meaningless, trivial, unimposing

slack
syn. sluggish, lax, loose, derelict, neglectful, remiss
ant. stiff, taut, rigid

slender
syn. bony, fleshless, lanky, lean, skinny, negligible
ant. cubby, overweight, plump

solitary
syn. detached, isolated, lonesome, secluded, reticent, singular
ant. accompanied, together, sociable

sophisticated
syn. cosmopolitan, worldly, intellectual, adulterated, thoughtful, cerebral
ant. rustic, rural, simple

spectacular
syn. dramatic, sensational, theatrical, breathtaking, astounding, dazzling
ant. ordinary, usual, plain

speculative
syn. contemplative, deliberative, meditative, pensive, abstract, theoretical
ant. practical, realistic, concrete

spendthrift
syn. prodigal, profligate, extravagant, lavish, profuse, wasteful
ant. miser, economical, thrifty

spontaneous
syn. impulsive, instinctive, volitional, natural, unrestrained, unpremeditated
ant. deliberate, intended, planned

stagnant
syn. dormant, lifeless, listless, inactive, static, still
ant. moving, active, lively

stalwart
syn. indomitable, sturdy, dauntless, courageous, stout, dependable
ant. coward, meek, weak

static
syn. immobile, gridlocked, stalled, stationary, inert, latent
ant. active, changeable, variable

staunch
syn. steadfast, firm, allegiant, loyal, true, constant
ant. irresolute, unreliable, undependable

steadfast
syn. determined, unbending, unflinching, unwavering, resolute, steady
ant. disloyal, unreliable, shaky

steep
syn. abrupt, bold, precipitous, stiff, lofty, elevated
ant. moderate, gentle, beneath

stern
syn. demanding, exacting, harsh, rigid, severe, unyielding
ant. lenient, tolerant, light

stingy
syn. close-fisted, niggard, parsimonious, penurious, exiguous, skimpy
ant. generous, unselfish, wasteful

stout
syn. audacious, dauntless, heroic, plucky, valiant, hulking
ant. skinny, underweight, thin

straightforward
syn. candid, downright, ingenuous, forthright, plainspoken, frank
ant. deceitful, devious, dishonest

stun
syn. daze, bemuse, stupefy, numb, petrify
ant. expect, calm, bore

subordinate
syn. inferior, lower, petty, collateral, dependent, subservient
ant. chief, vital, major

summit
syn. apex, crest, vertex, acme, pinnacle, zenith
ant. base, bottom, nadir

superficial
syn. cursory, shallow, sketchy, apparent, ostensible, seeming
ant. analytical, thorough, genuine

superfluous
syn. excess, extra, spare, supererogatory, supernumerary, surplus
ant. valuable, necessary, intrinsic

supplement
syn. accessory, adjunct, appendage, appurtenance, attachment, complement
ant. basic, fundamental, integral

sympathetic
syn. empathetic, compassionate, condolatory, understanding, pitying, commiserative
ant. callous, merciless, uncaring

swift
syn. breakneck, expeditious, fleet, hurried, rapid, speedy
ant. delayed, slow, sluggish

Exercise

Choose the word which is CLOSEST in meaning to the given word.

1. Stun
   (a) defend (b) stupefy (c) cleave (d) splinter
2. Shabby
   (a) bleak (b) cagey (c) trivial (d) decrepit
3. Savour
   (a) imagine (b) relish (c) stupor (d) suffocate

Choose the word which is MOST SIMILAR in meaning to the underlined word in the given sentence.

4. The Principal decided to take <u>stern</u> action against the defaulters.
   (a) precipitant (b) firm (c) lenient (d) rustic
5. Sumedha is a <u>staunch</u> supporter of feminism.
   (a) static (b) dauntless (c) steadfast (d) virile

Choose the word which is OPPOSITE in meaning to the given word.

6. Solitary
   (a) reticent (b) lonesome (c) sociable (d) cerebral
7. Swift
   (a) expeditious (b) sluggish (c) intrinsic (d) stunned
8. Supplement
   (a) adjunct (b) thorough (c) integral (d) redundant

Choose the word which is MOST OPPOSITE in meaning to the underlined word in the given sentence.

9. Rajesh Khanna was a <u>spontaneous</u> actor.
   (a) nervous (b) artificial (c) conformist (d) spectacular
10. Many employees in the company have become <u>slack</u>.
    (a) lax (b) lean (c) active (d) stealthy

T - U

tactless
syn. clumsy, gauche, impolitic, maladroit, brash, undiplomatic
ant. discreet, thoughtful, refined

talkative
syn. chatty, conversational, garrulous, loquacious, talky, voluble
ant. quiet, reserved, uncommunicative

tally
syn. enumerate, reckon, score, conform, correspond, harmonise
ant. differ, deviate, contrast

tame
syn. domesticate, moderate, soften, subdue, tone down, bust
ant. arouse, incite, stimulate

taunt
syn. gibe, insult, jeer, scoff, twit, banter
ant. compliment, praise, respect

tease
syn. annoy, bait, beleaguer, beset, pester, torment
ant. appease, mollify, gladden

tedious
syn. dreary, humdrum, monotonous, stuffy, weary, dry
ant. entertaining, exciting, interesting

tempting
syn. bewitching, enchanting, enticing, fascinating, winsome, alluring
ant. repulsive, revolting, disgusting

tender
syn. gentle, mild, soft, delicate, dainty, frail
ant. hard, rough, tough

terrorise
syn. alarm, frighten, panic, scare, startle, terrify
ant. assuage, assure, help

thorny
syn. prickly, spiny, thistly, nettlesome, barbed, stingy
ant. dull, smooth, soothing

thorough
syn. exhaustive, intensive, arrant, outright, downright, unmitigated
ant. partial, superficial, unfinished

thrifty
syn. canny, chary, frugal, prudent, sparing, economical
ant. extravagant, spendthrift, wasteful

thrilling
syn. electrifying, exhilarating, moving, stimulating, exciting, uplifting
ant. depressing, discouraging, upsetting

tidy
syn. orderly, spruce, taut, uncluttered, moderate, snug
ant. chaotic, messy, sloppy

toil
syn. labour, strain, strive, travail, plod, trudge
ant. laze, skip, rest

tolerant
syn. liberal, progressive, broad-minded, lenient, merciful, lax
ant. prejudiced, biased, disapproving

transparent
syn. crystalline, limpid, lucid, see-through, pellucid, vaporous
ant. opaque, cloudy, blocked

treaty
syn. accord, agreement, concord, convention, pact, bond
ant. disagreement, discord, disunity

tremendous
syn. enormous, gigantic, massive, mighty, monumental, marvellous
ant. insignificant, tiny, petty

tribute
syn. commendation, compliment, congratulation, salute, salvo, testimonial
ant. accusation, criticism, blame

tricky
syn. crafty, cunning, foxy, guileful, scheming, wily
ant. naïve, ingenuous, unassuming

triumph
syn. conquest, victory, win, exultation, jubilation, success
ant. defeat, forfeit, failure

ugly
syn. hideous, unsightly, horrid, roiled, rugged, cranky
ant. lovely, pleasing, attractive

ultimate
syn. underlying, utmost, transcendent, unsurpassable, fundamental, essential
ant. preliminary, trivial, auxiliary

undue
syn. exorbitant, excessive, inordinate, improper, inapt, forbidden
ant. moderate, reasonable, sensible

unearth
syn. dig, uncover, ferret, excavate, reveal, ascertain
ant. bury, conceal, hide

uniformity
syn. analogy, comparison, correspondence, resemblance, harmony, similarity
ant. discord, disagreement, difference

unify
syn. coalesce, conjoin, conjugate, consolidate, couple, meld
ant. disjoin, disperse, separate

unique
syn. singular, solitary, matchless, peerless, exemplary, unrivaled
ant. commonplace, usual, regular

universal
syn. cosmic, global, pandemic, planetary, ubiquitous, generic
ant. confined, local, partial

upset
syn. overthrow, topple, derange, unsettle, disarray, disrupt
ant. organise, arrange, ready

urge
syn. insist, press, appeal, call, demand, plead
ant. answer, reply, protest

urgent
syn. dire, emergent, exigent, importune, insistent, persistent
ant. moderate, unimportant, usual

usual
syn. average, common, general, ordinary, typical, wonted
ant. abnormal, atypical, irregular

Exercise

Choose the word which is CLOSEST in meaning to the given word.

1. Tame
(a) incite (b) domesticate (c) deviate (d) barter

2. Urge
(a) plod (b) plead (c) conjugate (d) elaborate

3. Tolerant
(a) pellucid (b) exemplary (c) lenient (d) prejudiced

Choose the word which is MOST SIMILAR in meaning to the underlined word in the given sentence.

4. The actor unearthed the secret of staying fit.
(a) concealed (b) denounced (c) stressed (d) revealed

5. Rashmi was given the tedious job of handling pamphlets to visitors.
(a) monotonous (b) exciting (c) adjucating (d) forensic

Choose the word which is OPPOSITE in meaning to the given word.

6. Unify
(a) conjoin (b) disarray (c) disperse (d) ascertain

7. Testify
(a) beleaguer (b) avenge (c) support (d) deny

8. Tidy
(a) taut (b) messy (c) crystalline (d) liberal

Choose the word which is MOST OPPOSITE in meaning to the underlined word in the given sentence.

9. The ultimate aim is to lead a healthy life.
(a) reasonable (b) ubiquitous (c) preliminary (d) peerless

10. Sakshi was terrorised on seeing a monkey in her room.
(a) assuaged (b) startled (c) revolted (d) panicked

V - Z

vacant
syn. empty, void, idle, inane, vacuous, otiose
ant. full, occupied, overflowing

vague
syn. inexplicit, nebulous, obscure, bleary, fuzzy, unresolved
ant. certain, definite, clear

vain
syn. futile, hollow, conceited, egoistic, narcissistic, otiose
ant. modest, diffident, useful

valiant
syn. courageous, doughty, gallant, heroic, intrepid, mettlesome
ant. cowardly, timid, weak

valid
syn. cogent, just, authentic, authoritative, convincing, credible
ant. unsound, unacceptable, invalid

valour
syn. courage, fortitude, gallantry, intrepidity, pluckiness, valiance
ant. cowardice, timidity, meekness

vanish
syn. disappear, evanesce, evaporate, fade, exit, dematerialise
ant. appear, arrive, come

variable
syn. alterable, mutable, capricious, fickle, ticklish, volatile
ant. steady, fixed, constant

vast
syn. enormous, giant, immense, heroic, monstrous, walloping
ant. bounded, limited, little

versatile
syn. all-round, multifaceted, protean, adaptable, ambidextrous, resourceful
ant. inflexible, limited, nonconforming

veteran
syn. experienced, skilled, seasoned, adept, expert, hardened
ant. amateur, inexperienced, greenhorn

vibrant
syn. mettlesome, vivacious, peppery, spirited, resonant, sparkling
ant. colourless, dull, dispirited

victimise
syn. bilk, cheat, defraud, gull, mulct, swindle
ant. assist, help, assist

vigilant
syn. alert, observant, open-eyed, wakeful, wary, watchful
ant. indiscreet, negligent, inattentive

vigour
syn. bounce, spirit, liveliness, verve, vim, energy
ant. lethargy, weakness, enervation

violate
syn. breach, contravene, infringe, transgress, flout, ravish
ant. obey, observe, comply

visionary
syn. farsighted, chimerical, delusive, illusive, fanciful, notional
ant. practical, real, realistic

vital
syn. animate, robust, sturdy, vigorous, fundamental, integral
ant. trivial, insignificant, petty

vivid
syn. bright, colourful, flamboyant, graphic, expressive, meaningful
ant. dull, inexpressive, vague

voluntary
syn. willing, spontaneous, unforced, uncompensated, deliberate, unintended
ant. obligatory, forced, involuntary

vulgar
syn. humble, ignoble, mean, boorish, crass, bawdy
ant. decent, inoffensive, polite

wayward
syn. aberrant, balky, capricious, erratic, fickle, forward
ant. controllable, manageable, disciplined

weaken
syn. decline, degenerate, fade, languish, sink, wane
ant. strengthen, boost, build

weld
syn. bond, combine, fix, join, solder, unite
ant. disconnect, separate, detach

whimsical
syn. arbitrary, capricious, freakish, mercurial, temperamental, ticklish
ant. behaving, sensible, reasonable

wicked
syn. evil, iniquitous, reprobate, malignant, spiteful, venomous
ant. decent, moral, nice

widen
syn. broaden, expand, extend, augment, enlarge, stretch
ant. cramp, narrow, restrict

widespread
syn. all-inclusive, comprehensive, expansive, extensive, sweeping, far-reaching
ant. concentrated, local, narrow

witch
syn. enchantress, sorceress, beldam, crone, siren, temptress
ant. disenchanting, repulsive, disgusting

withdraw
syn. remove, retract, draw in, shove off, abjure, disengage
ant. remain, fill, deposit

withhold
syn. abstain, forbear, hold, retain, reserve, refrain
ant. release, let go, free

witty
syn. comedic, facetious, humorous, jocular, scintillating, sparkling
ant. serious, grim, pensive

wordy
syn. verbal, diffuse, discursive, rambling, loquacious, prolix
ant. concise, restrained, subdued

zeal
syn. ardour, enthusiasm, fervor, passion, intentness, alacrity
ant. apathy, indifference, lethargy

zigzag
syn. crinkled, crooked, fluctuating, inclined, meandering, transverse
ant. straight, linear, plain

Exercise

Choose the word which is CLOSEST in meaning to the given word.

1. Valiant
   (a) egoistic (b) timid (c) heroic (d) honest
2. Zeal
   (a) fervour (b) apathy (c) meekness (d) valiance
3. Wayward
   (a) boorish (b) spiteful (c) capricious (d) expansive

Choose the word which is MOST SIMILAR in meaning to the underlined word in the given sentence.

4. Sonam is <u>witty</u> and charming.
   (a) rambling (b) dull
   (c) bold (d) amusing
5. It lists five <u>versatile</u> herbs that can be used to cure many ailments.
   (a) flexible (b) wild (c) limpid (d) gifted

Choose the word which is OPPOSITE in meaning to the given word.

6. Vigilant
   (a) wakeful (b) robust (c) indiscreet (d) insipid
7. Voluntary
   (a) obligatory (b) spontaneous (c) erroneous (d) crass
8. Withhold
   (a) forbear (b) restrain (c) release (d) abstain

Choose the word which is MOST OPPOSITE in meaning to the underlined word in the given sentence.

9. Good communication skills are <u>vital</u> for success.
   (a) trivial (b) fundamental (c) illusive (d) impudent
10. General Suman was decorated for <u>valour</u> in the Iraq war.
    (a) pluck (b) fortitude
    (c) preparedness (d) timidity

ANSWERS
to all the
Essential Exercises

A	1 (c)	2 (d)	3 (c)	4 (a)	5 (b)	6 (d)	7 (a)	8 (a)	9 (b)	10 (d)
	11 (c)	12 (d)	13 (b)	14 (a)						
B	1 (d)	2 (c)	3 (c)	4 (a)	5 (b)	6 (c)	7 (b)	8 (b)	9 (c)	10 (c)
C	1 (a)	2 (a)	3 (a)	4 (c)	5 (a)	6 (d)	7 (c)	8 (d)	9 (d)	10 (b)
	11 (b)	12 (d)	13 (d)	14 (b)						
D	1 (d)	2 (b)	3 (a)	4 (b)	5 (b)	6 (b)	7 (b)	8 (b)	9 (c)	10 (b)
E	1 (a)	2 (b)	3 (c)	4 (d)	5 (d)	6 (c)	7 (a)	8 (c)	9 (c)	10 (b)
	11 (a)	12 (c)	13 (a)	14 (a)						
F	1 (a)	2 (b)	3 (d)	4 (c)	5 (d)	6 (c)	7 (c)	8 (b)	9 (d)	10 (b)
G - H	1 (b)	2 (b)	3 (c)	4 (a)	5 (b)	6 (a)	7 (c)	8 (a)	9 (b)	10 (c)
	11 (c)	12 (d)	13 (d)	14 (a)						
I - K	1 (a)	2 (d)	3 (b)	4 (b)	5 (c)	6 (a)	7 (d)	8 (a)	9 (c)	10 (a)
L - M	1 (a)	2 (d)	3 (b)	4 (c)	5 (d)	6 (b)	7 (a)	8 (c)	9 (d)	10 (b)
N - O	1 (d)	2 (a)	3 (c)	4 (b)	5 (d)	6 (a)	7 (d)	8 (a)	9 (b)	10 (c)
P - Q	1 (b)	2 (a)	3 (c)	4 (d)	5 (d)	6 (a)	7 (c)	8 (d)	9 (a)	10 (b)
R	1 (a)	2 (c)	3 (d)	4 (b)	5 (b)	6 (a)	7 (c)	8 (d)	9 (b)	10 (a)
S	1 (b)	2 (d)	3 (b)	4 (b)	5 (c)	6 (c)	7 (b)	8 (a)	9 (b)	10 (c)
T - U	1 (b)	2 (b)	3 (c)	4 (d)	5 (a)	6 (c)	7 (d)	8 (b)	9 (c)	10 (a)
V - Z	1 (c)	2 (a)	3 (c)	4 (d)	5 (d)	6 (c)	7 (a)	8 (c)	9 (a)	10 (d)

PART II

INTERMEDIATE

A

abash
syn. humiliate, humble, denigrate, debase, mortify, reduce
ant. exalt, upgrade, dignify

abate
syn. diminish, dwindle, ebb, lessen, subside, decline
ant. augment, enhance, intensify

abhor
syn. despise, detest, loathe, abominate, dislike, execrate
ant. love, yearn, admire

abide
syn. accept, tolerate, stand for, withstand, bear, endure
ant. shun, quit, migrate

abort
syn. terminate, end, abandon, call off, stop, halt
ant. continue, keep, sustain

abscond
syn. decamp, escape, flee, break out, run away, get away
ant. remain, stay, emerge

abstain
syn. refrain, withhold, desist, withdraw, go without, curb
ant. persist, pursue, offer

accessible
syn. handy, nearby, available, reachable, manageable, convenient
ant. restricted, inaccessible, limited

accessory
syn. ancillary, assistant, auxiliary, collateral, subsidiary, supportive
ant. principal, unsupportive, main

accommodating
syn. agreeable, obliging, complaisant, willing, cooperating, helpful
ant. alienating, disobliging, estranged

accomplice
syn. assistant, accessory, collaborator, partner, abettor, coconspirator
ant. adversary, enemy, opponent

accord
syn. agreement, treaty, settlement, deal, concord, pact
ant. disagreement, denial, refusal

acquaint
syn. inform, apprise, notify, familiarise, enlighten, tell
ant. conceal, hide, withhold

acquit
syn. abso!ve, vindicate, free, release, exonerate, exculpate
ant. convict, sentence, damn

acme
syn. peak, top, zenith, pinnacle, culmination, apogee
ant. bottom, nadir, minimum

acrid
syn. bitter, harsh, sour, vitriolic, acerbic, caustic
ant. delicious, savory, complimentary

acumen
syn. insight, wisdom, expertise, shrewdness, sagacity, astuteness
ant. ineptness, stupidity, ignorance

adamant
syn. obstinate, obdurate, relentless, unyielding, steadfast, stubborn
ant. compliant, flexible, lax

adapt
syn. acclimatise, adjust, conform, reconcile, suit, alter
ant. misfit, differ, dislocate

adjacent
syn. close, nearby, next, contiguous, bordering, flanking
ant. distant, remote, apart

admonish
syn. rebuke, reprimand, reproach, chide, reprove, scold
ant. applaud, praise, approve

adore
syn. idolise, revere, venerate, worship, glorify, exalt
ant. abhor, despise, loathe

adulterate
syn. debase, pollute, taint, impure, soil, infect,
ant. cleanse, filter, purify

adverse
syn. opposing, unfavourable, contrary, hostile, antagonistic, confrontational
ant. favourable, propitious, advantageous

affluent
syn. moneyed, rich, wealthy, prosperous, well-off, well-to-do
ant. needy, impoverished, destitute

aggravate
syn. enhance, intensify, augment, annoy, bother, pester
ant. appease, mollify, relieve

agile
syn. brisk, facile, nimble, swift, sprightly, supple
ant. clumsy, stiff, brittle

agitate
syn. protest, stir, disturb, churn, perturb, ruffle
ant. quiet, lull, soothe

agony
syn. anguish, distress, misery, torment, woe, affliction
ant. peace, comfort, happiness

aid
syn. abet, boost, help, succour, facilitate, sustain
ant. block , hinder, obstruct

alight
syn. land, get off, descend, dismount, perch, settle
ant. board, take on, get on

alike
syn. analogous, comparable, identical, similar, uniform, equivalent
ant. distinct, diverse, dissimilar

allege
syn. assert, claim, charge, contend, declare, maintain
ant. contradict, deny, disagree

alleviate
syn. allay, assuage, ease, mitigate, relieve, palliate
ant. aggravate, intensify, magnify

allure
syn. entice, seduce, tempt, draw, charm, lure
ant. repel, reject, deter

aloof
syn. reticent, solitary, withdrawn, detached, snooty, standoffish
ant. friendly, sociable, concerned

alter
syn. change, modify, vary, amend, revise, rework
ant. maintain, preserve, retain

amateur
syn. dabbler, unprofessional, slapdash, shoddy, inept, clumsy
ant. professional, expert, proficient

amenity
syn. facility, convenience, comfort, cordiality, warmth, geniality
ant. inconvenience, misbehaviour, disruption

ambiguous
syn. vague, obscure, uncertain, cloudy, nebulous, hazy
ant. explicit, lucid, clear

analogous
syn. alike, comparable, corresponding, akin, consonant, parallel
ant. disparate, dissimilar, unlike

anguish
syn. distress, wretchedness, suffering, grief, sorrow, angst
ant. contentment, solace, happiness

animosity
syn. acrimony, antipathy, malevolence, bitterness, malice, rancour
ant. congeniality, harmony, benevolence

annex
syn. affix, append, attach, capture, seize, appropriate
ant. detach, relinquish, leave off

annoy
syn. exasperate, fret, irk, infuriate, upset, enrage
ant. gratify, gladden, delight

anomalous
syn. aberrant, deviant, jarring, inconsistent, unusual, atypical
ant. conforming, regular, standard

apex
syn. crest, crown, peak, summit, pinnacle, zenith
ant. nadir, lowest point, zero level

apparent
syn. distinct, obvious, evident, perceptible, visible, outward
ant. hazy, indistinct, vague

appease
syn. assuage, conciliate, mollify, pacify, placate, soothe
ant. aggravate, incite, provoke

applaud
syn. cheer, acclaim, commend, laud, root, compliment
ant. boo, hiss, disparage

apprise
syn. acquaint, advise, inform, enlighten, educate, notify
ant. depreciate, undervalue, mystify

apt
syn. appropriate, befitting, felicitous, pertinent, inclined, competent
ant. improper, gauche, maladroit

arbitrary
syn. random, illogical, capricious, indiscriminate, haphazard, discretionary
ant. consistent, logical, reasonable

archaic
syn. ancient, antique, hoary, prehistoric, outdated, dowdy
ant. contemporary, modern, recent

assert
syn. affirm, avow, contend, proclaim, stress, emphasise
ant. deny, reject, refuse

Exercise

Choose the word which is CLOSEST in meaning to the given word.

1. Abstain
   (a) intensity (b) interact (c) desist (d) hate
2. Abhor
   (a) debase (b) subside (c) debar (d) abominate
3. Affluent
   (a) prosperous (b) quick (c) prominent (d) handy

Choose the word which is MOST SIMILAR in meaning to the underlined word in the given sentence.

4. Rashi was trying to <u>appease</u> her friend after they had an argument.
   (a) harass (b) mollify (c) pursue (d) detract
5. The society lacked the basic <u>amenities</u>.
   (a) networks (b) safety (c) conveniences (d) novelties

Choose the word which is OPPOSITE in meaning to the given word.

6. Allure
   (a) repel (b) assure (c) pacify (d) decline
7. Anguish
   (a) angst (b) appreciation (c) solace (d) reprimand
8. Ambiguous
   (a) anonymous (b) amiable (c) hazy (d) lucid

Choose the word which is MOST OPPOSITE in meaning to the underlined word in the given sentence.

9. Fog <u>aggravated</u> the situation of high pallution levels in Delhi.
   (a) differ (b) appease (c) augmented (d) reprimand
10. The dish had a very <u>acid</u> taste.
   (a) harsh (b) savoury (c) severe (d) putrid

B

baleful

syn. deadly, evil, malevolent, harmful, noxious, sinister
ant. auspicious, favourable, promising

bane

syn. destruction, devastation, havoc, ruin, curse, evil
ant. blessing, advantage, fortune

banish

syn. deport, exile, expatriate, ostracise, dismiss, dispel
ant. allow, keep, welcome

bare

syn. unclad, naked, empty, blank, vacant, shorn
ant. clothed, robed, covered

barren

syn. childless, unfruitful, unproductive, futile, useless, devoid
ant. fertile, productive, useful

batter

syn. assail, assault, beat, drub, hammer, pound
ant. aid, assist, guard

belittle

syn. decry, denigrate, derogate, disparage, downgrade, slight
ant. praise, value, exaggerate

beloved

syn. darling, dear, loved, precious, intimate, cherished
ant. despised, disliked, hated

benediction

syn. blessing, thanks, favour, gratitude, approbation, grace
ant. anathema, disapproval, criticism

bicker

syn. argue, contend, dispute, quarrel, spat, tiff
ant. agree, concede, discuss

bizarre

syn. curious, eccentric, freakish, odd, queer, strange
ant. normal, reasonable, usual

blatant

syn. brazen, shameless, unabashed, boisterous, clamorous, vociferous
ant. quiet, subtle, inconspicuous

bleak
syn. dismal, gloomy, sombre, joyless, cheerless, dreary
ant. bright, pleasant, sunny

blemish
syn. bug, defect, flaw, imperfection, shortcoming, blot
ant. adornment, embellishment, decoration

blossom
syn. bloom, flourish, thrive, flower, burgeon, succeed
ant. fade, shrink, shrivel

bony
syn. lanky, skinny, slender, lean, slim, thin
ant. fat, heavy, plump

boom
syn. bang, blast, roar, thunder, barrage, rumble
ant. collapse, failure, loss

boon
syn. advantage, benefit, blessing, favour, gain, profit
ant. disadvantage, drawback, handicap

bountiful
syn. ample, generous, plentiful, substantial, voluminous, abundant
ant. insufficient, meager, sparse

brag
syn. boast, bluster, crow, gloat, praise, exaggerate
ant. be modest, be quiet, deprecate

breach
syn. break, gap, hole, perforation, rupture, violation
ant. bridge, connect, join

breathtaking
syn. amazing, exciting, magnificent, stunning, impressive, thrilling
ant. disgusting, ugly, dull

brevity
syn. crispness, conciseness, economy, succinctness, transience, condensation
ant. lengthiness, longevity, permanence

bulldoze
syn. flatten, raze, shove, thrust, crash, decimate
ant. build, construct, create

bustle
syn. dash, hurry, hustle, rush, trot, zoom
ant. laziness, relaxation, delay

Exercise

Choose the word which is CLOSEST in meaning to the given word.

1. Bane
   (a) havoc (b) blank
   (c) unproductive (d) assault

2. Brag
   (a) gloat (b) sombre
   (c) deprecate (d) roar

3. Benediction
   (a) gratitude (b) devastation
   (c) profit (d) concurrence

Choose the word which is MOST SIMILAR in meaning to the underlined word in the given sentence.

4. The hostage episode <u>blemished</u> his reputation.
   (a) escalated (b) proved
   (c) catapulted (d) tarnished

5. Isn't it <u>bizarre</u> to wear such a dress on this occasion?
   (a) clamorous (b) unabashed
   (c) blatant (d) queer

Choose the word which is OPPOSITE in meaning to the given word.

6. Bulldoze
   (a) flatten (b) construct
   (c) raze (d) repair

7. Boon
   (a) generosity (b) inadequate
   (c) plenty (d) drawback

Choose the word which is MOST OPPOSITE in meaning to the underlined word in the given sentence.

8. Samira was blessed with a <u>bony</u> girl on Tuesday.
   (a) plump (b) sordid
   (c) weak (d) premature

9. Vikas <u>breached</u> the terms of the contract.
   (a) honoured (b) connected
   (c) tore (d) created

10. To put it <u>bluntly</u>, we cannot invite him.
    (a) usually (b) harshly
    (c) slowly (d) indirectly

C

cajole
syn. blandish, coax, honey, wheedle, persuade, convince
ant. bully, force, repel

candid
syn. downright, forthright, honest, ingenuous, plainspoken, straight
ant. deceitful, devious, crafty

captivate
syn. beguile, bewitch, harm, allure, enchant, entrance
ant. disgust, disillusion, repulse

cessation
syn. closure, completion, end, termination, finish, discontinuation
ant. beginning, commencement, inception

chaste
syn. decent, modest, nice, pure, virgin, virtuous
ant. corrupt, lewd, wanton

chivalrous
syn. courtly, gallant, courageous, gracious, knightly, stately
ant. cowardly, frightened, humble

circuitous
syn. meandrous, circular, devious, indirect, oblique, tortuous
ant. straight, direct, in-line

coax
syn. blandish, cajole, honey, wheedle, persuade, convince
ant. bully, force, repel

coherent
syn. congruous, consistent, logical, meaningful, lucid, orderly
ant. illogical, irrational, unorganised

colloquial
syn. chatty, confabulatory, conversational, informal, demotic, popular
ant. formal, standard, stilted

colossal
syn. behemoth, elephantine, gigantic, immense, jumbo, massy
ant. small, teeny, tiny

combative
syn. bellicose, belligerent, contentious, hostile, quarrelsome, scrappy
ant. agreeable, compromising, peaceful

compendious
syn. brief, concise, laconic, succinct, summary, terse
ant. enlarged, unabridged, lengthened

complacent
syn. conceited, satisfied, content, serene, gratified, smug
ant. dissatisfied, discontented, concerned

comply
syn. abide by, adhere, conform, follow, obey, observe
ant. obstruct, prevent, block

concede
syn. acknowledge, admit, avow, confess, grant, accord
ant. contradict, repudiate, reject

concord
syn. accord, harmony, rapport, tune, symphony, pact
ant. discord, disunity, disagreement

condone
syn. excuse, forgive, pardon, remit, ignore, overlook
ant. censure, condemn, punish

confine
syn. circumscribe, limit, restrict, bar, closet, imprison
ant. free, liberate, release

confiscate
syn. grab, seize, snatch, annex, usurp, impound
ant. give, offer, release

congregate
syn. assemble, convene, cluster, muster, summon, gather
ant. divide, scatter, separate

constraint
syn. coercion, duress, circumscription, confinement, restriction, inhibition
ant. freedom, release, liberty

content
syn. gratified, happy, satisfied, complacent, fulfilled, pleased
ant. depressed, upset, wanting

conventional
syn. orthodox, recognised, sanctioned, traditional, formal, accepted
ant. exotic, unusual, strange

cordial
syn. affable, amiable, congenial, pleasant, sociable, warm
ant. hostile, indifferent, inhospitable

counterfeit
syn. bogus, fake, fraudulent, phony, spurious, sham
ant. genuine, real, true

cowardice
syn. cravenness, dastardliness, funk, pusillanimity, unmanliness, timidity
ant. bravery, courage, fearlessness

credible
syn. believable, plausible, authentic, convincing, true, trustworthy
ant. implausible, unlikely, improbable

crooked
syn. bending, curved, corrupt, venal, dishonest, mercenary
ant. straight, honest, simple

cumbersome
syn. heavy, lumpish, ponderous, hefty, inconvenient, unhandy
ant. graceful, adroit, elegant

Exercise

Choose the word which is CLOSEST in meaning to the given word.

1. Cajole
   (a) bewitch (b) terminate
   (c) coax (d) harass

2. Comply
   (a) adhere (b) blandish
   (c) remit (d) arow

3. Circuitous
   (a) knightly (b) oblique
   (c) downright (d) lucid

4. Crooked
   (a) dishonest (b) elegant
   (c) unhandy (d) straight

Choose the word which is MOST SIMILAR in meaning to the underlined word in the given sentence.

5. Is this story credible?
   (a) ponderous (b) authentic
   (c) funk (d) courage

6. Somit was captivated by her pleasant manners.
(a) repulsed (b) wheedled
(c) incited (d) enchanted

7. The President was in a combative mood today.
(a) belligerent (b) pregnant
(c) sombre (d) gratified

Choose the word which is OPPOSITE in meaning to the given word.

8. Cumbersome
(a) venal (b) plausible
(c) graceful (d) ponderous

9. Convential
(a) consummate (b) phony
(c) exotic (d) traditional

10. Condone
(a) closure (b) censure
(c) debar (d) circumscribe

11. Cowardice
(a) brief (b) adhere
(c) bravery` (d) observe

Choose the word which is MOST OPPOSITE in meaning to the underlined word in the given sentence.

12. The cordial invitation has been sent to you.
(a) hostile (b) coax
(c) exotic (d) scatter

13. Where are we supposed to congregate ?
(a) scatter (b) dismantle
(c) impound (d) stand

14. Rashmi conceded even before the votes were counted.
(a) confers (b) granted
(c) remitted (d) won

D

daredevil

syn. bold, daring, enterprising, adventurous, audacious, courageous
ant. cautious, meek, prudent

dazzle

syn. awe, overpower, stupefy, astonish, strike, surprise
ant. bore, calm, expect

dawdle

syn. loiter, linger, lag, fiddle, procrastinate, delay
ant. hasten, hurry, rush

deface

syn. contort, disfigure, distort, tarnish, trash, spoil
ant. adorn, decorate, mend

defame

syn. asperse, malign, slander, slur, vilify, backbite
ant. commend, praise, compliment

default

syn. failure, neglect, omission, delinquency, dereliction, error
ant. advantage, perfection, success

defend

syn. guard, protect, safeguard, preserve, shield, ward
ant. attack, quit, relinquish

defer

syn. adjourn, delay, block, hinder, prolong, procrastinate
ant. expedite, forward, hasten

deference

syn. honour, respect, compliance, amenability, submission, tractability
ant. disobedience, impoliteness, noncompliance

defiance

syn. challenge, contempt, resistance, contumacy, recalcitrance, provocation
ant. regard, respect, submission

degradation

syn. demotion, humiliation, reduction, abasement, debasement, mortification
ant. elevation, upgrade, promotion

deliberate
syn. intentional, purposeful, voluntary, calculated, considered, premeditated
ant. indeterminate, chance, unintentional

deplete
syn. drain, exhaust, impoverish, sap, use up, desiccate
ant. add, augment, fill

depreciate
syn. devalue, downgrade, denigrate, derogate, belittle, decry
ant. fain, raise, increase

derogatory
syn. disparaging, slighting, detractive, humiliating, disdainful
ant. appreciative, complimentary, flattering

descent
syn. decline, fall, downfall, slide, ancestry, lineage
ant. ascent, elevation, upgrade

despot
syn. dictator, totalitarian, authoritarian, tyrant, oppressor, martinet
ant. democrat, subordinate, underling

deter
syn. discourage, dissuade, divert, block, debar, obstruct
ant. encourage, promote, stimulate

detest
syn. abhor, abominate, despise, execrate, hate, loathe
ant. adore, cherish, like

detrimental
syn. deleterious, harmful, evil, adverse, inimical, pernicious
ant. assisting, beneficial, advantageous

devise
syn. concoct, hatch, fabricate, formulate, contrive, forge
ant. destroy, ruin, destruct

dexterous
syn. adroit, deft, artful, facile, skilful, nimble
ant. awkward, clumsy, inept

discrepancy
syn. difference, disparity, divergence, gap, inconsistency, incongruity
ant. concurrence, parity, consistency

discrete
syn. distinct, separate, singular, particular, individual, single
ant. attached, combined, joined

discriminate
syn. differentiate, discern, distinguish, mark, singularise, characterise
ant. associate, connect, group

disgrace
syn. humiliation, ignominy, disrepute, opprobrium, dishonour, shame
ant. esteem, honour, regard

dismal
syn. gloomy, depressing, sad, bleak, desolate, sombre
ant. bright, sunny, pleasant

dismantle
syn. disassemble, dismount, pulverise, rase, tear, wreck
ant. assemble, construct, build

disparity
syn. discrepancy, divergence, difference, gap, incongruity, inconsistency
ant. equality, similarity, sameness

dispel
syn. banish, dismiss, disperse, dissipate, repel, scatter
ant. accumulate, garner, recall

dissuade
syn. deter, discourage, divert, disincline, remonstrate, derail
ant. induce, advise, persuade

distress
syn. affliction, anguish, agony, angst, anxiety, concern
ant. comfort, happiness, pleasure

dogged
syn. bullheaded, mulish, obstinate, tenacious, headstrong, wilful
ant. willing, weak, yielding

dogmatic
syn. authoritarian, bossy, dictatorial, overbearing, imperious, masterful
ant. amenable, flexible, submissive

dormant
syn. inactive, latent, quiescent, abeyant, inert, inoperative
ant. active, lively, bustling

draconian
syn. brutal, cruel, oppressive, rough, severe, drastic
ant. kind, merciful, sympathetic

dreary
syn. bleak, dismal, gloomy, dark, sombre, monotonous
ant. bright, pleasant, cheerful

drudgery

syn. labour, toil, grind, chore, travail, workout
ant. entertainment, fun, pastime

dumbfound

syn. boggle, flabbergast, floor, stagger, amaze, overwhelm
ant. explicate, explain, clear up

dwindle

syn. abate, diminish, decrease, drain, taper, lessen
ant. enhance, intensify, magnify

Exercise

Choose the word which is CLOSEST in meaning to the given word.

1. Deplete
   (a) hinder (b) resist (c) abase (d) exhaust
2. Descent
   (a) demotion (b) dereliction (c) slide (d) vilification
3. Dexterous
   (a) detractive (b) deft (c) obtrusive (d) inmical

Choose the word which is MOST SIMILAR in meaning to the underlined word in the given sentence.

4. Why did you <u>defer</u> your appointment with the lawyer?
   (a) prolong (b) forward (c) impoverish (d) cancel
5. The children were <u>dawdling</u> to school.
   (a) hurrying (b) playing (c) lingering (d) talking

Choose the word which is OPPOSITE in meaning to the given word.

6. Disgrace
   (a) comfort (b) esteem (c) parity (d) divergence
7. Distress
   (a) comfort (b) bustle (c) regard (d) submission
8. Dissuade
   (a) banish (b) induce (c) discern (d) cherish

Choose the word which is MOST OPPOSITE in meaning to the underlined word in the given sentence.

9. There seems to be a <u>discrepancy</u> between press and radio reports.
   (a) incongruity (b) concurrence (c) ignomity (d) esteem
10. A number of investments in this bank have remained <u>dormant</u>.
    (a) inactive (b) stable (c) illegal (d) active

E

egotism
syn. pride, vanity, arrogance, boastfulness, immodesty, vainglory
ant. humility, meekness, servility

elaborate
syn. amplify, develop, enlarge, expand, expatiate, explain
ant. simplify, abridge, decipher

elated
syn. elevated, overjoyed, happy, cheerful, excited, stirred
ant. depressed, dejected, dismayed

elevate
syn. heightened, exalted, eloquent, noble, lofty, august
ant. condemned, denounced, humiliated

elicit
syn. draw, educe, evoke, summon, extract, bring out
ant. insert, repress, suppress

elite
syn. nobility, aristocracy, gentry, pick, quality, upper crust
ant. common, ordinary, mediocre

eloquent
syn. articulate, exalted, significant, meaningful, expressive, lofty
ant. dull, insignificant, meaningless

elucidate
syn. clarify, expound, illuminate, illustrate, explain, elucidate
ant. confuse, distract, obscure

elusive
syn. evasive, slippery, cagey, deceptive, baffling, intangible
ant. comprehensible, forthright, upright

emancipate
syn. discharge, free, liberate, release, loosen, spring
ant. hold, imprison, incarcerate

embittered
syn. acrimonious, bitter, rancorous, resentful, virulent, hard
ant. content, genial, pleasant

endeavour
syn. attempt, effort, exertion, pain, strain, struggle
ant. idleness, laziness, ease

endorse
syn. approve, authorise, consent, advocate, champion, recommend
ant. censure, reject, protest

enduring
syn. abiding, continuing, durable, lasting, persistent, permanent
ant. ephemeral, fleeting, transient

enervate
syn. attenuate, debilitate, weaken, undermine, unnerve, enfeeble
ant. energise, empower, invigorate

enigmatic
syn. mysterious, occult, puzzling, cabalistic, cryptic, arcane
ant. simple, plain, obvious

enmity
syn. animosity, antipathy, hostility, hatred, ill will, malice
ant. friendship, affinity, love

enthrall
syn. bewitch, charm, enchant, spellbind, mesmerise, rivet
ant. repel, bore, bother

entice
syn. allure, appeal, lure, seduce, tempt, pull
ant. dissuade, repulse, disgust

eradicate
syn. abolish, exterminate, extirpate, liquidate, uproot, purge
ant. establish, institute, fix

erode
syn. bite, corrode, wear, gnaw, consume, scour
ant. build, construct, fix

escalate
syn. aggrandise, amplify, burgeon, mount, proliferate, upsurge
ant. diminish, lower, weaken

esteem
syn. admiration, respect, appreciation, consideration, regard, favour
ant. abuse, ridicule, mock

eulogy
syn. acclamation, commendation, compliment, kudos, laudation, plaudit
ant. calumny, condemnation, criticism

evade

syn. avoid, dodge, fudge, circumvent, elude, eschew
ant. face, meet, confront

exertion

syn. application, endeavour, effort, pain, struggle, exercise
ant. idleness, laziness, relaxation

exhilarating

syn. bracing, refreshing, invigorating, stimulating, renewing, restorative
ant. agitating, depressing, boring

expedite

syn. accelerate, hasten, hurry, quicken, facilitate
ant. cease, hinder, halt

explicit

syn. categorical, definite, precise, specific, unambiguous, clear
ant. ambiguous, obscure, vague

exploit

syn. utilise, manipulate, actuate, abuse, maneuver, use
ant. cherish, revere, treasure

Exercise

Choose the word which is CLOSEST in meaning to the given word.

1. Escalate
(a) amplify (b) collaborate
(c) stack (d) purge

2. Enmity
(a) affinity (b) hostility
(c) gravity (d) brevity

3. Endeavour
(a) exertion (b) malice
(c) appeal (d) repeal

4. Exploit
(a) manipulate (b) genial
(c) strive (d) purge

Choose the word which is MOST SIMILAR in meaning to the underlined word in the given sentence.

5. The work should not be done in an <u>expedite</u> manner.
(a) effort (b) stimulating
(c) hurry (d) glib

6. Should students evade subjects they don't like?
(a) amplify (b) study
(c) avoid (d) detest

7. She has been talking explicitly about female hygiene.
(a) solemnly (b) shyly
(c) unknowingly (d) overtly

Choose the word which is OPPOSITE in meaning to the given word.

8. Elucidate
(a) confuse (b) illustrate
(c) liberate (d) strive

9. Embittered
(a) acrimonious (b) rile
(c) ambitious (d) content

10. Exhilarating
(a) boring (b) fearless
(c) stumble (d) viable

Choose the word which is MOST OPPOSITE in meaning to the underlined word in the given sentence.

11. Mr. Sharma is a man of esteem.
(a) respect (b) ridicule
(c) rivet (d) permanence

12. Hussain has an enigmatic personality.
(a) contemporary (b) obvious
(c) genial (d) cantankerous

13. One has to endure many things in one's life.
(a) criticise (b) praise
(c) resist (d) deal with

14. Raveena was elated on hearing her daughter's result.
(a) pestered (b) doubtful
(c) sad (d) worried

F

facile
syn. brisk, spry, nimble, slick, glib, deft
ant. arduous, laborious, profound

fainthearted
syn. chickenhearted, cowardly, craven, pusillanimous, gutless, unmanly
ant. brave, courageous, fearless

falter
syn. dither, stagger, waver, wobble, stumble, lurch
ant. persist, endure, maintain

fanatic
syn. extremist, radical, revolutionary, ultra, zealot, votary
ant. balanced, moderate, conservative

fatigued
syn. bleary, drained, exhausted, weary, worn-out, rundown
ant. lively, vivacious, refreshed

feasible
syn. possible, practicable, viable, workable, attainable, probable
ant. inconceivable, unreasonable, unlikely

feeble
syn. decrepit, fragile, frail, unsubstantial, flimsy, tenuous
ant. hardy, powerful, sound

felicitate
syn. commend, compliment, praise, honour, recommend, salute
ant. condemn, reject, criticise

fierce
syn. ferocious, inhuman, barbarous, intense, vehement, violent
ant. gentle, tender, tame

flabby
syn. flaccid, floppy, limp, drooping, sloppy, sagging
ant. firm, lean, slim

fleeting
syn. momentary, ephemeral, temporal, transient, fugacious, transitory
ant. long-lasting, permanent, staying

flimsy
syn. frail, infirm, feeble, incredible, unbelievable, unsubstantial
ant. sturdy, substantial, tough

flout
syn. break, defy, disobey, transgress, violate, refuse
ant. honour, respect, follow

foil
syn. balk, defeat, frustrate, thwart, checkmate, baffle
ant. abet, aid, assist

forbid
syn. ban, disallow, debar, inhibit, interdict, prohibit
ant. approve, authorise, sanction

forge
syn. beat, assemble, build, construct, mold, fake
ant. dismantle, raze, disjoint

formidable
syn. direful, arduous, scary, exacting, taxing, rigorous
ant. nice, light, easy

fracas
syn. affray, brawl, riot, broil, altercation, tumult
ant. harmony, calm, peace

fragile
syn. brittle, delicate, puny, weak, frail, unsubstantial
ant. durable, strong, firm

fragment
syn. scrap, shard, stub, crumb, iota, particle
ant. entirety, total, whole

frightful
syn. appalling, awful, dreadful, horrendous, direful, scary
ant. soothing, calming, encouraging

frugality
syn. economy, thrift, providence, moderation, parsimony, niggardliness
ant. generosity, lavishness, wastefulness

frustrate
syn. baffle, balk, checkmate, defeat, foil, stymie
ant. assist, facilitate, aid

fury
syn. ire, rage, wrath, ferocity, vehemence, violence
ant. calm, happiness, peace

fussy
syn. exacting, fastidious, finicky, meticulous, particular, squeamish
ant. careless, indiscriminate, undemanding

Exercise

Choose the word which is CLOSEST in meaning to the given word.

1. Feeble
   (a) frail (b) crave
   (c) deride (d) pugnacious

2. Falter
   (a) commend (b) stumble
   (c) trespass (d) thwart

Choose the word which is MOST SIMILAR in meaning to the underlined word in the given sentence.

3. Has Sunil <u>flouted</u> the rule?
   (a) drafted (b) obeyed
   (c) disregarded (d) sanctioned

4. Dalits were <u>forbidden</u> to visit the temples.
   (a) allowed (b) denied
   (c) advised (d) executed

5. What is this <u>fracas</u> all about?
   (a) battle (b) discussion
   (c) event (d) argument

Choose the word which is OPPOSITE in meaning to the given word.

6. Forge
   (a) dismantle (b) sanction
   (c) defy (d) trail

7. Fragment
   (a) part (b) subject
   (c) create (d) entirety

8. Frightful
   (a) approving (b) soothing
   (c) alluring (d) gaining

Choose the word which is MOST OPPOSITE in meaning to the underlined word in the given sentence.

9. Is Naman a <u>fussy</u> person?
   (a) fastidious (b) uncritical
   (c) feeble (d) reticent

10. Gaurav was <u>felicitated</u> in the literature meet.
    (a) appeased (b) condemned
    (c) pardoned (d) lauded

homage
syn. deference, honour, obeisance, esteem, reverence, tribute
ant. scorn, treachery, disloyalty

hospitable
syn. affable, warm, gracious, congenial, courteous, friendly
ant. alienating, estranged, rude

humbug
syn. charlatan, fake, fraud, impostor, phony, pretender
ant. genuine, truthful, original

humiliate
syn. abase, degrade, demean, humble, mortify, denigrate
ant. elevate, laud, praise

hypocrite
syn. pharisee, phony, charlatan, spurious, sham, pseudo
ant. genuine, real, sincere

hypothetical
syn. abstract, theoretical, conjectural, presumptive, suppositious, inferential
ant. factual, measured, proven

Exercise

Choose the word which is CLOSEST in meaning to the given word.

1. Gaudy
   (a) appalling (b) cranky
   (c) flagrant (d) garish

2. Hackneyed
   (a) banal (b) discerning
   (c) austere (d) flashy

3. Haughty
   (a) irresolute (b) intrepid
   (c) gleeful (d) overbearing

4. Hypothetical
   (a) fraud (b) sterile
   (c) launch (d) theoretical

Choose the word which is MOST SIMILAR in meaning to the underlined word in the given sentence.

5. Beware of those who are <u>hypocrite</u>.
   (a) factual (b) articulate
   (c) pseudo (d) edific

6. Kovid has a gluttonous appetite.
   (a) ravenous (b) moderate
   (c) egregious (d) abstract

7. She committed a grave mistake in her final exam.
   (a) frivolous (b) serious
   (c) ominous (d) tawdry

Choose the word which is OPPOSITE in meaning to the given word.

8. Grudge
   (a) rancour (b) growl
   (c) fondness (d) scorn

9. Homage
   (a) respect (b) disregard
   (c) animosity (d) regard

10. Gullible
   (a) astute (b) tributable
   (c) friendly (d) reckless

Choose the word which is MOST OPPOSITE in meaning to the underlined word in the given sentence.

11. The boy grumbled over not being given ice-cream.
   (a) praise (b) resolute
   (c) wavering (d) courteous

12. Freshers are usually hesitant in making friends with their seniors.
   (a) resolute (b) assorted
   (c) pendulous (d) wavering

13. Demonetisation hampered the progress of many industries.
   (a) shackled (b) vindicated
   (c) animated (d) facilitated

14. Vivekananda's voice galvanised many youngsters to realise their dreams.
   (a) enlisted (b) prodded
   (c) demotivated (d) deserted

I - K

illuminate
syn. lighten, clarify, elucidate, illustrate, enlighten, edify
ant. obscure, darken, cloud

illusive
syn. chimerical, deceptive, fallacious, hallucinatory, visionary, dreamlike
ant. real, factual, definite

immaculate
syn. spotless, perfect, stainless, unsullied, unsoiled, errorless
ant. foul, filthy, tainted

immerse
syn. dip, douse, submerge, soak, consume, engross
ant. dry, retrieve, surface

impair
syn. blemish, damage, tarnish, vitiate, flaw, mar
ant. mend, fix, heal

imperative
syn. pressing, urgent, obligatory, mandatory, emergent, requisite
ant. optional, voluntary, secondary

imposing
syn. grand, magnificent, princely, splendid, stately, noble
ant. drab, paltry, unimpressive

impotent
syn. powerless, inadequate, barren, weak, infertile, sterile
ant. productive, capable, strong

impulsive
syn. brash, hasty, reckless, slapdash, instinctive, spontaneous
ant. cautious, heedful, thoughtful

inarticulate
syn. dumb, mute, faltering, mum, voiceless, reticent
ant. communicative, effusive, articulate

inception
syn. beginning, commencement, inauguration, launch, onset, leadoff
ant. conclusion, end, finish

incessant
syn. ceaseless, interminable, eternal, everlasting, perpetual, relentless
ant. intermittent, interrupted, ceasing

incite
syn. excite, foment, impel, instigate, trigger, prod
ant. halt, dissuade, repress

inconsequential
syn. insignificant, trivial, petty, negligible, meager, irrelevant
ant. substantial, valuable, significant

incorporate
syn. integrate, embody, combine, weave, assimilate, merge
ant. exclude, divide, drop

incorrigible
syn. intractable, incurable, hardened, irreparable, hopeless, wanton
ant. manageable, obedient, reparable

indeed
syn. actually, certainly, genuinely, positively, truthfully, verily
ant. doubtfully, questionably, dubitably

indigenous
syn. aboriginal, native, endemic, ingrained, inherent, inbred
ant. alien, foreign, extrinsic

indiscriminate
syn. haphazard, random, unplanned, desultory, assorted, motley
ant. systematic, orderly, methodical

induce
syn. convince, persuade, effectuate, generate, trigger, bring about
ant. discourage, prevent, hinder

infamy
syn. notoriety, abomination, disrespect, ignominy, stigma, obloquy
ant. dignity, virtue, righteousness

infatuate
syn. allure, enamour, beguile, bewitch, fascinate, enthrall
ant. disillusion, repel, disgust

infer
syn. conclude, deduce, deduct, draw, guess, speculate
ant. doubt, misinterpret, misunderstand

infuriate
syn. anger, enrage, incense, provoke, aggravate, exasperate
ant. please, soothe, pacify

ingenious
syn. creative, innovative, inventive, original, resourceful, novel
ant. inept, dumb, customary

inherent
syn. elemental, inbred, innate, intrinsic, ingrained, congenital
ant. acquired, incidental, external

inhibit
syn. bridle, constrain, curb, block, forbid, debar
ant. approve, assist, aid

instigate
syn. goad, propel, spur, stimulate, motivate, incite
ant. halt, dissuade, discourage

integrity
syn. honesty, principle, honour, incorruptibility, strength, entirety
ant. corruption, disgrace, dishonesty

intense
syn. fierce, desperate, vehement, violent, furious, concentrated
ant. moderate, mild, low-key

intermittent
syn. fitful, occasional, sporadic, periodical, cyclic, alternate
ant. perpetual, continual, regular

intimidate
syn. frighten, threaten, menace, browbeat, bulldoze, bully
ant. assist, encourage, protect

instinctive
syn. intuitive, visceral, impulsive, involuntary, reflex, unpremeditated
ant. deliberate, conscious, mediated

intrinsic
syn. constitutional, inborn, indigenous, ingrained, innate, inherent
ant. accidental, acquired, extrinsic

irate
syn. furious, ireful, rabid, wrathful, fuming, incensed
ant. calm, cheerful, pleased

irk
syn. annoy, bother, exasperate, nettle, rile, ruffle
ant. delight, gratify, placate

ironic
syn. cynic, sardonic, wry, acrid, caustic, derisive
ant. considerate, deferential, flattering

jeer
syn. deride, gibe, jest, mock, ridicule, scoff
ant. commend, revere, appreciate

jeopardy
syn. danger, hazard, peril, risk, endangerment, precariousness
ant. protection, safety, surety

jest
syn. butt, joke, mockery, gag, quip, wit
ant. adulation, solemnity, seriousness

jettison
syn. discard, dispose of, junk, scrap, rid of, chuck
ant. retain, embrace, absorb

jiff
syn. instant, flash, moment, wink, twinkle, twinkling
ant. delay, pause, long-term

jilt
syn. deceive, ditch, dump, forsake, reject, oust
ant. adopt, accept, embrace

jostle
syn. nudge, push, shove, scramble, elbow, hustle
ant. aid, pull, build

kindle
syn. ignite, inspire, arouse, awaken, light
ant. extinguish, discourage, put out

Exercise

Choose the word which is CLOSEST in meaning to the given word.

1. Immaculate
   (a) fallacious (b) chimerical
   (c) filthy (d) unsullied

2. Jettison
   (a) gag (b) scrap
   (c) rile (d) propel

3. Inception
   (a) splendour (b) commencement
   (c) conclusion (d) hindrance

Choose the word which is MOST SIMILAR in meaning to the underlined word in the given sentences.

4. The crowd jostled to get inside the theatre.
(a) queued (b) gathered
(c) pushed (d) fought

5. Do you know what is ironic in this story?
(a) sarcastic (b) superficial
(c) interesting (d) climax

Choose the word which is OPPOSITE in meaning to the given word.

6. Kindle
(a) support (b) ignite
(c) extinguish (d) spoiled

7. Instigate
(a) awaken (b) retain
(c) dissuade (d) distract

Choose the word which is MOST OPPOSITE in meaning to the underlined word in the given sentence.

8. Do you know what irked Sunita?
(a) annoyed (b) spoiled
(c) pleased (d) disgusted

9. I have an intermittent issue with my laptop.
(a) continuous (b) serious
(c) complicated (d) random

10. The jilted lover was last seen in the park.
(a) prominent (b) gifted
(c) sad (d) cherished

L - M

laboured

syn. contrived, strained, ponderous, forced, effortful, heavy-handed
ant. relaxed, facile, easy

lack

syn. deficiency, inadequacy, paucity, scarcity, shortcoming, dearth
ant. abundance, plethora, surplus

lag

syn. dawdle, drag, linger, poke, procrastinate, detain
ant. push, expedite, hasten

lament

syn. grieve, mourn, sorrow, suffer, bemoan, deplore
ant. celebrate, compliment, gloat

languish

syn. decline, degenerate, fade, wane, fizzle, flag
ant. flourish, improve, develop

latent

syn. eventual, potential, abeyant, dormant, inactive, quiescent
ant. apparent, obvious, manifest

laud

syn. acclaim, eulogise, applaud, extol, glorify, commend
ant. blame, castigate, denounce

lax

syn. lenient, tolerant, derelict, negligent, remiss, slack
ant. rigid, careful, virtuous

lenient

syn. charitable, indulgent, forbearing, lax, clement, tolerant
ant. rigorous, surly, harsh

limit

syn. constraint, inhibition, stricture, ceiling, curb, restriction
ant. opening, infinity, expanse

listless

syn. eager, curious, ardent, indifferent, indolent, languid
ant. ardent, earnest, engaged

lofty
- ***syn.*** elevated, eminent, dignified, stately, haughty, towering
- ***ant.*** depressed, stunted, mean

lucid
- ***syn.*** resplendent, luminous, pellucid, rational, limpid, lucent
- ***ant.*** turbid, muddy, mystified

lucrative
- ***syn.*** gainful, advantageous, beneficial, useful, remunerative, productive
- ***ant.*** vain, disadvantageous, fruitless

lure
- ***syn.*** allure, entice, ensnare, entrap, seduce, tempt
- ***ant.*** guide, instruct, conduct

lurid
- ***syn.*** murky, lowering, wan, dismal, gloomy, sad
- ***ant.*** bright, luminous, bright

lusty
- ***syn.*** robust, vigorous, stout, burly, brawny, corpulent
- ***ant.*** infirm, ailing, effete

magnanimity
- ***syn.*** generosity, forbearance, clemency, chivalry, philanthropy, benevolence
- ***ant.*** meanness, pettiness, paltriness

malicious
- ***syn.*** spiteful, malignant, malevolent, vindictive, retaliatory, vicious
- ***ant.*** kind, benevolent, genial

malign
- ***syn.*** traduce, asperse, calumniate, vilify, defame, slander
- ***ant.*** praise, commend, eulogise

mandatory
- ***syn.*** binding, compulsory, indispensable, essential, obligatory, requisite
- ***ant.*** optional, voluntary, unnecessary

manifold
- ***syn.*** numerous, multifarious, varied, sundry, diverse, multiplied
- ***ant.*** scant, rare, scarce

marred
- ***syn.*** blemished, spoiled, defective, deficient, faulty, fallible
- ***ant.*** perfect, consummate, impeccable

meddle
- ***syn.*** interpose, intervene, interfere, arbitrate, mediate, insert
- ***ant.*** withdraw, retract, recede

meek
syn. mild, gentle, submissive, modest, yielding, unassuming
ant. bold, arrogant, proud

mend
syn. repair, restore, rectify, reform, amend, ameliorate
ant. impair, corrupt, pervert

mercurial
syn. buoyant, capricious, effervescent, expansive, fickle, impulsive
ant. tranquil, unvarying, calm

meritorious
syn. praiseworthy, commendable, honourable, creditable, exemplary, virtuous
ant. censurable, reprehensible, improper

messy
syn. blotchy, careless, disheveled, unorganised, grubby, raunchy
ant. uncluttered, clear, organised

microscopic
syn. puny, wee, tiny, diminutive, minuscule, negligible
ant. huge, gigantic, bulky

mingle
syn. compound, blend, confound, confuse, associate, amalgamate
ant. segregate, sift, sort

mirage
syn. delusion, fantasy, hallucination, illusion, apparition, fallacy
ant. reality, concreteness, actuality

miscreant
syn. rogue, vagabond, scamp, rascal, swindler, villain
ant. gentleman, honest, righteous

modest
syn. mild, gentle, submissive, polite, yielding, unassuming
ant. arrogant, self-asserting, bold

momentary
syn. instantaneous, fleeting, transitory, ephemeral, cursory, flashing
ant. permanent, staying, lasting

Exercise

Choose the word which is CLOSEST in meaning to the given word.

1. Lag
   (a) expedite (b) flag
   (c) retract (d) procrastinate

2. Messy
   (a) dishevelled (b) fickle
   (c) puny (d) expansive

3. Lucrative
   (a) remunerative (b) luminous
   (c) indolent (d) spontaneous

Choose the word which is MOST SIMILAR in meaning to the underlined word in the given sentence.

4. Is he <u>meddling</u> in your matter?
   (a) receding (b) intervening
   (c) differing (d) advising

5. Did you also download the <u>malicious</u> software?
   (a) aiding (b) harmful
   (c) latest (d) testing

Choose the word which is OPPOSITE in meaning to the given word.

6. Mingle
   (a) sift (b) settle
   (c) gather (d) amalgamate

7. Mend
   (a) ameliorate (b) defend
   (c) adopt (d) impair

8. Languid
   (a) clear (b) argumentative
   (c) relaxed (d) energetic

Choose the word which is MOST OPPOSITE in meaning to the underlined word in the given sentence.

9. <u>Miscreants</u> damaged public property to stop screening of Padmavat.
   (a) followers (b) artists
   (c) sticklers (d) communists

10. She showed a <u>lofty</u> disregard of her seniors.
    (a) noble (b) great
    (c) humble (d) haughty

N - O

nasty
syn. filthy, atrocious, repellent, foul, profane, spiteful
ant. magnificent, wonderful, delightful

notable
syn. celebrated, distinguished, illustrious, prominent, eminent, renowned
ant. commonplace, insignificant, inconsequential

noteworthy
syn. exceptional, extraordinary, outstanding, memorable, meaningful, prominent
ant. ordinary, unimportant, common

notorious
syn. infamous, scandalous, blatant, flagrant, glaring, opprobrious
ant. obscure, unknown, unremarkable

novice
syn. beginner, freshman, greenhorn, neophyte, tyro, fledgling
ant. expert, professional, veteran

nullify
syn. abolish, abrogate, annihilate, negate, validate, counteract
ant. sanctify, validate, affirm

obdurate
syn. callous, hardened, adamant, grim, remorseless, implacable
ant. amenable, susceptible, submissive

obligatory
syn. compulsory, imperative, mandatory, necessary, required, requisite
ant. optional, voluntary, nonessential

obliged
syn. beholden, bound, indebted, obligated, attached, favoured
ant. critical, let off, disparaged

obscene
syn. lewd, ribald, profane, scurrilous, vulgar, ridiculous
ant. moral, upright, decent

observant
syn. alert, vigilant, wakeful, weary, heedful, conscious
ant. inattentive, unaware, thoughtless

obstinate
syn. dogged, tenacious, mulish, indocile, obstreperous, recalcitrant
ant. cooperative, flexible, yielding

obstruct
syn. interfere, hold, bog, encumber, impede, block
ant. abet, boost, promote

oddity
syn. odd, curious, unusual, original, strange, different
ant. conventional, usual, normal

offbeat
syn. atypical, novel, unconventional, unusual, unwonted, odd
ant. expected, normal, usual

officious
syn. interfering, intrusive, meddlesome, meddling, obtrusive, impertinent
ant. laid-back, modest, shy

ominous
syn. apocalyptic, baneful, direful, grave, portentous, unlucky
ant. auspicious, propitious, promising

oppressive
syn. arduous, burdensome, demanding, laborious, taxing, severe
ant. gentle, relieving, facile

ostentatious
syn. flamboyant, pretentious, showy, splashy, splurgy, extravagant
ant. modest, plain, simple

ostracise
syn. blacklist, boycott, banish, exile, deport, expatriate
ant. embrace, welcome, accept

outdo
syn. exceed, excel, outmatch, outrun, surpass, transcend
ant. fail, lose, fall behind

outrageous
syn. atrocious, heinous, monstrous, preposterous, ridiculous, shocking
ant. sensible, reasonable, magnificent

outwit
syn. outmaneuver, outsmart, outthink, overreach, hoodwink, outfox
ant. give up, lose, fail

overlook
syn. scan, survey, command, dominate, oversee, superintend
ant. follow, obey, heed

oversight
syn. disregard, neglect, blunder, default, laxity
ant. attention, care, watchfulness

Exercise

Choose the word which is CLOSEST in meaning to the given word.

1. Notorious
   (a) obscure (b) atrocious
   (c) implacable (d) scandalous

2. Ostentatious
   (a) pretentious (b) modest
   (c) apocalyptic (d) yielding

Choose the word which is MOST SIMILAR in meaning to the underlined word in the given sentence.

3. The petition was <u>nullified</u> in the court.
   (a) accepted (b) highlighted
   (c) cancelled (d) deciphered

4. Ravi was as <u>obdurate</u> as his father.
   (a) pleasing (b) implacable
   (c) profane (d) ribald

5. Roma walked towards us with an <u>officious</u> stride.
   (a) hostile (b) awkward
   (c) intrusive (d) gentle

Choose the word which is OPPOSITE in meaning to the given word.

6. Ostracise
   (a) transcend (b) embrace
   (c) blacklist (d) expatriate

7. Obscene
   (a) upright (b) showy
   (c) aloof (d) vulgar

8. Ominous
   (a) imperative (b) critical
   (c) dire (d) propitious

Choose the word which is MOST OPPOSITE in meaning to the underlined word in the given sentence.

9. Rashu is a <u>novice</u> bird-watcher.
   (a) great (b) supportive
   (c) experienced (d) neophyte

10. He <u>outwitted</u> everyone in the declamation contest.
    (a) dominated (b) displeased
    (c) welcomed (d) guarded

P - Q

painstaking
syn. careful, fastidious, meticulous, punctilious, scrupulous, thoughtful
ant. careless, thoughtless, mindless

paltry
syn. negligible, petty, trifling, lousy, miserable, shoddy
ant. significant, substantial, wealthy

parody
syn. imitation, burlesque, farce, mock, sham, travesty
ant. reality, sobriety, solemnity

passionate
syn. amorous, lustful, lewd, ardent, fervent, impassioned
ant. cool, frigid, indifferent

paucity
syn. deficiency, inadequacy, lack, scarcity, shortcoming, defect
ant. abundance, affluence, plenty

pauper
syn. beggar, indigent, destitute, insolvent, bum, supplicant
ant. rich, wealthy, affluent

penchant
syn. disposition, leaning, predilection, propensity, tendency, trend
ant. dislike, hatred, indifference

pensive
syn. contemplative, cogitative, reflective, meditative, ruminative, thoughtful
ant. heedless, inconsiderate, inattentive

perceptible
syn. discernible, visible, appreciable, distinct, distinguishable, sensible
ant. ambiguous, obscure, vague

perennial
syn. abiding, continuing, enduring, lasting, permanent, persistent
ant. varying, intermittent, interrupted

perpetual
syn. ceaseless, everlasting, incessant, interminable, relentless, persistent
ant. ephemeral, fleeting, transient

perplexed
syn. addled, confounded, turbid, fuddled, foxed, confused
ant. unbaffled, clear, cognizant

persist
syn. insist, persevere, hang on, continue, survive, endure
ant. cease, quit, leave

pertinent
syn. applicable, apposite, apropos, germane, material, relevant
ant. inappropriate, unsuitable, irrelevant

perturb
syn. agitate, bother, flurry, rock, toss, upset
ant. soothe, please, calm

philanthropic
syn. altruistic, benevolent, charitable, benignant, humanitarian, magnanimous
ant. misanthropic, miserly, stingy

pilfer
syn. filch, purloin, snatch, steal, thieve, lift
ant. give, receive, contribute

pithy
syn. precise, terse, compact, crisp, succinct, epigrammatic
ant. verbose, wordy, loose

placate
syn. appease, assuage, conciliate, mollify, propitiate, pacify
ant. agitate, upset, disturb

placid
syn. peaceful, serene, tranquil, still, halcyon, calm
ant. agitated, excited, troubled

plausible
syn. believable, credible, tenable, probable, logical, conceivable
ant. improbable, unlikely, unbelievable

plethora
syn. deluge, extravagance, excess, overabundance, superfluity, surfeit
ant. rarity, scarcity, want

poignant
syn. affecting, impressive, moving, stirring, touching, piquant
ant. numb, soothing, pleasant

precarious
syn. shaky, tottering, wobbly, rickety, unstable, weak
ant. definite, firm, stable

pretentious
syn. grandiose, pompous, flamboyant, ostentatious, showy, splashy
ant. modest, tasteful, simple

primordial
syn. earliest, initial, maiden, original, pioneer, first
ant. last, latest, final

procure
syn. acquire, obtain, secure, gain, get, receive
ant. lose, forfeit, forsake

prodigy
syn. marvel, miracle, astonishment, sensation, phenomenon, wonder
ant. simpleton, buffoon, moron

profound
syn. abysmal, deep, intense, abstruse, esoteric, recondite
ant. lucid, plain, simple

proliferate
syn. propagate, augment, escalate, aggrandise, mount, upsurge
ant. decline, degrade, diminish

propriety
syn. decency, respectability, ethicality, morality, decorum, righteousness
ant. immorality, impropriety, wrong

provincial
syn. insular, rustic, pastoral, bucolic, limited, local
ant. liberal, metropolitan, modern

questionable
syn. debatable, uncertain, ambiguous, dubious, improbable, shady
ant. certain, definite, acknowledged

quip
syn. gap, jape, jest, joke, crack, dig
ant. compliment, flatter, praise

quixotic
syn. idealistic, romantic, unrealistic, utopian, visionary, chimerical
ant. practical, unromantic, real

Exercise

Choose the word which is CLOSEST in meaning to the given word.

1. Pauper
(a) affluent (b) audacious
(c) insolvent (d) ardent

2. Paltry
(a) punctilious (b) trifling
(c) substantial (d) terminal

3. Quixotic
(a) chimerical (b) certain
(c) bucolic (d) definite

Select the word which is MOST SIMILAR in meaning to the underlined word in the given sentence.

4. The snow was a <u>parody</u> on the current state of affairs.
(a) documentary (b) praise
(c) farce (d) comedy

5. Some of the stafs were <u>pilfering</u> when the owner was not around.`
(a) sleeping (b) talking
(c) complaining (d) filching

Choose the word which is OPPOSITE in meaning to the given word.

6. Prodigy
(a) buffoon (b) solemnly
(c) fallacy (d) tragedy

7. Placid
(a) agitated (b) serene
(c) pioneer (d) tenable

8. Persist
(a) endure (b) sustain
(c) cease (d) intervene

Choose the word which is MOST OPPOSITE in meaning to the underlined word in the given sentence.

9. There was a <u>plethora</u> of books on Ornithology in the library.
(a) surfeit (b) list
(c) calamity (d) shortage

10. The vehicles in Delhi are <u>proliferating</u> day by day.
(a) polluting (b) decreasing
(c) growing (d) De-escalating

R

rage
syn. animosity, fury, ire, wrath, passion, frenzy
ant. glee, calm, happiness

ragged
syn. tattered, coarse, cragged, harsh, jagged, battered
ant. eve, kempt, smooth

ratify
syn. adopt, affirm, approve, sanction, confirm, pass
ant. renounce, revoke, veto

ravage
syn. desolate, devastate, pillage, plunder, ransack, depredate
ant. cultivate, protect, assist

raze
syn. demolish, destroy, dismantle, pulverise, wreck, level
ant. build, construct, develop

recede
syn. ebb, retract, retreat, retrocede, retrograde, retrogress
ant. forge, forward, advance

reckless
syn. heedless, unconcerned, brash, foolhardy, impetuous, slapdash
ant. cautious, responsible, wary

redundant
syn. verbose, prolix, inordinate, periphrastic, padded, wordy
ant. concise, essential, reasonable

refrain
syn. abstain, forbear, keep, withhold, abjure, abnegate
ant. indulge, use, partake

rejoice
syn. delight, exult, celebrate, revel, enjoy, make merry
ant. grieve, mourn, dislike

relentless
syn. adamant, unbending, unyielding, ceaseless, perpetual, incessant
ant. sympathetic, fleeting, transient

relinquish
syn. abandon, cede, waive, forswear, forgo, yield
ant. hold, keep, claim

relish
syn. enjoy, savour, adore, appreciate, devour, feast on
ant. dislike, hate, detest

remit
syn. condone, pardon, subside, abandon, relinquish, postpone
ant. remain, stay, hold

render
syn. abdicate, demit, cede, portray, rephrase, construe
ant. assume, retain, guard

renounce
syn. disown, reject, repudiate, relinquish, disavow, yield
ant. allow, approve, condone

remonstrate
syn. challenge, demur, expostulate, object, protest, oppose
ant. agree, concede, consent

repeal
syn. rescind, revoke, reverse, nullify, annul, abrogate
ant. enact, validate, enact

repentant
syn. contrite, regretful, remorseful, sorry, apologetic, penitent
ant. satisfied, content, happy

reprimand
syn. admonish, castigate, chastise, chide, reprove, reproach
ant. forgive, praise, reward

resentment
syn. dudgeon, huff, miff, pique, umbrage, acrimony
ant. delight, pleasure, happiness

resolute
syn. decisive, determined, firm, steadfast, unflinching, unwavering
ant. cautious, cowardly, infirm

respite
syn. reprieve, breather, break, adjournment, intermission, recess
ant. continuation, blame, rest

resurgence
syn. resumption, revival, renewal, resurrection, continuation, reactivation
ant. exhaustion, cessation, halt

retaliate
syn. counter, reciprocate, retort, settle, strike back, hit back
ant. forgive, pardon, surrender

retard
syn. delay, detain, lag, stall, check, choke
ant. advance, push, unblock

retreat
syn. recede, retrograde, backtrack, renege, retrogress, pull back
ant. advance, arrive, forward

retrograde
syn. ebb, decline, descend, backpedal, atrophy, sink
ant. push, forward, flourish

revamp
syn. fix, mend, overhaul, patch, furbish, rejuvenate
ant. preserve, sustain, retain

revoke
syn. lift, recall, repeal, rescind, reverse, annul
ant. approve, enforce, authorise

rift
syn. chink, fissure, cleft, crevice, alienation, rupture
ant. closure, joint, unity

rot
syn. decay, decompose, putrefy, taint, spoil, disintegrate
ant. germinate, improve, purify

rouse
syn. awaken, stir, kindle, raise, stimulate, excite
ant. deaden, bore, hypnotise

rugged
syn. coarse, uneven, roiled, turbulent, stormy, strenuous
ant. flat, smooth, easy

rustic
syn. provincial, pastoral, bucolic, unadorned, artless, rural
ant. metropolitan, urban, liberal

Exercise

Choose the word which is CLOSEST in meaning to the given word.

1. Refrain
   (a) exult (b) abstain
   (c) cease (d) swear

2. Repentant
   (a) content (b) steadfast
   (c) proud (d) remorseful

Choose the word which is MOST SIMILAR in meaning to the underlined word in the given sentence.

3. Many coastal villages were <u>ravaged</u> in the storm.
   (a) derailed (b) warned
   (c) monitored (d) plundered

4. Manisha had to sign the <u>relinquishment</u> deed in the court.
   (a) approval (b) fulfilment
   (c) abdication (d) mandatory

5. There was a <u>resurgence</u> in terrorist activities after Republic Day.
   (a) cessation (b) reappearance
   (c) adjournment (d) improvement

Choose the word which is OPPOSITE in meaning to the given word.

6. Retaliate
   (a) renounce (b) revoke
   (c) attack (d) pardon

7. Repeal
   (a) nullify (b) condone
   (c) enact (d) reveal

8. Resolute
   (a) cowardly (b) unflinching
   (c) penitent (d) contrite

Choose the word which is MOST OPPOSITE in meaning to the underlined word in the given sentence.

9. We went to a <u>rustic</u> resort in our holidays.
   (a) urban (b) modern
   (c) rural (d) simple

10. The administrator is allowed to <u>revoke</u> the rights of any user.
   (a) grant (b) enforce
   (c) remove (d) access

S

salvage
syn. reclaim, recover, redeem, rescue, glean, regain
ant. endanger, hurt, lose

sane
syn. rational, commonsensical, judicious, prudent, sapient, reasonable
ant. crazy, unsound, unstable

sarcastic
syn. derisive, jeering, mocking, satiric, scoffing, sneering
ant. humble, believing, praising

scary
syn. appalling, dire, dreadful, redoubtable, formidable
ant. calming, soothing, encouraging

scintillating
syn. animated, glittering, dazzling, ebullient, twinkling, flashing
ant. dull, drab, boring

scrutinise
syn. examine, check, inspect, peruse, traverse, observe
ant. ignore, neglect, forget

seclude
syn. insulate, isolate, segregate, cloister, confine, embargo
ant. join, mingle, socialise

sedentary
syn. settled, inactive, sluggish, idle, sitting, torpid
ant. energetic, mobile, active

shackle
syn. chain, fetter, hamper, hobble, leash, manacle
ant. loosen, unbind, untie

shun
syn. avoid, burke, bypass, circumvent, dodge, eschew
ant. face, meet, confront

solace
syn. comfort, consolation, alleviation, condolence, pity, relief
ant. discord, disharmony, indifference

soothe
syn. appease, assuage, conciliate, dulcify, placate, propitiate
ant. agitate, distress, upset

sovereign
syn. autonomous, free, independent, imperial, overbearing, ascendant
ant. inferior, submissive, subservient

sparing
syn. canny, chary, economical, frugal, thrifty, prudent
ant. squandering, wasteful, reckless

spat
syn. altercation, bicker, contention, dispute, squabble, spank
ant. concord, harmony, unity

sporadic
syn. fitful, intermittent, occasional, periodic, infrequent, rare
ant. constant, continuous, regular

spurious
syn. bogus, counterfeit, fraudulent, phony, sham, fallacious
ant. authentic, genuine, real

squander
syn. devour, dissipate, waste, fritter away, consume, trifle away
ant. hoard, save, set aside

stall
syn. arrest, hinder, cease, check, discontinue, halt
ant. advance, further, allow

stark
syn. austere, bleak, dour, grim, harsh, severe
ant. bright, cheerful, sunny

stifle
syn. repress, strangle, smother, dampen, deaden, censor
ant. encourage, persuade, facilitate

stipulate
syn. specify, detail, particularise, designate, postulate, impose
ant. generalise, withhold, imply

strenuous
syn. knockabout, dynamic, lively, sprightly, vigorous, forceful
ant. enervated, lethargic, inactive

stringency
syn. austerity, hardness, harshness, rigour, severity, rigidity
ant. blandness, gentility, mildness

strive
syn. labour, moil, strain, toil, sweat, endeavour
ant. skip, retreat, surrender

stubborn
syn. adamant, implacable, intransigent, relentless, obdurate, unyielding
ant. complacent, complying, yielding

sturdy
syn. robust, stalwart, stable, substantial, vigorous, burly
ant. weak, wobbly, unstable

suave
syn. bland, smooth, urban, civilized, cultured, courteous
ant. awkward, clumsy, unsophisticated

subside
syn. abate, ebb, lapse, moderate, slacken, wane
ant. grow, develop, flourish

substantial
syn. concrete, corporeal, phenomenal, tangible, plentiful, voluminous
ant. insignificant, unimportant, minor

subtle
syn. delicate, fine, nice, refined, exquisite, implied
ant. harsh, coarse, unsophisticated

succumb
syn. bow, buckle, capitulate, yield, surrender, expire
ant. conquer, overcome, withhold

suppress
syn. crush, extinguish, quell, put down, muffle, throttle
ant. encourage, stimulate, release

surpass
syn. exceed, overreach, overstep, transcend, outmatch, better
ant. fall behind, lose, fail

sustain
syn. maintain, preserve, support, bolster, abide, tolerate
ant. halt, stop, discontinue

Exercise

Choose the word which is CLOSEST in meaning to the given word.

1. Scary
   (a) scoffing (b) dreadful
   (c) ebullient (d) overbearing

2. Spat
   (a) strain (b) moil
   (c) altercation (d) rigour

3. Shun
   (a) confront (b) dodge
   (c) hobble (d) dilute

Choose the word which is MOST SIMILAR in meaning to the underlined word in the given sentence.

4. Sarika somehow managed to <u>salvage</u> his pride.
   (a) prolong (b) cloister
   (c) increase (d) redeem

5. Is it a good thing to <u>squander</u> your resources?
   (a) expend (b) hoard
   (c) donate (d) manage

Choose the word which is OPPOSITE in meaning to the given word.

6. Stubborn
   (a) courteous (b) sporadic
   (c) adroit (d) complacent

7. Subside
   (a) flourish (b) abstract
   (c) subsume (d) steady

8. Suave
   (a) bland (b) clumsy
   (c) tangible (d) moderate

Choose the word which is MOST OPPOSITE in meaning to the underlined word in the given sentence.

9. Were the attacks on the camps <u>sporadic</u>?
   (a) continuous (b) intermittent
   (c) justified (d) unjustified

10. <u>Sovereign</u> power is said to lie with people in democratic countries.
    (a) maximum (b) medium
    (c) minimum (d) local

T - U

tainted

syn. decayed, decomposed, stained, contaminated, corrupt, defiled
ant. flourishing, clean, ripening

tangle

syn. ensnarl, complicate, enmesh, entrap, bicker, spat
ant. order, solve, clarify

tardy

syn. belated, overdue, laggard, sluggish, delinquent, loitering
ant. prompt, ready, punctual

tarnish

syn. blemish, impair, mar, prejudice, besmear, denigrate
ant. clean, polish, uncorrupt

taxing

syn. arduous, burdensome, demanding, exigent, exacting, onerous
ant. motivating, facile, trivial

tenacious

syn. dogged, mulish, obstinate, pertinacious, perverse, wilful
ant. weak, yielding, surrendering

tentative

syn. sketchy, conditional, provisional, hesitant, indecisive, timid
ant. certain, decisive, definite

tepid

syn. halfhearted, lukewarm, apathetic, lifeless, temperate, unenthusiastic
ant. lively, warm, enthusiastic

terse

syn. brief, concise, laconic, succinct, summary, compendious
ant. prolific, wordy, elaborate

thriving

syn. booming, flourishing, prosperous, roaring, developing, burgeoning
ant. languishing, declining, failing

tiff

syn. altercation, bicker, contention, dispute, spat, squabble
ant. agreement, harmony, concurrence

timid
syn. coy, demure, modest, bashful, indecisive, diffident
ant. bold, audacious, daring

tirade
syn. diatribe, fulmination, harangue, censure, ranting, revilement
ant. praise, harmony, commendation

tiresome
syn. dreary, humdrum, monotonous, tedious, dull, weary
ant. facile, stimulating, interesting

torment
syn. torture, agonise, afflict, scourge, haunt, annoy
ant. please, gladden, assist

tranquility
syn. hush, peace, lull, placidity, serenity, quietude
ant. chaos, turbulence, wildness

transitory
syn. evanescent, fleeting, fugacious, momentary, temporal, ephemeral
ant. permanent, enduring, everlasting

translucent
syn. clear, crystalline, limpid, lucid, pellucid, see-through
ant. blocked, opaque, cloudy

trifle
syn. frivolity, trivia, bauble, crumb, fragment, modicum
ant. lot, entirety, whole

trivial
syn. inconsequent, insignificant, flimsy, meager, diminutive, incidental
ant. valuable, worthwhile, significant

turbulence
syn. agitation, commotion, agitation, frenzy, tumult, unruliness
ant. calmness, tranquility, stillness

turmoil
syn. flutter, upset, tumult, disturbance, perturbation, ferment
ant. calm, harmony, peace

tyrannical
syn. autocratic, despotic, arbitrary, totalitarian, dictatorial, absolutistic
ant. submissive, democratic, docile

unabated

syn. incessant, persistent, tenacious, unflagging, unfaltering, sustained

ant. intermittent, relenting, yielding

underdog

syn. loser, miserable, underprivileged, unfortunate, wretch, small fry

ant. favourite, prized, winner

undermine

syn. attenuate, debilitate, unnerve, weaken, sabotage, subvert

ant. strengthen, support, assist

undo

syn. annul, efface, unbind, expunge, undermine, obliterate, wreck

ant. retain, validate, construct

unfold

syn. expand, extend, stretch, unroll, develop, evolve

ant. fold, wrap, cover

unruffled

syn. composed, detached, imperturbable, nonchalant, possessed, unflappable

ant. discomposed, stormy, nervous

unruly

syn. disorderly, lawless, obstreperous, refractory, untoward, wild

ant. compliant, obedient, yielding

upright

syn. perpendicular, honest, incorruptible, righteous, forthright, upstanding

ant. fallen, corrupt, dishonest

uprising

syn. insurgence, mutiny, rebellion, revolt, mounting, insurrection

ant. tranquility, peace, harmony

uproar

syn. brouhaha, turbulence, commotion, tumult, pandemonium, clamour

ant. quietude, repose, stillness

urbane

syn. smooth, suave, civilized, cultured, refined, polished

ant. uncouth, uncivilized, unsophisticated

utter

syn. pronounce, convey, vent, express, declare, state

ant. bumble, keep mum, hold

Exercise

Choose the word which is CLOSEST in meaning to the given word.

1. Tardy
   (a) prompt (b) delinquent
   (c) exigent (d) perverse

2. Transitory
   (a) enduring (b) flourishing
   (c) fleeting (d) frivolous

Choose the word which is MOST SIMILAR in meaning to the underlined word in the given sentence.

3. Anju got a tepid response to her suggestion.
   (a) mild (b) exciting
   (c) biased (d) bold

4. Alvira pursued her work with unabated zeal.
   (a) diminished (b) intermittent
   (c) reluctant (d) undiminished

5. Karan Thapar is regarded as a tenacious interviewer.
   (a) dogged (b) derilish
   (c) calm (d) complacent

Choose the word which is OPPOSITE in meaning to the given word.

6. Unfold
   (a) evolve (b) enhance
   (c) wrap (d) mystery

7. Urbane
   (a) suave (b) righteous
   (c) uncouth (d) weakling

Choose the word which is MOST OPPOSITE in meaning to the underlined word in the given sentence.

8. The underdogs went on to win the contest.
   (a) dark horses (b) outsiders
   (c) pacifists (d) favourites

9. She wanted to get rid off her tyrannical husband.
   (a) incompetent (b) dormant
   (c) despotic (d) docile

10. The tranquility of the valley attracted him.
    (a) serenity (b) chaos
    (c) depth (d) surroundings

V - Z

vagabond
syn. itinerant, nomadic, peripatetic, vagrant, migrant, pastoral
ant. settled, native, endemic

validate
syn. attest, authenticate, corroborate, justify, testify, endorse
ant. contradict, disclaim, refute

vanquish
syn. beat, conquer, defeat, overcome, subdue, rout
ant. fail, lose, surrender

vanity
syn. ego, conceit, pride, narcissism, vainness, futility
ant. modesty, humility, propriety

vehemence
syn. ferocity, fury, intensity, pitch, severity, force
ant. frigidity, coldness, apathy

venomous
syn. toxic, virulent, malevolent, malignant, spiteful, wicked
ant. benign, harmless, affectionate

venturesome
syn. adventurous, audacious, daring, enterprising, hazardous, perilous
ant. afraid, cowardly, cautious

verbose
syn. long-winded, periphrastic, pleonastic, prolix, redundant
ant. concise, succinct, sporadic

versatile
syn. all-round, many-sided, multifaceted, protean, adept, proficient
ant. inflexible, limited, inept

viable
syn. feasible, practical, doable, usable, workable, possible
ant. impossible, unpractical, unreasonable

vice
syn. bestiality, depravity, immorality, perversion, turpitude, villainy
ant. propriety, virtue, morality

virtuous
syn. ethical, moral, principled, righteous, chaste, decent
ant. sinful, vile, wicked

vitiate
syn. blemish, damage, impair, tarnish, canker, debase
ant. polish, uncorrupt, adorn

vivacious
syn. animated, bouncy, chipper, dashing, lively, pert
ant. boring, unattractive, dull

void
syn. empty, vacant, vacuous, barren, destitute, hollow
ant. full, occupied, overflowing

volatile
syn. capricious, erratic, changeable, freakish, unpredictable, variable
ant. stable, steadfast, firm

vulnerable
syn. liable, prone, susceptible, attackable, defenseless, pregnable
ant. guarded, protected, secure

wag
syn. clown, comedian, farceur, humourist, jester, zany
ant. tragedian, dramatist, serious

waive
syn. abandon, abdicate, cede, demit, relinquish, renounce
ant. retain, treasure, usurp

wander
syn. drift, meander, ramble, rove, saunter, stroll
ant. stay, halt, remain

wane
syn. abate, remit, slacken, subside, decline, languish
ant. grow, increase, raise

wary
syn. vigilant, wakeful, cautious, chary, circumspect, prudent
ant. careless, indiscreet, reckless

wax
syn. aggrandise, amplify, augment, burgeon, proliferate, soar
ant. shrink, constrict, decline

weary
syn. drained, exhausted, worn-out, dreary, humdrum, tiresome
ant. activated, energetic, lively

weird
syn. eerie, uncanny, cranky, outlandish, quaint, singular
ant. conventional, standard, habitual

wholesome
syn. healthy, hygienic, salubrious, decent, modest, hale
ant. impure, indecent, unhealthy

wither
syn. sear, shrivel, wizen, languish, pine, petrify
ant. bloom, grow, germinate

withstand
syn. resist, abide, bear, endure, sustain, tolerate
ant. surrender, yield, give up

woe
syn. affliction, agony, anguish, distress, torment, torture
ant. happiness, joy, pleasure

woo
syn. court, pursue, spark, caress, chase, beg
ant. ignore, disregard, lose

wrath
syn. furor, fury, ire, rage, acrimony, asperity
ant. happiness, glee, cheer

wretched
syn. abominable, contemptible, despicable, nefarious, obnoxious, repugnant
ant. comfortable, fortunate, happy

yearn
syn. covet, desire, hanker, long, pine, wish
ant. dislike, hate, disgust

yield
syn. produce, crop, revenue, earning, output, turnout
ant. bills, debt, payment

zenith
syn. acme, apogee, crest, culmination, pinnacle, summit
ant. bottom, nadir, base

Exercise

Choose the word which is CLOSEST in meaning to the given word.

1. Vagabond
(a) nomadic (b) spiteful
(c) honourable (d) social

2. Wander
(a) languish (b) ramble
(c) cede (d) shrivel

3. Weafy
(a) eevie (b) decent
(c) lively (d) dreamy

Choose the word which is MOST SIMILAR in meaning to the underlined word in the given sentence.

4. Few people share their vulnerabilities with others.
(a) strengths (b) values
(c) feelings (d) weaknesses

5. Pushpa suddenly became very vehement and agitated.
(a) fierce (b) humble
(c) gentle (d) kindred

Choose the word which is CLOSEST in meaning to the given word.

6. Vivacious
(a) boring (b) attractive
(c) scholarly (d) deceptive

7. Wrath
(a) rage (b) glee
(c) kindness (d) belief

8. Yield
(a) relinquish (b) forgo
(c) withhold (d) surfeit

Choose the word which is OPPOSITE in meaning to the underlined word in the given sentence.

9. Didn't he behave in a weird way today?
(a) simple (b) honest
(c) strange (d) normal

10. I yearn to have a house in Delhi cantt.
(a) wish (b) hanker
(c) yield (d) despise

ANSWERS
to all the
Intermediate Exercises

A	1 (c)	2 (d)	3 (a)	4 (b)	5 (c)	6 (a)	7 (c)	8 (d)	9 (c)	10 (b)
B	1 (a)	2 (b)	3 (a)	4 (d)	5 (d)	6 (b)	7 (d)	8 (a)	9 (a)	10 (d)
C	1 (c)	2 (a)	3 (b)	4 (a)	5 (b)	6 (d)	7 (a)	8 (c)	9 (c)	10 (b)
	11 (c)	12 (a)	13 (a)	14 (d)						
D	1 (d)	2 (c)	3 (b)	4 (a)	5 (c)	6 (b)	7 (a)	8 (b)	9 (b)	10 (d)
E	1 (a)	2 (b)	3 (a)	4 (a)	5 (c)	6 (c)	7 (d)	8 (a)	9 (d)	10 (a)
	11 (b)	12 (b)	13 (c)	14 (c)						
F	1 (a)	2 (b)	3 (c)	4 (b)	5 (d)	6 (a)	7 (d)	8 (b)	9 (b)	10 (b)
G - H	1 (d)	2 (a)	3 (d)	4 (d)	5 (c)	6 (a)	7 (b)	8 (c)	9 (b)	10 (a)
	11 (a)	12 (a)	13 (d)	14 (c)						
I - K	1 (d)	2 (b)	3 (b)	4 (c)	5 (a)	6 (c)	7 (c)	8 (c)	9 (a)	10 (d)
L - M	1 (d)	2 (a)	3 (a)	4 (b)	5 (a)	6 (d)	7 (d)	8 (d)	9 (c)	10 (c)
N - O	1 (d)	2 (a)	3 (c)	4 (b)	5 (c)	6 (b)	7 (a)	8 (d)	9 (c)	10 (d)
P - Q	1 (c)	2 (b)	3 (a)	4 (c)	5 (d)	6 (a)	7 (a)	8 (c)	9 (d)	10 (b)
R	1 (b)	2 (d)	3 (d)	4 (c)	5 (b)	6 (d)	7 (c)	8 (a)	9 (a)	10 (b)
S	1 (b)	2 (c)	3 (b)	4 (d)	5 (a)	6 (d)	7 (a)	8 (b)	9 (a)	10 (c)
T - U	1 (b)	2 (c)	3 (a)	4 (d)	5 (a)	6 (c)	7 (c)	8 (d)	9 (d)	10 (b)
V - Z	1 (a)	2 (b)	3 (c)	4 (d)	5 (a)	6 (a)	7 (b)	8 (c)	9 (d)	10 (d)

PART III
ADVANCED

abdicate
syn. cede, demit, relinquish, renounce, abandon, render
ant. hold, retain, maintain

aberration
syn. divergence, anomaly, eccentricity, deviance, peculiarity, derangement
ant. conformity, regularity, sameness

abet
syn. connive, incite, succour, boost, aid, urge
ant. hinder, inhibit, block

aboriginal
syn. native, indigenous, endemic, autochthonous, original, local
ant. foreigner, outsider, immigrant

accede
syn. comply, grant, acquiesce, assent, subscribe, nod
ant. demur, denounce, protest

acclaim
syn. commend, eulogise, exalt, extol, glorify, laud
ant. berate, damn, vituperate

accolade
syn. distinction, honour, tribute, award, laurel, kudos
ant. criticism, blame, accusation

acquisition
syn. accession, accomplishment, procurement, possession, gain, attainment
ant. loss, dearth, lack

acrimonious
syn. bitter, rancorous, resentful, virulent, discordant, hostile
ant. affable, benign, forgiving

adept
syn. proficient, skilled, adroit, dexterous, masterly, crack
ant. awkward, clumsy, inept

adherent
syn. enthusiast, follower, aficionado, cohort, disciple, minion
ant. opponent, cynic, disbeliever

adroit
syn. deft, nimble, competent, neat, artful, slick
ant. inept, unskilled, stupid

advent
syn. initiation, beginning, dawn, appearance, arrival, coming
ant. departure, end, culmination

adversary
syn. antagonist, opponent, rival, foe, challenger, resister
ant. ally, backer, supporter

affinity
syn. empathy, sympathy, kinship, resemblance, correspondence, likeness
ant. dislike, hatred, dissimilarity

affliction
syn. illness, infirmity, disorder, indisposition, burden, scourge
ant. aid, comfort, relief

affray
syn. brawl, scuffle, commotion, tussle, tumult, melee
ant. agreement, harmony, peace

aghast
syn. afraid, horrified, shocked, appalled, apprehensive, funky
ant. unsurprised, unaffected, calm

agog
syn. ardent, avid, eager, enthusiastic, curious, agape
ant. incurious, uninterested, indifferent

ail
syn. concern, distress, trouble, worry, afflict, upset
ant. excite, comfort, cheer

alienate
syn. disunite, estrange, distance, isolate, cede, separate
ant. disarm, be friendly, conciliate

allay
syn. alleviate, assuage, lull, palliate, calm, dispel
ant. worsen, aggravate, provoke

altercation
syn. argument, bicker, contention, dispute, squabble, row
ant. agreement, concord, harmony

altruistic
syn. beneficent, benevolent, benign, selfless, philanthropic, noble
ant. selfish, unsacrificing, mercenary

amalgamate
syn. merge, mingle, mix, integrate, fuse, blend
ant. divide, separate, branch

amass
syn. accrue, accumulate, garner, hoard, stockpile, assemble
ant. disperse, dissipate, scatter

ameliorate
syn. amend, improve, upgrade, enrich, enhance, better
ant. worsen, deteriorate, degenerate

amenable
syn. compliant, docile, obedient, willing, docile, pliable
ant. defiant, noncompliant, recalcitrant

amicable
syn. friendly, warmhearted, harmonious, good-humored, polite, neighbourly
ant. hostile, unfriendly, acrimonious

amnesty
syn. forgiveness, pardon, remission, reprieve, absolution, exoneration
ant. censure, denunciation, conviction

amorous
syn. erotic, lewd, lustful, passionate, ardent, infatuated
ant. unloving, detached, indifferent

ample
syn. extensive, copious, substantial, abundant, bounteous, generous
ant. insufficient, meager, paltry

anarchy
syn. disorder, lawlessness, chaos, mayhem, riot, misrule
ant. order, rule, lawfulness

annul
syn. abolish, abrogate, void, rescind, negate, invalidate
ant. retain, validate, keep

antagonism
syn. antipathy, animosity, enmity, hostility, resentment, contradiction
ant. accord, rapport, agreement

antithesis
syn. contrast, opposition, antagonism, polarity, contrariety, converse
ant. same, conformity, uniformity

apathy
syn. indifference, lassitude, ennui, droopiness, listlessness, stolidity
ant. care, concern, sympathy

appalling
syn. awful, dreadful, ghastly, horrendous, outrageous, atrocious
ant. comforting, reassuring, pleasing

apprehension
syn. dread, fright, panic, trepidation, detention, capture
ant. calmness, contentment, happiness

ardent
syn. fervent, passionate, avid, sizzling, fiery, dedicated
ant. cold, dispassionate, frigid

arduous
syn. laborious, demanding, exacting, rigorous, severe, strenuous
ant. easy, facile, effortless

arid
syn. dry, parched, scorched, barren, unfertile, drab
ant. damp, moist, humid

articulate
syn. eloquent, lucid, vocal, fecund, expressive, coherent
ant. unintelligible, unclear, misrepresented

aspersion
syn. slander, slur, calumny, vilification, smear, disparagement
ant. calmness, mildness, happiness

assent
syn. consent, nod, sanction, approbation, acquiescence, approval
ant. dissent, rejection, disagreement

assuage
syn. appease, mitigate, conciliate, placate, dulcify, propitiate
ant. upset, exacerbate, agitate

astounding
syn. astonishing, phenomenal, prodigious, stupendous, wondrous, amazing
ant. boring, dull, satisfying

astute
syn. perceptive, judicious, perspicacious, cagey, canny, shrewd
ant. idiotic, stupid, unintelligent

atrocious
syn. vile, heinous, horrid, nauseating, awful, hideous
ant. inoffensive, innocuous, unobtrusive

audacious
syn. foolhardy, impudent, heroic, intrepid, plucky, undaunted
ant. meek, mild, timid

augment
syn. amplify, intensify, mount, proliferate, aggrandise, upsurge
ant. decrease, degrade, belittle

avarice

syn. covetousness, cupidity, avidity, acquisitiveness, greed, avariciousness

ant. generosity, philanthropy, charity

aversion

syn. abhorrence, detestation, abomination, loathing, repugnance, revulsion

ant. attachment, fondness, liking

avid

syn. keen, fervent, agog, rapacious, ardent, solicitous

ant. dispassionate, indifferent, unenthusiastic

awe

syn. reverence, veneration, admiration, esteem, dread, fright

ant. calmness, familiarity, expectation

Exercise

Choose the word which is CLOSEST in meaning to the given word.

1. Accolades

(a) tribute (b) gain
(c) kudos (d) profit

2. Amnesty

(a) hostility (b) domesticity
(c) acrimony (d) pardon

3. Aberration

(a) anomaly (b) conformity
(c) legality (d) accusation

4. Awe

(a) keen (b) avid
(c) dread (d) fright

Choose the word which is MOST SIMILAR in meaning to the underlined word in the given sentence.

5. I have an aversion to alcohol.

(a) liking (b) esteem
(c) detest (d) frigid

6. I went to the arduous pilgrimage on my own.

(a) strennuous (b) distant (c) closest (d) easy

7. Sumit was charged with causing an affray.

(a) promotion (b) brawl (c) assault (d) offence

Choose the word which is OPPOSITE in meaning to the given word.

8. Acrimonious

(a) acrid (b) dexterous
(c) pleasant (d) apathetic

9. Atrocious

(a) rigorous (b) parched
(c) wonderful (d) tardy

10. Avarice

(a) dedicated (b) charity
(c) mildness (d) capture

Choose the word which is MOST OPPOSITE in meaning to the underlined word in the given sentence.

11. Generally, soldiers are <u>audacious</u> in nature.

(a) timid (b) abhorrence
(c) profitable (d) humble

12. Rupin was <u>alienated</u> by his friends.

(a) isolated (b) conciliated
(c) scolded (d) warned

13. It was <u>appalling</u> to see the condition of her shanty.

(a) shocking (b) revealing
(c) pleasing (d) difficult

14. Neha did not <u>abet</u> in the crime.

(a) incite (b) aid
(c) react (d) discourage

B

baleful
syn. malign, sinister, calamitous, pernicious, foreboding, dire
ant. auspicious, favourable, promising

banal
syn. commonplace, hackneyed, stereotyped, corny, overused, trite
ant. fresh, new, original

bashful
syn. diffident, modest, shy, timid, copy, demure
ant. confident, unabashed, bold

bedlam
syn. chaos, commotion, furor, hubbub, tumult, pandemonium
ant. calm, peace, quiet

befit
syn. agree, correspond, match, serve, suit, behoove
ant. misfit, mismatch, disagree

beguile
syn. betray, deceive, dupe, fool, mislead, hoodwink
ant. dissuade, repel, turn off

belie
syn. distort, falsify, pervert, twist, mislead, warp
ant. attest, prove, counsel

bellicose
syn. belligerent, contentious, combative, hostile, pugnacious, truculent
ant. calm, easygoing, peaceful

bemoan
syn. bewail, complain, cry, deplore, lament, rue
ant. delight, rejoice, revel

bemuse
syn. daze, benumb, stun, stupefy, blunt, deaden
ant. enlighten, illuminate, clear up

benign
syn. benevolent, kind, altruistic, fortunate, propitious, good
ant. hostile, malignant, hurtful

bestow
syn. give, present, contribute, confer, grant, accord
ant. deprive, refuse, take

bewitch
syn. charm, enchant, enthrall, spellbind, voodoo, beguile
ant. disenchant, disgust, turn off

bigoted
syn. intolerant, prejudiced, dogmatic, narrow-minded, chauvinistic, fanatical
ant. tolerant, liberal, lenient

blandish
syn. cajole, coax, adulate, flatter, wheedle, butter up
ant. bully, force, repel

boisterous
syn. blatant, clamorous, strident, vociferous, loudmouthed, effervescent
ant. calm quiet, restrained

bolster
syn. buoy, prop, sustain, support, hold, cushion
ant. hinder, obstruct, prevent

boorish
syn. crass, crude, uncouth, rude, vulgar, philistine
ant. cultured, refined, sophisticated

bottleneck
syn. barrier, hindrance, obstruction, snag, jam, block
ant. help, push, assistance

brash
syn. impetuous, reckless, slapdash, impudent, pert, maladroit
ant. cautious, discreet, careful

brazen
syn. pushy, audacious, nervy, blatant, presumptuous, assuming
ant. shy, meek, humble

browbeat
syn. bludgeon, intimidate, menace, threaten, bully, cow
ant. compliment, coax, praise

buffoon
syn. droll, fool, jester, zany, joker, wag
ant. charmer, enthusiast, exciter

bungle
syn. blunder, flounder, fudge, fumble, muddle, boggle
ant. fix, manage, succeed

buoy
syn. bolster, prop, support, elate, exhilarate, lift
ant. hinder, undermine, obstruct

Exercise

Choose the word which is CLOSEST in meaning to the given word.

1. Benign
   (a) enlightened (b) benevolent (c) enchanting (d) dogmatic

2. Boisterous
   (a) restricted (b) prejudiced (c) clamorous (d) subtle

Choose the word which is MOST SIMILAR in meaning to the underlined word in the given sentence.

3. Sonam was <u>beguiled</u> into purchasing the flat by her friend.
   (a) duped (b) dissuaded (c) repelled (d) stunned

4. As time progresses we tend to be less <u>bashful</u> with our acquaintances.
   (a) bold (b) modest
   (c) sincere (d) stereotyped

5. The PM made some <u>bellicose</u> statements about our military strengths.
   (a) distorted (b) apathetic
   (c) rigid (d) hostile

Choose the word which is OPPOSITE in meaning to the given word.

6. Bedlam
   (a) peace (b) tumult (c) rowdy (d) prosperity

7. Boorish
   (a) vulgar (b) refined (c) rude (d) exciting

Choose the word which is MOST OPPOSITE in meaning to the underlined word in the given sentence.

8. They <u>browbeat</u> him into accepting the offer.
   (a) threatened (b) complimented
   (c) assisted (d) simplified

9. She was <u>buoyed</u> up by the warm wishes.
   (a) guided (b) cheered
   (c) fumbled (d) depressed

10. I was told a <u>brazen</u> lie by Sameer.
    (a) enchanting (b) bold
    (c) brave (d) meek

C

callous

syn. hardened, heartless, obdurate, unfeeling, apathetic, careless
ant. compassionate, sensitive, sympathetic

camouflage

syn. disguise, dissemble, dissimulate, mask, masquerade, deceptive
ant. reveal, show, uncover

canker

syn. infect, poison, brutalise, debase, vitiate, pervert
ant. bless, elevate, upgrade

censorious

syn. captious, carping, critical, faultfinding, hypercritical, belittle
ant. laudatory, praising, flattering

chary

syn. cautious, circumspect, prudent, wary, sparing, thrifty
ant. heedless, rash, careless

chastise

syn. castigate, penalise, discipline, admonish, rebuke, reprimand
ant. cheer, comfort, encourage

cede

syn. abandon, abdicate, demit, renounce, demit, waive
ant. defend, guide, fight

chide

syn. admonish, castigate, rebuke, reprimand, reproach, scold
ant. compliment, laud, praise

circumspect

syn. careful, cautious, chary, wary, prudent, gingerly
ant. indiscreet, rash, audacious

clamorous

syn. blatant, boisterous, obstreperous, strident, vociferous, noisy
ant. quiet, restrained, silent

clandestine

syn. covert, secret, closet, concealed, stealthy, surreptitious
ant. forthright, truthful, open

clemency

syn. charity, grace, lenience, mercy, compassion, forbearance
ant. cruelty, harshness, meanness

cognizant
syn. alive, awake, aware, sensible, sentient, wise
ant. ignorant, unaware, uninformed

comely
syn. attractive, gorgeous, pretty, ravishing, stunning, decent
ant. disgusting, ugly, plain

conciliate
syn. appease, assuage, calm, mollify, placate, pacify
ant. aggravate, incite, provoke

concoct
syn. contrive, devise, fabricate, formulate, hatch, invent
ant. divide, separate, detach

conducive
syn. contributive, helpful, leading, productive, accessory, promoting
ant. adverse, hindering, unfavorable

conform
syn. accord, chime, square, tally, match, befit
ant. differ, fight, refuse

confound
syn. befuddle, bewilder, dizzy, jumble, muddle, discomfit
ant. clarify, enlighten, clear

confront
syn. accost, encounter, face, dare, defy, stand up
ant. back, surrender, yield

congenial
syn. affable, amiable, cordial, genial, pleasant, grateful
ant. incompatible, unfriendly, ill-suited

congruity
syn. accordance, agreement, conformity, harmony, congruence, consistency
ant. conflict, difference, variation

contravene
syn. breach, break, infringe, violate, contradict, negate
ant. concur, consent, endorse

converge
syn. close, centre, channel, focalise, focus, meet
ant. disperse, diverge, scatter

copious
syn. abundant, ample, bounteous, generous, plentiful, substantial
ant. meager, needy, scarce

cozy
syn. comfortable, easy, snug, comfy, cushy, secure
ant. uncomfortable, afflictive, distressing

crave
syn. hunger, itch, lust, desire, implore, plead
ant. abjure, dislike, spurn

cryptic
syn. arcane, enigmatic, mysterious, hidden, secret, puzzling
ant. obvious, plain, seen

curt
syn. abrupt, blunt, brief, brusque, crusty, gruff
ant. gracious, lengthy, polite

cynical
syn. ironic, sardonic, distrustful, acrid, burlesque, caustic
ant. considerate, deferential, savoury

Exercise

Choose the word which is CLOSEST in meaning to the given word.

1. Cynical
(a) savoury (b) sardonic
(c) gruff (d) arcane

2. Curt
(a) brusque (b) gracious
(c) acrid (d) cushy

3. Cozy
(a) crusty (b) ravishing
(c) sentient (d) snug

4. Crave
(a) desire (b) aware
(c) wise (d) biased

Choose the word which is MOST SIMILAR in meaning to the underlined word in the given sentence.

5. The store has copious amount of ration.
(a) gorgeous (b) plentiful (c) pretty (d) appeased

6. Did you check the cryptic clues in the crossword?
(a) obvious (b) detailed (c) quick (d) confusing

7. The company knew that its health drink contravened safety standards.
(a) endorsed (b) exhibited (c) infringed (d) confused

Choose the word which is OPPOSITE in meaning to the given word.

8. Comely
(a) ravishing (b) stealthy
(c) disgusting (d) gorgeous

9. Confront
(a) dare (b) defy
(c) encounter (d) yield

10. Congenial
(a) incompatible (b) abundant
(c) puzzling (d) iconic

11. Converge
(a) savory (b) brief
(c) obvious (d) diverge

Choose the word which is MOST OPPOSITE in meaning to the underlined word in the given sentence.

12. There is no congruity between your sayings and deed.
(a) difference (b) match
(c) sophistication (d) irony

13. Is your home environment conducive to creativity?
(a) hindering (b) restrained
(c) grateful (d) stunning

14. Abhay spoke in a nervous and conciliating voice.
(a) placating (b) provoking
(c) appeasing (d) forboding

D

dainty
syn. delicate, elegant, exquisite, fine, finicky, meticulous
ant. clumsy, coarse, harsh

damn
syn. condemn, doom, sentence, curse, imprecate, cuss
ant. bless, commend, laud

dampen
syn. moisten, deaden, muffle, wet, sprinkle, stifle
ant. dry, scorch, shrivel

dastardly
syn. chickenhearted, cowardly, craven, pusillanimous, unmanly, faint-hearted
ant. brave, courageous, audacious

daunt
syn. appal, consternate, dismay, horrify, shake, shock
ant. assist, embolden, incite

dearth
syn. absence, lack, want, deficit, depletion, paucity
ant. abundance, affluence, plenty

debase
syn. cheapen, degrade, demean, downgrade, adulterate, stain
ant. laud, praise, upgrade

debilitate
syn. attenuate, devitalise, enervate, enfeeble, undermine, undo
ant. assist, invigorate, energise

deceit
syn. deception, duplicity, guile, cunningness, craftiness, chicanery
ant. frankness, openness, uprightness

decrepit
syn. feeble, flimsy, fragile, frail, decaying, dilapidated
ant. durable, tough, sound

decry
syn. belittle, denigrate, depreciate, detract, disparage, slight
ant. applaud, compliment, exalt

deft
syn. adroit, artful, dexterous, facile, slick, nimble
ant. awkward, clumsy, inept

defunct
syn. dead, extinct, lifeless, vanquished, deceased, departed
ant. existent, operative, functioning

defy
syn. brave, challenge, dare, flout, disobey, violate
ant. obey, surrender, yield

demean
syn. abase, degrade, humble, humiliate, degrade, downgrade
ant. enhance, improve, upgrade

denounce
syn. censure, condemn, deplore, accuse, arraign, charge
ant. approve, commend, compliment

deplore
syn. reprehend, reprobate, rue, regret, repent, denounce
ant. approve, rejoice, revel

deprecate
syn. disapprove, derogate, discountenance, detract, disfavour, discount
ant. commend, endorse, compliment

deride
syn. gibe, jeer, jest, mock, ridicule, scoff
ant. flatter, revere, regard

desist
syn. abandon, quit, relinquish, remit, discontinue, break off
ant. endure, persevere, resume

deviate
syn. depart, digress, stray, swerve, veer, wander
ant. stay, keep, remain

devoid
syn. barren, destitute, empty, lacking, void, wanting
ant. occupied, full, filled

diehard
syn. adamant, grim, incompliant, stubborn, relentless, unyielding
ant. merciful, amenable, facile

diffidence
syn. bashful, coy, demure, timid, modest, retiring
ant. bold, confident, aggressive

diminutive
syn. dwarf, pygmy, tiny, wee, minuscule, miniature
ant. huge, giant, large

dingy
syn. shabby, shoddy, sleazy, tattered, decrepit, mangy
ant. immaculate, spotless, preserved

dire
syn. baneful, grave, ominous, portentous, critical, apocalyptic
ant. cheerful, promising, happy

discerning
syn. discriminating, perceptive, clear, tactful, critical, percipient
ant. negligent, overlooking, unobservant

discordant
syn. contradictory, disagreeing, divergent, incongruous, antagonistic, discrepant
ant. harmonious, agreeing, reconciled

disgruntle
syn. disappoint, discontent, dissatisfy, annoy, irritate, irk
ant. delight, excite, please

disguise
syn. cloak, façade, pretense, sham, semblance, masquerade
ant. honesty, truth, openness

dismay
syn. anxiety, apprehension, fright, consternation, trepidation, panic
ant. assurance, confidence, calmness

dismissive
syn. disdainful, contemptuous, cavalier, egotistic, haughty, overbearing
ant. meek, modest, humble

dissent
syn. confrontation, contention, discord, friction, strife, variance
ant. endorsement, ratification, approval

dissipate
syn. dispel, disperse, scatter, consume, squander, waste
ant. accumulate, gather, hoard

distraught
syn. demented, maniac, dotty, insane, disordered, distracted
ant. untroubled, gladdened, calm

divest
syn. deprive, dispossess, rob, strip, bare, expose
ant. confer, bestow, cover

divulge

syn. expose, reveal, uncover, betray, blab
ant. conceal, hide, suppress

dour

syn. austere, bleak, harsh, severe, stark, gloomy
ant. bright, appealing, cheerful

dunce

syn. blockhead, dullard, buffoon, chump, dolt, clod
ant. brilliant, genius, charmer

Exercise

Choose the word which is CLOSEST in meaning to the given word.

1. Devoid
(a) deplore (b) arraign (c) denounce (d) wanting

2. Daunting
(a) muffling (b) ostracising (c) appalling (d) inciting

3. Diminutive
(a) coy (b) tiny (c) relentless (d) sleazy

Choose the word which is MOST SIMILAR in meaning to the underlined word in the given sentence.

4. Saroj got debilitated due to his old age.
(a) downgraded (b) decayed (c) enervated (d) criticised

5. He gifted her a dainty necklace on her birthday.
(a) exquisite (b) precious (c) sturdy (d) gleaming

Choose the word which is OPPOSITE in meaning to the given word.

6. Dingy
(a) ominous (b) grave (c) gloomy (d) immaculate

7. Dissipate
(a) hoard (b) deprive (c) expose (d) betray

8. Divulge
(a) accumulate (b) ratify (c) reject (d) conceal

Choose the word which is MOST OPPOSITE in meaning to the underlined word given in the sentence.

9. It is believed that the great scientist was a dunce at school.
(a) negligent (b) genius (c) stupid (d) alert

10. Neha was disgruntled on hearing her result.
(a) disturbed (b) sober (c) delighted (d) praised

E

earnest
syn. grave, sedate, serious, sombre, solemn, momentous
ant. flippant, frivolous, funny

eccentric
syn. bizarre, freaky, erratic, quaint, weird, idiosyncratic
ant. plain, regular, unusual

ecstatic
syn. delirious, entranced, frenzied, crazy, elated, euphoric
ant. tormented, sorrowful, despaired

eerie
syn. uncanny, weird, mysterious, scary, unearthly, spectral
ant. funny, normal, silly

efface
syn. annul, obliterate, cancel, erase, expunge, delete
ant. retain, validate, keep

effuse
syn. decant, draw, pour, emanate, radiate, gush
ant. fill, close, stop

elude
syn. avoid, bypass, duck, shun, escape, eschew
ant. encounter, entice, invite

emaciated
syn. feeble, debilitated, drained, gaunt, cadaverous, shrunken
ant. heavy, overweight, plump

empathy
syn. sympathy, pity, compassion, condolence, concord, rapport
ant. apathy, discord, disdain

emulate
syn. copy, follow, imitate, contend, contest, rival
ant. abandon, desert, leave

enchant
syn. bewitch, charm, enthrall, spellbind, captivate, fascinate
ant. disgust, repel, repulse

ennui
syn. boredom, monotony, listlessness, jadedness, fatigue, lassitude
ant. excitement, liveliness, vigour

euphemism
syn. pomposity, floridness, grandiloquence, pretense, hedge, circumlocution
ant. conciseness, terseness, directness

evict
syn. dismiss, expel, oust, chuck, eject, bump
ant. admit, include, welcome

evince
syn. demonstrate, display, exhibit, manifest, proclaim, reveal
ant. conceal, hide, cover

exacerbate
syn. annoy, embitter, enrage, inflame, aggravate, provoke
ant. calm, comfort, soothe

exculpate
syn. absolve, clear, exonerate, vindicate, acquit, purge
ant. blame, condemn, sentence

exalt
syn. glorify, uplift, eulogise, extol, laud, exhilarate
ant. castigate, debase, denounce

exasperate
syn. annoy, bother, bug, irk, peeve, provoke
ant. placate, please, soothe

exhort
syn. press, urge, encourage, goad, prick, prod
ant. approve, commend, compliment

exigency
syn. distress, necessity, juncture, need, trouble, want
ant. easy, calmness, ordinariness

exonerate
syn. absolve, vindicate, clear, exculpate, purge, free
ant. accuse, incriminate, condemn

exorbitant
syn. excessive, immoderate, inordinate, undue, overabundant, extravagant
ant. moderate, inexpensive, reasonable

expunge
syn. cancel, delete, efface, undo, wipe, obliterate
ant. build, construct, create

exquisite
syn. dainty, delicate, elegant, fine, graceful, ethereal
ant. flawed, crude, inferior

exterminate
syn. abolish, annihilate, eradicate, erase, obliterate, extirpate
ant. establish, institute, enact

extol
syn. exalt, eulogise, panegyrise, honour, laud, glorify
ant. blame, criticise, calumniate

extraneous
syn. alien, extrinsic, foreign, impertinent, inapplicable, peripheral
ant. native, integral, appropriate

extricate
syn. untangle, extract, liberate, detach, release, liberate
ant. entangle, involve, insert

extrinsic
syn. alien, foreign, outward, superficial, outer, exotic
ant. intrinsic, integral, interior

Exercise

Choose the word which is CLOSEST in meaning to the given word.

1. Expunge
(a) efface (b) absolve
(c) vindicate (d) calumniate

2. Extraneous
(a) superficial (b) integral
(c) foreign (d) concise

3. Earnest
(a) flippant (b) sombre
(c) frivolous (d) weird

4. Extrinsic
(a) alien (b) interior
(c) truthful (d) gross

Choose the word which is MOST SIMILAR in meaning to the underlined word given in the sentence.

5. The kite was extricated by the boy.
(a) pretended (b) untangled
(c) mistaken (d) distrait

6. It was eerie to see him speaking in his dreams.
(a) delirious (b) idiosyncratic
(c) silly (d) mysterious

7. The team was ecstatic on hearing the news.
   (a) frensied (b) bizarre
   (c) tormented (d) freaky

Choose the word which is OPPOSITE in meaning to the given word.

8. Empathy
   (a) jadedness (b) discord
   (c) vigour (d) compassion

9. Exquisite
   (a) peripheral (b) crude
   (c) exotic (d) cryptic

10. Exasperating
   (a) entangling (b) erasing
   (c) placating (d) betraying

11. Extol
   (a) false (b) moderate
   (c) blame (d) innocent

Choose the word which is MOST OPPOSITE in meaning to the underlined word given in the sentence.

12. The press exalted the deeds of the boy.
   (a) hedged (b) covered
   (c) created (d) debase

13. I am quite sure that you would be exonerated.
   (a) commended (b) accused
   (c) placated (d) allured

14. Andre evinced an interest in Tennis at an early age.
   (a) ousted (b) revealed
   (c) enraged (d) hided

F

fallacious

syn. false, illogical, invalid, erroneous, mistaken, deceptive
ant. correct, real, truthful

faraway

syn. distant, far, far-flung, remote, bemused, distrait
ant. close, near, attentive

fastidious

syn. meticulous, punctilious, scrupulous, painstaking, persnickety, exacting
ant. indifferent, informal, uncaring

fathom

syn. apprehend, comprehend, grasp, understand, follow, conceive
ant. misunderstand, misinterpret, confound

feign

syn. fake, pretend, sham, pose, simulate, profess
ant. authenticate, corroborate, substantiate

fervent

syn. ardent, blazing, fervid, passionate, zealous, enthusiastic
ant. dispirited, impassive, discouraged

fervour

syn. ardour, passion, zeal, fire, enthusiasm, heat
ant. apathy, calmness, pessimism

fickle

syn. capricious, erratic, freakish, inconsistent, mercurial, temperamental
ant. constant, reliable, stable

fidelity

syn. faithfulness, loyalty, allegiance, devotion, accuracy, veracity
ant. disloyalty, treachery, infidelity

flag

syn. droop, wilt, sag, decline, degenerate, languish
ant. rise, strengthen, increase

flagrant

syn. offensive, arrant, egregious, glaring, gross, atrocious
ant. mild, moral, restrained

flamboyant

syn. florid, ornate, ostentatious, pretentious, showy, splashy
ant. modest, moderate, restrained

fledgling
syn. beginner, greenhorn, novice, neophyte, tyro, abecedarian
ant. expert, veteran, professional

forestall
syn. avert, obviate, preclude, prevent, forfend, stave off
ant. aid, help, permit

forsake
syn. abandon, desert, leave, quit, desolate, abdicate
ant. rediscover, return, revert

forthright
syn. candid, direct, honest, plainspoken, straightforward, ingenuous
ant. devious, dishonest, truthful

fortify
syn. brace, forearm, gird, ready, confirm, strengthen
ant. hurt, weaken, injure

fortitude
syn. bravery, courage, mettle, pluck, valour, intrepidity
ant. cowardice, weakness, helplessness

foster
syn. cultivate, nourish, nurse, nurture, feed, promote
ant. condemn, discourage, neglect

foxy
syn. crafty, cunning, guileful, scheming, sly, sharp
ant. naive, unintelligent, honest

fractious
syn. disorderly, intractable, refractory, unruly, untoward, recalcitrant
ant. complaisant, agreeable, pleasant

freak
syn. vagary, whim, fanatic, maniac, caprice, notion
ant. regular, ordinary, constant

fret
syn. aggravate, annoy, bother, bug, irritate, peeve
ant. calm, comfort, soothe

frigid
syn. frosty, wintry, icy, gelid, inhibited, arctic
ant. hot, warm, aggressive

frivolous
syn. frothy, giddy, silly, gaga, trivial, scatterbrained
ant. grave, sensible, solemn

Exercise

Choose the word which is CLOSEST in meaning to the given word.

1. Forthright
   (a) devious (b) ingenuous (c) giddy (d) candid

2. Fallacious
   (a) remote (b) erroneous (c) authentic (d) remorseful

Choose the word which is MOST SIMILAR in meaning to the underlined word in the given sentence.

3. Are you worried about his frivolous remark?
   (a) aggressive (b) grave (c) sad (d) silly

4. Jasmine has become a fitness freak now.
   (a) candid (b) hater (c) maniac (d) finder

5. The fledgling company needed a lot of funds.
   (a) experienced (b) budding (c) enterprising (d) fraudulent

Choose the word which is OPPOSITE in meaning to the given word.

6. Fathom
   (a) misinterpret (b) droop (c) witty (d) sham

7. Fortitude
   (a) mettle (b) cowardice (c) condemnation (d) neglect

8. Flagrant
   (a) moral (b) splashy (c) tyro (d) desolate

Choose the word which is OPPOSITE in meaning to the underlined word in the given sentence.

9. The country was swept by patriotic fervour.
   (a) ardour (b) zeal (c) feeling (d) apathy

10. Karna's knowledge forsook him when he needed it the most.
    (a) preclude (b) forearm (c) reverted (d) girded

G - H

gainsay
syn. contradict, contravene, deny, negate, disaffirm, oppugn
ant. concede, concur, reconcile

garner
syn. extract, glean, harvest, accrue, cumulate, aggregate
ant. dissipate, spread, disperse

garrulous
syn. talkative, loquacious, voluble, chatty, eloquent, chattering
ant. taciturn, reserved, uncommunicative

gay
syn. blithe, mirthful, jocund, merry, vivid, lesbian
ant. depressed, upset, worried

genteel
syn. courteous, polite, well-bred, prim, prudish, puritanical
ant. boorish, callous, rugged

gibe
syn. insult, jeer, scoff, taunt, twit, ridicule
ant. commendation, appreciation, compliment

giddy
syn. dizzy, reeling, frivolous, frothy, woozy, silly
ant. sensible, mature, grave

glee
syn. gaiety, hilarity, joviality, merriment, mirth, blitheness
ant. sadness, dullness, solemnity

glib
syn. facile, slick, artful, insincere, flip, suave
ant. inarticulate, stuttering, tongue-tied

glitch
syn. bug, hitch, flaw, setback, malfunction, setback
ant. perfection, achievement, advantage

glut
syn. excess, fat, surplus, superfluity, overflow, overrun
ant. insufficiency, lack, want

grandiose
syn. imposing, magnificent, regal, royal, sublime, pompous
ant. moderate, unpretentious, calm

gratuitous
syn. complimentary, gratis, free, wanton, supererogatory, uncalled-for
ant. costly, expensive, essential

greenhorn
syn. abecedarian, tyro, novice, neophyte, fledgling, tenderfoot
ant. expert, professional, veteran

grievous
syn. deplorable, lamentable, rueful, woeful, mournful, severe
ant. cheerful, delightful, excellent

gritty
syn. coarse, grainy, granular, rough, abrasive, lumpy
ant. fine, smooth, refined

grueling
syn. difficult, taxing, demanding, arduous, backbreaking, rigorous
ant. effortless, smooth, easy

gruesome
syn. ghastly, grim, grisly, hideous, lurid, macabre
ant. pleasant, bright, sunny

guile
syn. artifice, craft, cunningness, foxiness, slyness, deception
ant. frankness, naivety, openness

hapless
syn. ill-fated, luckless, unfortunate, cursed, jinxed, untoward
ant. fortuitous, lucky, well-off

harrowing
syn. agonising, anguishing, excruciating, tormenting, tortuous, frightening
ant. calming, pleasant, straight

headstrong
syn. bullheaded, dogged, mulish, obstinate, perverse, tenacious
ant. docile, submissive, tolerant

heartrending
syn. agonising, distressing, pitiful, doleful, harrowing, tragic
ant. delightful, endurable, soothing

heinous
syn. atrocious, monstrous, outrageous, scandalous, shocking, disgraceful
ant. glorious, wonderful, pleasing

heretic
syn: dissident, nonconformist, schismatic, sectarian, separatist, dissenter
ant. adherent, faithful, loyalist

hideous
syn. ugly, displeasing, grim, gruesome, lurid, macabre
ant. pleasing, attractive, cheerful

hoary
syn. ancient, antiquated, olden, archaic, venerable, timeworn
ant. modern, recent, forward-looking

hone
syn. acuminate, edge, sharpen, whet, grind, taper
ant. blunt, dull, round

hubbub
syn. tumult, clamour, din, hullabaloo, pandemonium, rumpus
ant. calm, order, peace

hyperbole
syn. exaggeration, overstatement, baloney, hogwash, elaboration, boasting
ant. understatement, condensation, suppression

Exercise

Choose the word which is CLOSEST in meaning to the given word.

1. Guile
(a) perfection (b) slyness (c) naivety (d) macabre
2. Horrendous
(a) savoury (b) compliment (c) gaiety (d) unpleasant

Choose the word which is MOST SIMILAR in meaning to the underlined word in the given sentence.

3. Elvira is a garrulous old woman.
(a) submissive (b) taciturn (c) mature (d) loquacious
4. There was a glitch in the office network today.
(a) perfection (b) flip (c) interruption (d) increase
5. No one knew who was behind the hideous crime.
(a) grim (b) tortuous (c) scandalous (d) perverse

Choose the word which is OPPOSITE in meaning to the given word.

6. Heretic
(a) sectarian (b) loyalist (c) nonconformist (d) socialist
7. Hapless
(a) gruesome (b) abrasive (c) fortuitous (d) taxing
8. Glut
(a) lack (b) hitch (c) mirth (d) superfluity

Choose the word which is MOST OPPOSITE in meaning to the underlined word in the given sentence.

9. Is paying your bills a harrowing experience for you?
(a) excruciating (b) tenacious (c) chaotic (d) pleasant
10. Are you a greenhorn in this venture?
(a) veteran (b) novice (c) stranger (d) participant

I - K

idiosyncrasy

syn. eccentricity, peculiarity, quirk, singularity, abnormality, freakishness

ant. normality, standard, regularity

illusory

syn. fallacious, unreal, dreamlike, misleading, delusive, hallucinatory

ant. real, certain, definite

imbibe

syn. sip, guzzle, consume, absorb, assimilate, digest

ant. abstain, ignore, evade

imminent

syn. impending, momentary, proximate, forthcoming, expectant, approaching

ant. distant, doubtful, later

immune

syn. impervious, insusceptible, resistant, exempt, clear, safe

ant. unguarded, vulnerable, susceptible

impart

syn. carry, communicate, convey, disclose, transmit, tell

ant. conceal, hide, withhold

impassioned

syn. ardent, blazing, fervent, glowing, passionate, scorching

ant. frigid, uncaring, indifferent

impel

syn. galvanise, spur, mobilise, propel, actuate, drive

ant. dissuade, repress, suppress

implicate

syn. embroil, involve, incriminate, inculpate, entangle, mire

ant. defend, pardon, release

implicit

syn. inferred, tacit, unsaid, unfaltering, absolute, wholehearted

ant. specific, explicit, restricted

impoverish
syn. bankrupt, bust, pauperise, ruin, deplete, exhaust
ant. enrich, stabilise, strengthen

impudence
syn. audacity, boldness, effrontery, pertness, insolence, pushiness
ant. shyness, uncertainty, modesty

inadvertent
syn. unintentional, unplanned, meant, accidental, contingent, fortuitous
ant. deliberate, intentional, attentive

inanimate
syn. dead, insensate, defunct, extinct, inert, lifeless
ant. living, functioning, operative

inbred
syn. native, natural, congenital, constitutional, elemental, innate
ant. extra, additional, foreign

incisive
syn. acute, keen, penetrating, sharp, probing, trenchant
ant. stupid, dull, blunt

incredulous
syn. disbelieving, questioning, skeptical, dubious, hesitant, suspicious
ant. convinced, credulous, believing

indefatigable
syn. tireless, unfailing, unflagging, untiring, weariless, inexhaustible
ant. tired, weary, fatigued

indict
syn. accuse, arraign, charge, denounce, incriminate, tax
ant. absolve, acquit, exonerate

indignation
syn. anger, ire, exasperation, fury, pique, rage
ant. glee, comfort, happiness

indeterminate
syn. ambiguous, dubious, clouded, indecisive, equivocal, indefinite
ant. definite, measurable, determined

indolent
syn. lazy, slothful, sluggish, inert, sluggard, lethargic
ant. diligent, energetic, intent

inept
syn. incongruous, infelicitous, incompetent, maladroit, lumpish, clumsy
ant. adroit, dexterous, competent

infringe
syn. breach, break, contravene, transgress, violate, encroach
ant. comply, obey, observe

ingenuous
syn. guileless, naive, candid, downright, unsophisticated, forthright
ant. deceitful, sly, dishonest

inimical
syn. hostile, unfriendly, adverse, noxious, pernicious, repugnant
ant. friendly, hospitable, kind

iniquity
syn. wickedness, unjustness, diablerie, immorality, misdeed, offence
ant. virtue, goodness, ethicality

innate
syn. hereditary, inborn, congenital, intrinsic, elemental, ingrained
ant. extrinsic, acquired, superficial

innocuous
syn. harmless, inoffensive, insipid, jejune, vapid, washy
ant. destructive, injurious, harmful

inordinate
syn. excessive, exorbitant, extravagant, overmuch, undue, immoderate
ant. moderate, reasonable, warranted

insatiate
syn. avaricious, avid, covetous, craving, hoggish, desirous
ant. abstemious, benevolent, generous

insidious
syn. astute, crafty, crooked, cunning, deceitful, adroit
ant. fair, sincere, open

insinuate
syn. imply, intimate, suggest, foist, infiltrate, edge
ant. conceal, withhold, hide

insipid
syn. bland, savoury, innocuous, vapid, jejune, watery
ant. exciting, exhilarating, pleasing

insolent
syn. haughty, overbearing, supercilious, brazen, presumptuous, sassy
ant. modest, servile, humble

insurgent
syn. rebellious, mutinous, revolutionary, riotous, seditious, anarchical
ant. obedient, subordinate, compliant

intangible
syn. impalpable, imperceptible, invisible, unnoticeable, indiscernible, insensible
ant. palpable, perceptible, tangible

intrepid
syn. audacious, dauntless, gallant, mettlesome, plucky, valiant
ant. meek, timid, cowardly

irrelevant
syn. extraneous, immaterial, impertinent, inapplicable, digressive, unsuitable
ant. appropriate, relevant, pertinent

irresolute
syn. halting, hesitant, indecisive, pendulous, tentative, timid
ant. definite, unyielding, obstinate

jittery
syn. edgy, fidgety, nervous, restless, tense, twitchy
ant. assured, content, cool

juncture
syn. connection, seam, coupling, joint, crisis, exigency
ant. disconnection, disjoint, anticlimax

kinetic
syn. brisk, dynamic, sprightly, strenuous, vigorous, lively
ant. lethargic, sluggish, dull

knack
syn. trick, adeptness, technique, proficiency, bent, instinct
ant. ineptitude, lack, want

knave
syn. fraud, miscreant, rogue, scoundrel, swindler, reprobate
ant. gentleman, reputable, virtuous

Exercise

Choose the word which is CLOSEST in meaning to the given word.

1. Knack
   (a) bent (b) swindle (c) exigency (d) vigour

2. Idiosyncrasy
   (a) effrontery (b) assimilation
   (c) proximity (d) freakishness

Choose the word which is MOST SIMILAR in meaning to the underlined word in the given sentence.

3. Rakshit was feeling <u>jittery</u> before the commencement of his interview.
   (a) defunct (b) fidgety
   (c) fervent (d) mired

4. What values did Shankar <u>imbibe</u> from his experiences?
   (a) evade (b) validate
   (c) ascertain (d) assimilate

5. One student had the <u>impudence</u> to use his cellphone during the exam.
   (a) prohibition (b) ingenuity
   (c) effrontery (d) knowledge

Choose the word which is OPPOSITE in meaning to the given word.

6. Intrepid
   (a) diligent (b) timid (c) adroit (d) frightened

7. Knave
   (a) virtuous (b) lively (c) cunning (d) lazy

Choose the word which is MOST OPPOSITE in meaning to the underlined word in the given sentence.

8. Shweta was known for her <u>incisive</u> remarks.
   (a) inept (b) probing
   (c) audacious (d) stupid

9. Nelson Mandela fought against the <u>iniquities</u> of apartheid.
   (a) wickedness (b) virtues
   (c) survivors (d) detractors

10. I was always rather <u>inept</u> at art.
    (a) inert (b) dexterous
    (c) grumpy (d) great

L - M

laggard
syn. loiterer, saunterer, dawdler, sluggard, drone, procrastinator
ant. quick, focused, hardworking

lambaste
syn. assail, assault, batter, admonish, castigate, thrash
ant. defend, resist, praise

lanky
syn. lean, meager, gangly, slim, feeble, bony
ant. robust, brawny, sturdy

levity
syn. inconstancy, volatility, fitfulness, caprice, wavering, indecision
ant. persistence, steadfastness, tenacity

licentious
syn. voluptuous, dissolute, rakish, debauched, profligate, unbridled
ant. temperate, sober, ascetic

limpid
syn. transparent, crystalline, pure, lucid, clear, explicit
ant. opaque, muddy, hazy

linger
syn. tarry, loiter, saunter, lag, hesitate, wait
ant. haste, press, push

livid
syn. lurid, pale, pallid, dusky, bloodless, haggard
ant. lively, sanguine, incarnadine

loathe
syn. abominate, detest, execrate, hate, despise, dislike
ant. desire, long for, love

lonesome
syn. forlorn, dreary, forsaken, solitary, desolate, lonely
ant. befriended, animated, bustling

long
syn. desire, aspire, yearn, wish, crave, want
ant. aver, abhor, loathe

lop

syn. prune, curtail, shorten, retrench, amputate, truncate
ant. grow, elongate, trail

lull

syn. quiet, assuagement, cessation, tranquil, subsidence, quiescence
ant. tumult, tempest, storm

luscious

syn. sweet, delicious, appetising, delightful, savoury, tasty
ant. sour, tart, bitter

lustrous

syn. gleaming, glossy, radiant, refulgent, luminous, shiny
ant. dull, leaden, opaque

maladroit

syn. awkward, clumsy, lumpish, gauche, inept, brash
ant. dexterous, skilful, adroit

malaise

syn. distress, infirmity, angst, melancholy, debility, doldrums
ant. wellbeing, vigour, health

manifest

syn. evince, convey, proclaim, embody, incarnate, express
ant. conceal, harbour, hide

maverick

syn. radical, nonconformist, bohemian, dissenter, unorthodox, original
ant. conformist, orthodox, standard

measly

syn. exiguous, puny, negligible, nugatory, inconsiderate, trifling
ant. abundant, plenty, sufficient

melancholy

syn. depression, despondency, glum, dumps, funks, dejection
ant. joy, cheerfulness, happiness

menacing

syn. dangerous, threatening, intimidating, endangering, impending, fearsome
ant. aiding, helping, assisting

menial

syn. obsequious, servile, slavish, subservient, demeaning, base
ant. superior, talented, skilled

metamorphosis
syn. changeover, conversion, mutation, transformation, shift, transmutation
ant. stagnation, maintenance, deactivation

mettle
syn. bravery, courage, gallantry, intrepidity, nerve, valiancy
ant. cowardice, diffidence, timidity

minuscule
syn. diminutive, dwarf, miniature, minute, pigmy, tiny
ant. huge, big, tall

mitigate
syn. allay, alleviate, assuage, palliate, relieve, lessen
ant. aggravate, incite, irritate

modicum
syn. crumb, dot, fragment, iota, shred, whit
ant. lot, plenty, whole

mollify
syn. appease, conciliate, propitiate, soothe, dulcify, placate
ant. exasperate, provoke, irk

momentous
syn. earnest, severe, grave, weighty, fatal, significant
ant. trivial, insignificant, petty

morose
syn. sullen, glum, saturnine, sour, sulky, surly
ant. optimistic, cheerful, joyous

mournful
syn. rueful, woeful, dolorous, grievous, lugubrious, plaintive
ant. hopeful, optimistic, pleasant

mundane
syn. earthen, secular, tellurian, temporal, terrene, worldly
ant. exciting, supernatural, extraordinary

myopic
syn. biased, astigmatic, shortsighted, blind, prejudiced, partial
ant. farsighted, provident, fair

myriad
syn. legion, many, numerous, multitudinous, countless, immeasurable
ant. limited, measurable, finite

Exercise

Choose the word which is CLOSEST in meaning to the given word.

1. Malaise
(a) angst (b) subsidence (c) dissent (d) glum

2. Mitigate
(a) incite (b) palliate (c) harbour (d) increase

3. Menacing
(a) servile (b) saturnine (c) impending (d) conciliatory

Choose the word which is MOST SIMILAR in meaning to the underlined word in the given sentence.

4. Josh is a <u>laggard</u>. Isn't he?
(a) unscrupulous (b) dawdler (c) pessimist (d) feminist

5. Saksham never <u>longed</u> to be in the Army.
(a) hated (b) tried (c) yearned (d) liked

Choose the word which is OPPOSITE in meaning to the given word.

6. Loathe
(a) detest (b) despise (c) desire (d) execrate

7. Maverick
(a) conformist (b) trifling (c) veteran (d) nugatory

8. Myriad
(a) miraculous (b) sullen (c) varied (d) limited

Choose the word which is MOST OPPOSITE in meaning to the underlined word in the given sentence.

9. Peehu treated the matter with <u>levity</u>.
(a) sense (b) caprice (c) brevity (d) lull

10. Adam tried to <u>mollify</u> Eve by gifting her a present.
(a) dulcify (b) exasperate (c) placate (d) conquer

N - O

nadir

syn. base, bottom, lowest, floor, minimal, zero level
ant. top, zenith, highest

nag

syn. fuss, scold, carp at, nudge, annoy, badger
ant. assuage, praise, please

nauseating

syn. atrocious, disgusting, revolting, sickening, repulsive, vile
ant. alluring, appealing, likeable

nefarious

syn. abhorrent, despicable, disgusting, loathsome, lousy, mean
ant. respectable, honorable, virtuous

negate

syn. nullify, abolish, annul, invalidate, contravene, traverse
ant. approve, permit, allow

noisome

syn. fetid, foul, malodorous, mephitic, reeky, stinking
ant. upright, moral, just

nonpartisan

syn. impartial, neutral, uncommitted, dispassionate, equitable, impartial
ant. partial, biased, prejudiced

noxious

syn. baneful, malignant, pernicious, pestilent, virulent, deadly
ant. hygienic, sterile, wholesome

nudge

syn. dig, jab, jog, poke, prod, shove
ant. aid, gratify, soothe

oblique

syn. biased, slanted, circuitous, devious, tortuous, indirect
ant. direct, forthright, straightforward

obliterate

syn. eradicate, extirpate, liquidate, erase, exterminate, efface
ant. build, construct, create

oblivious
syn. forgetful, ignorant, unconscious, unfamiliar, unwitting, amnesic
ant. aware, conscious, mindful

obnoxious
syn. contemptible, detestable, loathsome, lousy, nefarious, rotten
ant. admirable, respectable, worthy

obscure
syn. foggy, indistinct, insular, unobtrusive, nebulous, vague
ant. apparent, explicit, perceptible

obtrusive
syn. interfering, intrusive, meddlesome, meddling, officious, nosy
ant. unconcerned, avoiding, modest

obtuse
syn. dumb, stupid, blockheaded, dimwitted, stolid, insensitive
ant. intelligent, smart, quick

offhand
syn. extempore, impromptu, improvised, unrehearsed, informal, laidback
ant. deliberate, calculated, planned

oft
syn. generally, habitually, regularly, often, frequently, customarily
ant. rarely, seldom, occasionally

opportune
syn. auspicious, favourable, propitious, prosperous, timely, well-timed
ant. unlucky, unsuitable, disadvantageous

optimal
syn. best, optimum, superlative, unsurpassed, choicest, matchless
ant. flawed, imperfect, problematic

ostensible
syn. apparent, external, ostensive, outward, seeming, superficial
ant. improbable, obscure, unlikely

outmoded
syn. antique, archaic, bygone, dated, dowdy, fusty
ant. current, modern, popular

overbearing
syn. arrogant, haughty, insolent, dictatorial, authoritarian, imperious
ant. humble, modest, shy

overt
syn. manifest, apparent, definite, public, observable, visible
ant. concealed, secret, hidden

overwhelming
syn. awesome, staggering, towering, mind-blowing, mind-boggling, intense
ant. average, dull, reasonable

Exercise

Choose the word which is CLOSEST in meaning to the given word.

1. Nag
(a) nudge (b) negate (c) revolt (d) agree

2. Outmoded
(a) improbable (b) dowdy (c) haughty (d) meek

3. Obtuse
(a) stolid (b) lousy (c) amnesic (d) impromptu

Choose the word which is MOST SIMILAR in meaning to the underlined word in the given sentence.

4. She was found to be involved in <u>nefarious</u> activities.
(a) virtuous (b) illusive (c) simple (d) despicable

5. It was an <u>oblique</u> reference to his parents' life.
(a) indirect (b) direct (c) pernicious (d) sullen

Choose the word which is OPPOSITE in meaning to the given word.

6. Noxious
(a) hygienic (b) fetid (c) attractive (d) pestilent

7. Oft
(a) rarely (b) openly (c) regularly (d) habitually

8. Nebulous
(a) attractive (b) ambiguous (c) narrow (d) clear

Choose the word which is MOST OPPOSITE in meaning to the underlined word in the given sentence.

9. Karni Sena <u>overtly</u> supported the ban on the movie.
(a) openly (b) secretly (c) steadily (d) wisely

10. Was Smita <u>oblivious</u> to her surroundings?
(a) forgetful (b) conscious (c) vague (d) close

P - Q

palliate

syn. allay, alleviate, assuage, extenuate, mitigate, lighten
ant. accuse, blame, condemn

palpable

syn. tactile, appreciable, detectable, discernible, perceivable, perceptible
ant. elusive, subtle, imperceptible

pandemonium

syn. babel, clamour, din, hubbub, racket, rumpus
ant. quiet, silence, peace

pariah

syn. deportee, derelict, expatriate, fugitive, vagabond, tramp
ant. confronting, permanent, caring

parity

syn. equality, par, sameness, affinity, conformity, consistency
ant. inequality, variation, irregularity

parsimonious

syn. cheap, niggard, pinching, penurious, miserly, stingy
ant. generous, lavish, liberal

partake

syn. contribute, engage, indulge, participate, conduce, ingest
ant. abstain, refrain, distress

pedantic

syn. academic, bookish, donnish, literary, scholastic, formal
ant. informal, ignorant, illiteracy

peeve

syn. aggravate, annoy, bother, exasperate, fret, nettle
ant. comfort, soothe, calm

perpetuate

syn. bolster, eternise, immortalise, conserve, maintain, preserve
ant. cease, prevent, stop

pervade
syn. imbue, impregnate, permeate, saturate, suffuse, transfuse
ant. deplete, drain, exhaust

petite
syn. bantam, diminutive, miniature, slight, dainty, tiny
ant. giant, huge, tall

phlegmatic
syn. apathetic, detached, impassive, stolid, indifferent, listless
ant. ardent, friendly, warm

piquant
syn. pungent, sharp, spicy, zesty, poignant, spirited
ant. bland, dull, boring

ponderous
syn. heavy, hefty, cumbersome, lumpish, elephantine, weighty
ant. airy, buoyant, delicate

pragmatic
syn. prosaic, realistic, sober, down-to-earth, logical, utilitarian
ant. romantic, idealistic, unrealistic

prate
syn. babble, chatter, gabble, blather, jabber, prattle
ant. sense, wisdom, drawl

predicament
syn. corner, dilemma, hot spot, plight, quagmire, trouble
ant. solution, fix, boon

preempt
syn. arrogate, assume, engage, monopolise, seize, usurp
ant. give, offer, release

preposterous
syn. ridiculous, idiotic, insane, lunatic, moronic, outrageous
ant. reasonable, sensible, sane

presumptuous
syn. rude, brash, brazen, impertinent, impudent, insolent
ant. humble, modest, meek

primeval
syn. earliest, early, primary, primitive, pristine, original
ant. modern, current, present

pristine
syn. purified, refined, immaculate, unadulterated, sterile, stainless
ant. impure, stained, dirty

procrastinate
syn. dally, dawdle, linger, loiter, tarry, trail
ant. accelerate, advance, quicken

prod
syn. foment, goad, impel, incite, instigate, prompt
ant. repress, suppress, dissuade

profane
syn. blasphemous, sacrilegious, temporal, ribald, scurrilous
ant. sacred, pious, reverent

profligate
syn. dissipated, dissolute, licentious, unbridled, wanton, extravagant
ant. chaste, moral, innocent

promulgate
syn. announce, proclaim, propagate, disseminate, enact, legislate
ant. conceal, hide, hinder

propitious
syn. advantageous, beneficial, auspicious, opportune, benign, fortunate
ant. inauspicious, unpromising, unfavourable

puerile
syn. childish, immature, infantile, juvenile, naive, inane
ant. mature, adult, intelligent

quandary
syn. puzzle, perplexity, bewilderment, predicament, dilemma, bind
ant. certainty, solution, fix

quarantine
syn. detention, seclusion, segregation, separation, disjunction, estrangement
ant. freedom, liberation, release

quarry
syn. aim, chase, game, objective, victim, prey
ant. attacker, subjective, culprit

quash
syn. crush, extinguish, quell, suppress, quench, squash
ant. aid, assist, help

quench
syn. douse, choke, gag, muffle, repress, smother, throttle
ant. set, release, free

Exercise

Choose the word which is CLOSEST in meaning to the given word.

1. Pandemonium
   (a) din (b) affinity (c) distress (d) calm

2. Pariah
   (a) saint (b) judge
   (c) foster (d) fugitive

3. Quash
   (a) prattle (b) suppress (c) suffuse (d) bother

Choose the word which is MOST SIMILAR in meaning to the underlined word in the given sentence.

4. Tension was palpable on the skipper's face.
   (a) discernible (b) elusive (c) confronting (d) often

5. Babita was in such a great quandary.
   (a) insecurity (b) limelight (c) perplexity (d) levity

Choose the word which is OPPOSITE in meaning to the given word.

6. Profane
   (a) temporal (b) reverent (c) unbridled (d) stained

7. Querulous
   (a) good-natured (b) victim (c) petulant (d) protagonist

Choose the word which is MOST OPPOSITE in meaning to the underlined word in the given sentence.

8. The saint promulgated the teachings of Buddhism.
   (a) disseminated (b) enacted (c) supported (d) hindered

9. His great asset was his calm and phlegmatic manner.
   (a) stolid (b) proper (c) nervous (d) scholastic

10. Bheem behaved in a puerile way.
    (a) juvenile (b) unpromising (c) childlike (d) mature

R

radical

syn. fundamental, primary, extremist, underlying, rabid, fanatic
ant. extrinsic, conservative, moderate

rakish

syn. licentious, profligate, wanton, dissolute, unbridled, dissipated
ant. upright, gentleman, moral

ramble

syn. drift, meander, roam, stray, wander, saunter
ant. direct, guide, stay

rancid

syn. frowzy, fusty, moldy, musty, putrid, rotten
ant. perfumed, fresh, pleasant

rankle

syn. exasperate, bother, embitter, pester, rile, vex
ant. delight, lease, placate

rant

syn. bellow, harangue, rave, clamour, agitate, outrage
ant. calm soothe, forbear

ravenous

syn. famished, starving, voracious, edacious, rapacious, avid
ant. satisfied, indifferent, generous

recalcitrant

syn. defiant, indocile, obstreperous, refractory, untoward, wild
ant. amenable, obedient, accommodating

recapitulate

syn. abstract, epitomise, review, summarise, synopsise, outline
ant. disperse, scatter, conceal

reconcile

syn. reunite, resolve, acclimatise, conform, adapt, attune
ant. dissent, object, estrange

redoubtable

syn. appalling, direful, scary, illustrious, formidable, prominent
ant. comforting, soothing, unremarkable

redress
syn. amend, rectify, reform, remedy, repay, vindicate
ant. accuse, damage, punish

refractory
syn. fractious, indocile, intractable, recalcitrant, disorderly, unruly
ant. manageable, obedient, amenable

refurbish
syn. refresh, recreate, rejuvenate, renovate, revamp, renew
ant. demolish, destroy, ruin

relegate
syn. commend, commit, confide, consign, entrust, hand over
ant. assume, hold, keep

remiss
syn. derelict, lax, neglectful, negligent, slack, careless
ant. mindful, scrupulous, thoughtful

remorseful
syn. compunctious, contrite, penitent, regretful, repentant, sorry
ant. callous, merciless, ruthless

repercussion
syn. force, impact, impression, influence, echo, reverberation
ant. cause, question, ineffectuality

replete
syn. brimming, bursting, chockablock, full, packed, teeming
ant. empty, needy, wanting

repress
syn. choke, gag, block, muffle, smother, stifle
ant. permit, allow, let go

reprove
syn. admonish, castigate, chastise, reprimand, reproach, criticise
ant. applaud, commend, extol

repulse
syn. repel, parry, fend, beat off, keep off, rebuff
ant. attract, enchant, draw

requisite
syn. essential, indispensable, necessary, mandatory, obligatory, compulsory
ant. optional, non-essential, voluntary

restive

syn. edgy, fidgety, jittery, nervous, restless, twitchy
ant. calm, patient, relaxed

retort

syn. respond, riposte, counter, reciprocate, retaliate, reply
ant. question, request, corroborate

retract

syn. abjure, recant, withdraw, recede, retreat, retrogress
ant. emphasise, reaffirm, corroborate

retrench

syn. conserve, curtail, cut down, reduce, scrimp, trim
ant. extend, lengthen, prolong

retrieve

syn. recoup, recover, regain, salvage, redeem, fetch
ant. give, offer, relinquish

revel

syn. bask, indulge, roll, rollick, wallow, rejoice
ant. disappoint, succeed, distress

reverent

syn. admiring, deferential, reverential, upholding, worshipping, regardful
ant. insincere, immodest, inconsiderate

rickety

syn. precarious, shaky, tottering, unstable, wobbly, unsteady
ant. stable, steady, certain

rivet

syn. enthrall, fascinate, grip, mesmerise, spellbind, transfix
ant. distract, repel, disenchant

rout

syn. conquer, overcome, prevail, subdue, vanquish, surmount
ant. lose, surrender, fail

rudimentary

syn. basic, elementary, initial, primary, simple, undeveloped
ant. additional, derivative, nonessential

ruffian

syn. hoodlum, rowdy, delinquent, hooligan, thug, bully
ant. restrained, sophisticate, police

Exercise

Choose the word which is CLOSEST in meaning to the given word.

1. Rant
   (a) soothe (b) scatter (c) estrange (d) clamour

2. Reconcile
   (a) attune (b) disperse (c) rejuvenate (d) consign

Choose the word which is MOST SIMILAR in meaning to the underlined word in the given sentence.

3. History is <u>replete</u> with examples of wars fought to prove one's supremacy over the other.
   (a) teeming (b) fidgety
   (c) wobbly (d) lacking

4. Would you stop <u>rambling</u>?
   (a) bellowing (b) embittering
   (c) playing (d) wandering

5. She resigned when she was <u>relegated</u> to a desk job.
   (a) assumed (b) consigned
   (c) laxed (d) derelicted

Choose the word which is OPPOSITE in meaning to the given word.

6. Restive
   (a) twitchy (b) mandatory
   (c) sluggish (d) patient

7. Rickety
   (a) steady (b) reverential
   (c) temporary (d) immodest

Choose the word which is MOST OPPOSITE in meaning to the underlined word in the given sentence.

8. Was Somit <u>reproved</u> today as well?
   (a) extolled (b) reprimanded
   (c) soothed (d) questioned

9. Many companies had to <u>retrench</u> these days.
   (a) recant (b) increase
   (c) extend (d) salvage

10. Kavita has <u>rudimentary</u> knowledge on this subject.
    (a) primitive (b) additional
    (c) archaic (d) rigid

S

sagacious

syn. wise, balanced, judicious, rational, sane, sapient
ant. stupid, ignorant, careless

satiate

syn. cloy, engorge, glut, pall, sate, surfeit
ant. deprive, dissatisfy, perturb

scoff

syn. deride, gibe, jeer, mock, ridicule, taunt
ant. respect, regard, praise

scrupulous

syn. careful, fastidious, meticulous, painstaking, punctilious, detailed
ant. negligent, careless, shallow

seduce

syn. allure, entice, inveigle, lure, tempt, debauch
ant. disenchant, repel, dissuade

serene

syn. placid, tranquil, calm, halcyon, quiet, still
ant. agitated, disturbed, troubled

sinister

syn. baleful, malign, malicious, deleterious, apocalyptic, foreboding
ant. benevolent, inauspicious, aiding

slipshod

syn. messy, sloppy, slovenly, disheveled, unkempt, untidy
ant. polished, refined, meticulous

slothful

syn. indolent, lazy, shiftless, sluggard, idle, lethargic
ant. active, lively, enthusiastic

slur

syn. asperse, backbite, calumniate, defame, malign, slander
ant. compliment, flatter, praise

sly

syn. crafty, cunning, foxy, guileful, scheming, wily
ant. honest, straightforward, dull

sneer
syn. affront, belittle, disdain, disparage, ridicule, jeer
ant. appease, compliment, respect

snob
syn. elitist, braggart, highbrow, pretender, parvenu, name-dropper
ant. social, polite, introvert

snub
syn. rebuff, shun, spurn, humiliate, offend, burr
ant. welcome, include, laud

solicitous
syn. anxious, agog, ardent, bursting, considerate, courteous
ant. unworried, laid-back, lukewarm

sombre
syn. cheerless, desolate, dreary, sedate, solemn, staid
ant. cheerful, lively, joyful

soporific
syn. opiate, slumberous, somnolent, drowsy, nodding, dozy
ant. awake, invigorating, stimulating

spurn
syn. decline, dismiss, refuse, reject, rebuff, shun
ant. embrace, welcome, want

squeamish
syn. dainty, exacting, fastidious, finicky, meticulous, persnickety
ant. willing, desirous, ready

staid
syn. earnest, grave, sedate, demure, composed, dignified
ant. adventurous, frivolous, sporting

stealthy
syn. feline, furtive, slinky, sneaking, clandestine, covert
ant. forthright, candid, upright

stilted
syn. wooden, pedantic, conceited, spurious, phony, edgy
ant. genuine, unimpaired, resilient

stodgy
syn. aseptic, lackluster, lifeless, prosaic, sterile, stumpy
ant. adventurous, fascinating, classy

stoic
syn. apathetic, detached, dispassionate, impassive, indomitable, phlegmatic
ant. passionate, concerned, responsive

strident

syn. boisterous, clamorous, jarring, raspy, raucous, vociferous
ant. restrained, circumspect, soothing

subdued

syn. hushed, unobtrusive, whispery, quiet, restrained, tasteful
ant. boisterous, communicative, roused

subjugate

syn. conquer, defeat, overcome, surmount, vanquish, enthrall
ant. liberate, relinquish, capitulate

submissive

syn. acquiescent, amenable, compliant, docile, tractable, passive
ant. intractable, resistant, unyielding

sulky

syn. dour, gloomy, morose, saturnine, sour, sullen
ant. content, joyous, gratified

sullen

syn. glum, morose, sour, churlish, fretful, perverse
ant. grinning, genial, uplifting

sumptuous

syn. lavish, luxuriant, opulent, palatial, gorgeous, grand
ant. mean, inferior, crude

surge

syn. flow, gush, pour, run, rush, stream
ant. abate, dwindle, stagnate

surly

syn. morose, grouchy, crabby, peevish, petulant, querulous
ant. gentle, please, animated

swindle

syn. cozen, defraud, gull, mulct, rook, victimise
ant. donate, give, be forthright

sycophant

syn. adulator, courtier, flatterer, fawner, minion, puppet
ant. leader, superior, proud

Exercise

Choose the word which is CLOSEST in meaning to the given word.

1. Soporific
   (a) drowsy (b) invigorating (c) bursting (d) insane

2. Stodgy
   (a) passionate (b) jarring (c) jovial (d) lacklustre

Choose the word which is MOST SIMILAR in meaning to the underlined word in the given sentence.

3. Isn't Kavya such a snob?
   (a) introvert (b) pretender
   (c) extrovert (d) saviour

4. They kept on grinning slyly.
   (a) sluggardly (b) loudly
   (c) openly (d) artfully

5. Amandeep walked stridently towards the CEO's office.
   (a) awkwardly (b) slowly
   (c) boisterously (d) shyly

Choose the word which is OPPOSITE in meaning to the given word.

6. Satiate
   (a) glut (b) deride
   (c) deprive (d) debauch

7. Seduce
   (a) lure (b) perturb
   (c) disenchant (d) prod

Choose the word which is MOST OPPOSITE in meaning to the underlined word in the given sentence.

8. Ankita was in a sulky mood today.
   (a) morose (b) jovial
   (c) saturnine (d) philanthropic

9. The arrangements were made in slipshod manner.
   (a) slovenly (b) meticulous
   (c) lively (d) exciting

10. There was a surge in petrol prices after the budget.
    (a) gush (b) stability
    (c) decrease (d) subsidy

T - U

tacit
syn. silent, unsaid, unuttered, implicit, inferred
ant. explicit, specific, clamorous

taciturn
syn. incommunicative, reserved, reticent, tightlipped, restrained, incommunicable
ant. communicative, talkative, wordy

tangible
syn. palpable, concrete, material, phenomenal, physical, substantial
ant. abstract, conceptual, imperceptible

tantalise
syn. bait, tease, annoy, badger, baffle, thwart
ant. disenchant, repulse, turn off

taut
syn. stiff, firm, snug, stressed, tidy, tense
ant. droopy, flabby, slack

tenable
syn. defensible, excusable, justifiable, logical, plausible, fit
ant. invalid, unjustifiable, unreasonable

tenuous
syn. feeble, flimsy, insubstantial, subtle, sketchy, slender
ant. significant, substantial, stable

testy
syn. peppery, touchy, crabbed, cranky, irascible, peevish
ant. happy, pleasant, gentle

thaw
syn. deliquesce, dissolve, fuse, flux, liquefy, melt
ant. freeze, concentrate, thicken

threadbare
syn. decrepit, dingy, shoddy, hackneyed, tattered, trite
ant. fresh, unused, new

thwart
syn. baffle, balk, check, foil, frustrate, stymie
ant. forward, encourage, assist

ticklish

syn. capricious, erratic, fickle, inconsistent, unsteady, volatile
ant. straightforward, stable, constant

tinker

syn. fiddle, meddle, mess, tamper, fidget, twiddle
ant. relax, dodge, ignore

torpid

syn. numb, stuporous, lethargic, unresponsive, sluggish, insensitive
ant. energetic, lively, active

torrid

syn. ardent, blistering, broiling, scorching, fervent, passionate
ant. freezing, frigid, dispassionate

tortuous

syn. flexuous, meandrous, sinuous, serpentine, devious, oblique
ant. direct, straight, untwisted

totter

syn. sway, teeter, waver, wobble, stagger, stumble
ant. ascend, scale, rise

traitorous

syn. disloyal, perfidious, recreant, treacherous, cheater, faithless
ant. ethical, moral, principled

transient

syn. evanescent, fleeting, fugacious, momentary, temporal, transitory
ant. enduring, incessant, persistent

travail

syn. drudgery, toil, labour, moil, strain, childbearing
ant. entertainment, fun, pastime

treacherous

syn. unfaithful, traitorous, recreant, chancy, hazardous, perilous
ant. forthright, true, guarded

trite

syn. banal, corny, hackneyed, stereotyped, timeworn, stale
ant. original, relevant, pertinent

truant

syn. astray, away, hooky, missing, absent, adrift
ant. staying, on course, available

tumultuous
syn. stormy, tempestuous, turbulent, raging, roiled, wild
ant. orderly, peaceful, moderate

tyro
syn. beginner, fledgling, greenhorn, learner, neophyte, novice
ant. veteran, expert, professional

unbridled
syn. dissolute, berserk, profligate, rakish, uninhibited, turbulent
ant. justified, restrained, reasonable

uncanny
syn. eerie, unearthly, weird, incredible, mystifying, scary
ant. natural, usual, common

uncouth
syn. boorish, churlish, crude, philistine, uncultured, vulgar
ant. cultivated, refined, sophisticated

undaunted
syn. audacious, courageous, gallant, heroic, mettlesome, valiant
ant. meek, coward, timid

unwarranted
syn. baseless, bottomless, groundless, idle, unfounded, gratuitous
ant. justifiable, reasonable, warranted

ungainly
syn. awkward, clumsy, gawky, inept, lumpish, maladroit
ant. agile, graceful, coordinated

unleash
syn. discharge, free, release, vent, liberate, let go
ant. block, restrain, jail

untold
syn. countless, manifold, immense, monstrous, innumerous, gigantic
ant. few, little, tiny

uphold
syn. boost, elevate, bolster, sustain, endorse, champion
ant. weaken, obstruct, undermine

utilitarian
syn. functional, handy, practical, useful, serviceable, pragmatic
ant. impractical, useless, unnecessary

Exercise

Choose the word which is CLOSEST in meaning to the given word.

1. Tangible
   (a) feeble (b) reticent
   (c) concrete (d) clamorous
2. Threadbare
   (a) capricious (b) peevish
   (c) tattered (d) cold
3. Torrid
   (a) stuporous (b) dispassionate
   (c) devious (d) fervent

Choose the word which is MOST SIMILAR in meaning to the underlined word in the given sentence.

4. The seminar aimed at unleashing the potential of the participants.
   (a) venting (b) blocking
   (c) failing (d) unlocking
5. Isn't that a tenuous argument?
   (a) strong (b) feeble
   (c) long (d) irritating

Choose the word which is OPPOSITE in meaning to the given word.

6. Testy
   (a) gentle (b) peppery
   (c) invalid (d) droopy
7. Transient
   (a) incessant (b) recreant
   (c) meandrous (d) blistering

Choose the word which is MOST OPPOSITE in meaning to the underlined word in the given sentence.

8. Bablu was warned to be cautious of his treacherous behaviour.
   (a) hazardous (b) forthright
   (c) pompous (d) gloomy
9. Watching the sun rise gave him an unbridled joy.
   (a) licentious (b) weird
   (c) limited (d) unwelcome
10. The share market is tottering.
    (a) staggering (b) profitable
    (c) upfront (d) ascending

V - Z

vagary
syn. conceit, caprice, freak, impulse, notion, whim
ant. constancy, dependability, steadfastness

vagrant
syn. itinerant, nomadic, peripatetic, vagabond, drifter, wanderer
ant. determined, resolute, motivated

variance
syn. difference, conflict, confrontation, discord, dissension, strife
ant. agreement, peace, concord

venerate
syn. adore, idolise, revere, worship, deify, esteem
ant. abhor, condemn, despise

vengeful
syn. spiteful, vindictive, inimical, punitive, antagonistic, rancorous
ant. condoning, forgiving, liking

vex
syn. aggravate, annoy, bother, bug, chafe, exasperate
ant. soothe, please, assist

vicarious
syn. delegated, empathetic, eventual, pretended, substitute, surrogate
ant. concrete, real, authentic

vicious
syn. immoral, iniquitous, peccant, reprobate, malevolent, bestial
ant. gentle, right, nice

vie
syn. compete, contend, contest, emulate, rival, challenge
ant. retreat, leave, desert

vindicate
syn. absolve, exculpate, exonerate, defend, avenge, redress
ant. accuse, convict, punish

vindictive
syn. revengeful, spiteful, vengeful, malicious, venomous, grim
ant. forgiving, compassionate, charitable

virtuoso
syn. ace, adept, authority, champ, prodigy, expert
ant. amateur, greenhorn, rookie

virulent
syn. baneful, noxious, pernicious, mephitic, embittered, rancorous
ant. harmless, beneficent, advantageous

vitriolic
syn. acrid, mordacious, scathing, stinging, trenchant, truculent
ant. kind, pleasant, uncritical

vivify
syn. animate, quicken, vitalise, invigorate, refresh, revive
ant. deaden, discourage, kill

vociferous
syn. blatant, boisterous, clamorous, obstreperous, strident, loudmouthed
ant. quiet, silent, subtle

voluble
syn. chatty, conversational, talkative, garrulous, loquacious, talky
ant. reserved, reticent, unfriendly

voluminous
syn. ample, capacious, abundant, bountiful, copious, plentiful
ant. little, slight, tiny

votary
syn. devotee, enthusiastic, fanatic, aficionado, zealot, supporter
ant. detractor, opponent, disinterested

vouch
syn. attest, certify, testify, confirm, cosign, guarantee
ant. disavow, refute, reject

wail
syn. bawl, blubber, howl, weep, moan, sob
ant. exalt, gloat, vaunt

wakeful
syn. awake, alert, observant, vigilant, wary, watchful
ant. sleepy, unaware, careless

warranted
syn. baseless, gratuitous, indefensible, undue, unfair, unjustified
ant. reasonable, justifiable, called-for

weave
syn. sway, teeter, falter, meander, stumble, entwine
ant. divide, stay, unravel

wee
syn. diminutive, dwarf, midget, miniature, minuscule, teeny
ant. big, giant, large

weighty
syn. hefty, massive, ponderous, portly, corpulent, gross
ant. small, thin, unsubstantial

wily
syn. crafty, cunning, foxy, guileful, scheming, sly
ant. ingenuous, naive, unskilled

windy
syn. airy, blowy, breezy, gusty, brisk, blustering
ant. calm, frozen, still

winsome
syn. attractive, bewitching, enchanting, engaging, enticing, alluring
ant. repulsive, repellent, unattractive

wisecrack
syn. crack, dig, quip, farce, retort, laugh
ant. question, request, praise

wistful
syn. dejected, depressed, desolate, downcast, melancholic, sad
ant. cheerful, joyous, happy

wobble
syn. sway, teeter, totter, falter, reel, stagger
ant. endure, persist, stay

wrangle
syn. altercation, bicker, contention, dispute, quarrel, bicker, squabble
ant. agreement, consideration, accord

zealot
syn. enthusiastic, sectary, votary, fanatic, maniac, radical
ant. apathetic, doubting, opponent

zest
syn. flavour, relish, savour, gusto, smack, tang
ant. blandness, dullness, listlessness

Exercise

Choose the word which is CLOSEST in meaning to the given word.

1. Vagary
(a) whim (b) conflict
(c) reverence (d) steadfastness

2. Wily
(a) ingenuous (b) timid
(c) sly (d) enticing

Choose the word which is MOST SIMILAR in meaning to the underlined word in the given sentence.

3. Snakes are venerated in India.
(a) condemned (b) despised
(c) beaten (d) revered

4. I can vouch that Shahid is the best editor.
(a) criticise (b) deny
(c) disavow (d) testify

5. Kajal was waylaid on her way to office.
(a) felicitated (b) ambushed
(c) sleeping (d) going

Choose the word which is OPPOSITE in meaning to the given word.

6. Winsome
(a) bewitching (b) repellent
(c) assuming (d) encashing

7. Vindicate
(a) convict (b) exculpate
(c) assist (d) emulate

Choose the word which is MOST OPPOSITE in meaning to the underlined word in the given sentence.

8. Dev Anand always used to be full of zest.
(a) accord (b) farce
(c) enthusiasm (d) blandness

9. Watching a movie gives one a vicarious pleasure.
(a) substitute (b) iniquitous
(c) authentic (d) gentle

10. He launched a vitriolic attack on the team's manager.
(a) garrulous (b) gentle
(c) hurtful (d) reticent

ANSWERS

to all the

Advanced Exercises

A	1 (c)	2 (d)	3 (a)	4 (d)	5 (c)	6 (a)	7 (b)	8 (c)	9 (c)	10 (b)
	11 (a)	12 (b)	13 (c)	14 (d)						
B	1 (b)	2 (c)	3 (a)	4 (b)	5 (d)	6 (a)	7 (b)	8 (b)	9 (d)	10 (d)
C	1 (b)	2 (a)	3 (d)	4 (a)	5 (b)	6 (d)	7 (c)	8 (c)	9 (d)	10 (a)
	11 (d)	12 (a)	13 (a)	14 (b)						
D	1 (d)	2 (c)	3 (b)	4 (c)	5 (a)	6 (d)	7 (a)	8 (d)	9 (b)	10 (c)
E	1 (a)	2 (c)	3 (b)	4 (a)	5 (b)	6 (d)	7 (a)	8 (b)	9 (b)	10 (c)
	11 (c)	12 (d)	13 (b)	14 (d)						
F	1 (d)	2 (b)	3 (d)	4 (c)	5 (b)	6 (a)	7 (b)	8 (a)	9 (d)	10 (c)
G - H	1 (b)	2 (d)	3 (d)	4 (c)	5 (a)	6 (b)	7 (c)	8 (a)	9 (d)	10 (a)
I - K	1 (a)	2 (d)	3 (b)	4 (d)	5 (c)	6 (c)	7 (a)	8 (d)	9 (b)	10 (b)
L - M	1 (a)	2 (b)	3 (c)	4 (b)	5 (c)	6 (c)	7 (a)	8 (d)	9 (a)	10 (b)
N - O	1 (a)	2 (b)	3 (a)	4 (d)	5 (a)	6 (a)	7 (a)	8 (d)	9 (b)	10 (b)
P - Q	1 (a)	2 (d)	3 (b)	4 (a)	5 (c)	6 (b)	7 (a)	8 (d)	9 (c)	10 (d)
R	1 (d)	2 (a)	3 (a)	4 (d)	5 (b)	6 (d)	7 (a)	8 (a)	9 (b)	10 (b)
S	1 (a)	2 (d)	3 (b)	4 (d)	5 (c)	6 (c)	7 (c)	8 (b)	9 (b)	10 (c)
T - U	1 (c)	2 (c)	3 (d)	4 (d)	5 (b)	6 (a)	7 (a)	8 (b)	9 (c)	10 (d)
V - Z	1 (a)	2 (c)	3 (d)	4 (d)	5 (b)	6 (b)	7 (a)	8 (d)	9 (c)	10 (b)

PART IV
SUPER NUTS

abase

syn. demean, belittle, degrade, mortify, subjugate, denigrate
ant. dignify, extol, respect

abecedarian

syn. beginner, greenhorn, fledgling, neophyte, tyro, novice
ant. professional, expert, veteran

abject

syn. dismal, gloomy, servile, meek, subservient, self-effacing
ant. commendable, exalted, magnificent

abjure

syn. shun, repudiate, retract, abnegate, disavow, refrain
ant. assume, hold, maintain

abominate

syn. despise, abhor, detest, loathe, execrate, hate
ant. cherish adore, admire

abracadabra

syn. gibberish, mumbo jumbo, jabberwocky, double talk, hocus-pocus, presto
ant. reality, truth, fact

abrade

syn. fret, excoriate, chafe, scrape, scuff, rasp
ant. gratify, please, soothe

absolve

syn. forgive, liberate, vindicate, remit, exonerate, dispense
ant. impeach, incriminate, sentence

abstemious

syn. abstaining, abstinent, temperate, sober, forbearing, reasonable
ant. gluttonous, greedy, hungry

abstruse

syn. profound, recondite, esoteric, subtle, obscure, enigmatical
ant. lucid, obvious, plain

abyss

syn. deep, gulf, chasm, pit, chaos, hell
ant. incline, mound, mountain

ace

syn. champion, star, expert, authority, wizard, proficient
ant. inept, unskilled, amateur

accrue
syn. accumulate, grow, swell, inflate, escalate, parlay
ant. decrease, lose, dwindle

acerbity
syn. acrimony, mordancy, sarcasm, acridity, bitterness, trenchancy
ant. mellowness, mildness, sweetness

acquiesce
syn. agree, accede, assent, concur, consent, nod
ant. dissent, object, disagree

actuate
syn. move, induce, compel, persuade, start, cause
ant. impede, stop, hinder

adduce
syn. present, bring forward, cite, mention, attest, quote
ant. hesitate, withdraw, stop

adjourn
syn. defer, postpone, discontinue, put off, suspend, retard
ant. convene, further, summon

adjunct
syn. addition, appendix, appendage, annex, accessory, extension
ant. subtraction, detriment, lessening

adjure
syn. charge, bind, command, implore, plead, beseech
ant. disclaim, renounce, retract

ado
syn. bustle, activity, commotion, movement, agitation, stir
ant. aid, convenience, help

adulation
syn. flattery, cajolery, wheedling, praise, fawning, blandishment
ant. abuse, criticism, condemnation

agglomerate
syn. accrue, aggregate, amass, cumulate, garner, gather
ant. dissipate, squander, waste

aggrandise
syn. dignify, exalt, glorify, soar, burgeon, brag
ant. belittle, debase, degrade

agnate
syn. alike, allied, cognate, connate, kindred, affiliated
ant. alien, disconnected, unrelated

agnostic
syn. uncertain, skeptical, doubtful, dubious, hesitant, unconvinced
ant. believer, undoubting, certain

alacrity
syn. readiness, quickness, promptness, swiftness, rapidity, zeal
ant. aversion, reluctance, disinclination

align
syn. line up, range, ally, affiliate, confederate, league
ant. divide, separate, disjoin

allegiance
syn. loyalty, fidelity, commitment, adherence, steadfastness, constancy
ant. disloyalty, enmity, sedition

amative
syn. amorous, lecherous, lascivious, lewd, lustful, prurient
ant. platonic, chaste, moral

amble
syn. stroll, saunter, wander, meander, ramble, promenade
ant. run, stay, be direct

amorous
syn. lustful, enamored, passionate, erotic, doting, ardent
ant. frigid, pure, chaste

ambush
syn. trap, surprise, ambuscade, ensnarement, bushwalk, waylay
ant. retreat, shelter, surrender

amiss
syn. erroneous, mistaken, awry, astray, sour, afield
ant. good, right, on course

anathema
syn. abhorrence, aversion, abomination, loathing, denunciation, bugbear
ant. love, fondness, affection

anaemic
syn. feeble, insipid, pallid, bland, lackluster, sickly
ant. strong, healthy, powerful

animate
syn. living, sentient, alive, vital, conscious, moving
ant. dead, unconscious, deceased

annihilate
syn. destroy, obliterate, extinguish, rout, uproot, liquidate
ant. preserve, revive, save

antidote
syn. remedy, cure, solution, medicine, answer, countermeasure
ant. disease, problem, doubt

aplomb
syn. assurance, composure, confidence, nonchalance, equanimity, poise
ant. gaucheness, perturbedness, discomposure

apocryphal
syn. doubtful, dubious, mysterious, equivocal, fictitious, spurious
ant. authentic, credible, undisputed

apogee
syn. climax, culmination, crest, meridian, pinnacle, summit
ant. nadir, base, bottom

apposite
syn. pertinent, apropos, relevant, suitable, apt, applicable
ant. inappropriate, irrelevant, unsuitable

approbation
syn. consent, esteem, regard, commendation, approval, authorisation
ant. criticism, disapproval, reprimand

aquiver
syn. quaky, shaky, shivery, tremulant, twittery, tremulous
ant. steady, unwavering, firm

arcane
syn. esoteric, mysterious, cryptic, inscrutable, puzzling, occult
ant. commonplace, normal, regular

ardour
syn. fervour, zeal, dedication, passion, enthusiasm, commitment
ant. coldness, frigidity, indifference

asperity
syn. severity, sternness, brusqueness, rigour, vicissitude, stringency
ant. calmness, softness, gentility

assiduous
syn. diligent, sedulous, industrious, studious, preserving, hardworking
ant. lazy, negligent, neglectful

assimilate
syn. conform, espouse, imbibe, equate, soak, blend in
ant. reject, forsake, abstain

atone
syn. redress, apologise, expiate, recompense, compensate, make amends
ant. defy, confront, flout

atrophy
syn. wither, degenerate, shrivel, deteriorate, retrograde, worsen
ant. flourish, grow, germinate

attenuate
syn. debilitate, devitalise, undo, undermine, sap, enervate
ant. expand, intensify, strengthen

austere

syn. dour, bleak, sombre, sparse, unembellished, grim
ant. bland, luxurious, elaborate

avow

syn. acknowledge, concede, grant, avouch, aver, affirm
ant. condemn, deny, disclaim

Exercise

Choose the word which is CLOSEST in meaning to the given word.

1. Abyss
(a) chasm (b) authority (c) mound (d) bitterness

2. Apogee
(a) pertinent (b) crest (c) base (d) regret

Choose the word which is MOST SIMILAR in meaning to the underlined word in the given sentence.

3. Kohli was dismayed at the abject performance of his team in the final.
(a) fledgling (b) exalted (c) gibberish (d) dismal

4. He atoned by apologising to her sister.
(a) ammended (b) espoused (c) pleaded (d) defied

5. Sampada is the object of his amorous desire.
(a) lustful (b) platonic (c) creative (d) hidden

Choose the word which is OPPOSITE in meaning to the given word.

6. Approbation
(a) reprimand (b) irrelevance (c) guidance (d) training

7. Agglomerate
(a) entrepreneur (b) dissipate (c) garner (d) belittle

Choose the word which is MOST OPPOSITE in meaning to the underlined word in the given sentence.

8. Kabir has a deep rooted anathema to foreign goods.
(a) aversion (b) charm (c) fondness (d) denunciation

9. The ascetic decided to live an austere life.
(a) disparaging (b) understated (c) global (d) luxurious

10. He was accosted by the people after the conference was over.
(a) criticised (b) felicitated (c) ignored (d) bullied

B

balk
syn. baffle, check, checkmate, frustrate, stymie, thwart
ant. aid, help, assist

bamboozle
syn. beguile, betray, deceive, cozen, dupe, mislead
ant. defend, protect, support

base
syn. ignoble, mean, sordid, lousy, squalid, sleazy
ant. noble, moral, good

bawdy
syn. coarse, dirty, filthy, lewd, nasty, ribald
ant. chaste, clean, decent

behemoth
syn. giant, jumbo, mammoth, monster, titan, leviathan
ant. dwarf, midget, runt

beleaguer
syn. harass, harry, hound, pester, tease, torment
ant. socialise, assist, please

berate
syn. reprimand, castigate, bawl out, reproach, revile, scotch
ant. compliment, hail, praise

beseech
syn. appeal, crave, implore, plead, pray, supplicate
ant. give, offer, spurn

besmirch
syn. cloud, denigrate, smudge, stain, sully, tarnish
ant. approve, commend, exalt

bestial
syn. cruel, feral, ferocious, inhuman, savage, truculent
ant. generous, gentle, humane

bilk
syn. cheat, defraud, swindle, cozen, victimise, rook
ant. give, give away, be honest

blight
syn. affliction, bane, canker, curse, rot, scourge
ant. blessing, boon, prosperity

bonkers
syn. crazy, insane, distraught, maniac, daft, loony
ant. sane, balanced, rational

braggadocio
syn. boaster, braggart, vaunter, blowhard, exhibitionist, bigmouth
ant. humble, meek, servile

bravura
syn. audacity, dash, grit, guts, daring, heroism
ant. cowardice, timidity, meekness

bridle
syn. brake, leash, restraint, control, hold, rein, constrain
ant. release, set free, let go

brio
syn. dash, bounce, sparkle, verve, vigour, vivaciousness
ant. dullness, inactivity, lethargy

brusque
syn. abrupt, blunt, crusty, gruff, short, brief
ant. kind, polite, tactful

budge
syn. move, stir, propel, push, roll, shift
ant. hold, remain, stay

bum
syn. idler, loafer, sluggard, lazybones, wastrel, layabout
ant. workaholic, overachiever, industrious

bumble
syn. blunder, stumble, flounder, limp, muddle, stagger
ant. correct, fix, restore

burgeon
syn. augment, boost, proliferate, mount, multiply, expand
ant. shrink, decline, decrease

burlesque
syn. imitation, farce, mockery, sham, irony, parody
ant. tragedy, solemnity, seriousness

burnish
syn. furbish, glaze, gloss, polish, shine, buff
ant. tarnish, mar, deform

buttress
syn. back, corroborate, support, reinforce, endorse, sustain
ant. weaken, debilitate, impoverish

Exercise

Choose the word which is CLOSEST in meaning to the given word.

1. Bonkers
   (a) braggart (b) insane (c) audacious (d) insincere
2. Bamboozle
   (a) frustrate (b) betray (c) stymie (d) defend

Choose the word which is MOST SIMILAR in meaning to the underlined word in the given sentence.

3. Did she budge from there?
   (a) agree (b) sacrifice
   (c) move (d) dupe
4. He wanted to buttress some of his arguments by showing the facts collected by him from the Internet.
   (a) shine (b) oppose
   (c) understand (d) strengthen
5. The accusations served to besmirch the General's reputation.
   (a) supplicate (b) interfere
   (c) denigrate (d) hinder

Choose the word which is OPPOSITE in meaning to the given word.

6. Balk
   (a) assist (b) deceive
   (c) baffle (d) measure
7. Bridle
   (a) release (b) leash
   (c) sparkle (d) knot
8. Burnish
   (a) reinforce (b) substantiate
   (c) tarnish (d) implore

Choose the word which is MOST OPPOSITE in meaning to the underlined word in the given sentence.

9. Peehu was berated by everyone in the event.
   (a) hounded (b) hailed
   (c) pestered (d) assisted
10. Didn't Rashi behave in a bestial way today?
    (a) sullied (b) distraught
    (c) gentle (d) arrogant

C

cacophony
syn. discord, harshness, noise, clamour, bedlam, boisterousness
ant. harmony, quiet, silence

callow
syn. crude, guileless, unrefined, puerile, sophomore, jejune
ant. experienced, mature, sophisticated

cantankerous
syn. cranky, fretful, grouchy, irascible, petulant, snappish
ant. happy, pleasant, good-natured

capacious
syn. ample, commodious, roomy, spacious, voluminous, wide
ant. cramped, squeezed, tiny

capricious
syn. changeable, fickle, inconsistent, mercurial, variable, volatile
ant. constant, staid, steadfast

carp
syn. cavil, niggle, nitpick, pettifog, quibble, criticise
ant. ignore, let go, concede

cavalier
syn. condescending, curt, disdainful, haughty, insolent, scornful
ant. humble, reticent, shy

celerity
syn. dispatch, expedition, fleetness, hustle, rapidity, swiftness
ant. slowness, sluggishness, lethargy

charlatan
syn. fake, fraud, humbug, impostor, phony, quack
ant. original, reality, genuine

chicanery
syn. craftiness, dishonesty, shadiness, slyness, sneakiness, trickery
ant. forthrightness, truthfulness, honesty

churlish
syn. barbaric, boorish, crass, philistine, uncouth, vulgar
ant. gentle, nice, polite

clarion
syn. blaring, inspiring, loud, ringing, shrill, strident
ant. dull, fuzzy, gloomy

comity
syn. benevolence, concord, cordiality, harmony, togetherness, friendliness
ant. discord, hostility, enmity

coagulate
syn. clot, congeal, curdle, jell, coalesce, consolidate
ant. dilute, dissolve, melt

coalesce
syn. combine, compound, conjoin, conjugate, unify, wed
ant. divide, separate, disharmonise

cognate
syn. agnate, akin, allied, connate, consanguine, kindred
ant. disassociated, dissimilar, unlike

connive
syn. collude, conspire, intrigue, machinate, plot, scheme
ant. disagree, divorce, part

connoisseur
syn. adept, aficionado, buff, critic, epicure, judge
ant. ignoramus, dimwit, moron

consummate
syn. absolute, downright, outright, thorough, flawless, impeccable
ant. incomplete, partial, superficial

contemptible
syn. abhorrent, despicable, disgusting, loathsome, obnoxious, repugnant
ant. admirable, respectable, worthy

contort
syn. deform, disfigure, distort, misshape, twist, convolute
ant. beautify, smooth, shape

contrite
syn. compunctious, penitent, regretful, remorseful, repentant, apologetic
ant. hurtful, indifferent, unashamed

conundrum
syn. enigma, mystery, perplexity, puzzle, riddle, poser
ant. known, clarity, certainty

convoluted
syn. complicated, daedal, intricate, knotty, tangled, labyrinthine
ant. uncoiled, simple, plain

coquet
syn. dally, toy, flirt, trifle, philander, titillate
ant. be shy, be faithful, take seriously

corpulent
syn. fat, fleshy, obese, porcine, portly, stout
ant. skinny, slender, slight

cozen
syn. beguile, betray, delude, dupe, mulct, swindle
ant. aid, help, defend

crass
syn. barbarian, boorish, churlish, gross, crude, philistine
ant. delicate, refined, sensitive

crestfallen
syn. dejected, depressed, despondent, dispirited, downcast, inconsolable
ant. elated, excited, heartened

cupidity
syn. acquisitiveness, avarice, avidity, covetousness, graspingness, greed
ant. dislike, distaste, generosity

Exercise

Choose the word which is CLOSEST in meaning to the given word.

1. Coalesce
   (a) conjugate (b) quibble
   (c) distort (d) machinate

2. Comity
   (a) hostility (b) slyness
   (c) reality (d) concord

3. Churlish
   (a) quack (b) reticent
   (c) crass (d) genuine

4. Cupidity
   (a) greed (b) clot
   (c) akin (d) wed

Choose the word which is MOST SIMILAR in meaning to the underlined word in the given sentence.

5. Your crass behaviour may land you in trouble.
(a) boorish (b) distaste
(c) generous (d) smooth

6. Isn't Sakshi a food connoisseur?
(a) moron (b) buff
(c) supplier (d) hater

7. Samar connived with Abha in stealing the company's data.
(a) conjoined (b) curdled
(c) commenced (d) colluded

Choose the word which is OPPOSITE in meaning to the given word.

8. Capacious
(a) commodious (b) wide
(c) squeezed (d) variable

9. Contemptible
(a) worthy (b) abhorrent
(c) loathsome (d) obnoxious

10. Crestfallen
(a) despondent (b) boorish
(c) elated (d) strident

11. Cozen
(a) clear (b) help
(c) twisted (d) down cast

Choose the word which is MOST OPPOSITE in meaning to the underlined word in the given sentence.

12. These days, many boys are no better than a coquet.
(a) worthy (b) shy
(c) greedy (d) crude

13. Solving this issue is considered a conundrum by many.
(a) riddle (b) distortion
(c) ridicule (d) certainty

14. The Principal was a corpulent lady.
(a) lazy (b) slender
(c) wise (d) fat

D

dabbler

syn. amateur, dilettante, neophyte, apprentice, novice, tyro
ant. professional, veteran, mentor

daft

syn. distraught, dotty, unsound, demented, maniacal, insane
ant. rational, reasonable, sane

debark

syn. disembark, land, descend, alight, set down, get off
ant. embark, get on, leave

decoy

syn. allurement, camouflage, deception, lure, pretense, seducement
ant. uprightness, frankness, honesty

defile

syn. besmirch, contaminate, corrupt, desecrate, smutch, infect
ant. purify, sanctify, cleanse

delineate

syn. depict, describe, express, portray, render, present
ant. distort, confuse, mix up

deleterious

syn. detrimental, harmful, evil, hurtful, injurious, ill, mischievous
ant. assist, aid, help

delusion

syn. illusion, mirage, hallucination, fallacy, fantasy, figment
ant. certainty, actuality, reality

demure

syn. reticent, reserved, bashful, coy, diffident, timid
ant. aggressive, bold, outgoing

denigrate

syn. befoul, besmear, smudge, smut, taint, sully
ant. cleanse, enhance, improve

depravity

syn. immorality, perversion, turpitude, vice, villainy, bestiality
ant. uprightness, virtue, nobility

derange

syn. disarray, disrupt, jumble, tumble, muddle, upset
ant. calm, comfort, arrange

derelict
syn. bereft, desolate, forlorn, lax, remiss, negligent
ant. careful, thoughtful, preserved

desecrate
syn. defile, profane, violate, pollute, sacrilege, blaspheme
ant. honour, sanctify, praise

desolate
syn. forlorn, lonesome, forsaken, downcast, bereft, melancholic
ant. cultivated, populated, cheerful

despise
syn. contempt, disdain, scorn, abominate, detest, loathe
ant. admire, appreciate, love

despondent
syn. despairing, desperate, forlorn, hopeless, dejected, doleful
ant. elated, spirited, cheerful

desultory
syn. aimless, haphazard, chaotic, erratic, unstable, random
ant. pointed, purposeful, resolute

destitute
syn. barren, devoid, lacking, wanting, impoverished, indigent
ant. prosperous, wealthy, secure

devious
syn. sneaky, circuitous, oblique, erratic, stray, guileful
ant. direct, straight, in line

diatribe
syn. tirade, harangue, fulmination, jeremiad, onslaught, vituperation
ant. praise, recommendation, flattery

didactic
syn. moral, academic, expository, pedantic, preachy, sermonic
ant. amoral, informal, practical

diddle
syn. idle, laze, bum, loaf, loiter, lounge
ant. hurry, rush, vamoose

disarray
syn. scramble, chaos, confusion, disorder, jumble, mess
ant. arrangement, harmony, order

discomfit
syn. abash, chagrin, confound, embarrass, faze, mortify
ant. please, gladden, assure

discursive
syn. digressive, excursive, parenthetic, rambling, tangential, meandering
ant. apparent, obvious, evident

disdain
syn. contempt, despite, scorn, derision, aversion, ridicule
ant. admiration, esteem, respect

disparage
syn. belittle, denigrate, detract, slight, derogate, discount
ant. sanction, laud, flatter

disparate
syn. divergent, diverse, unlike, variant, different, dissimilar
ant. alike, equal, similar

dissonance
syn. clash, conflict, confrontation, dissent, schism, strife
ant. agreement, concord, harmony

distend
syn. augment, inflate, expand, enlarge, dilate, bloat
ant. constrict, deflate, shrink

dither
syn. falter, halt, hesitate, pause, stagger, waver
ant. carry on, continue, go on

dodder
syn. teeter, totter, tremble, shudder, shiver, wobble
ant. go, move, run

dodge
syn. avoid, bypass, circumvent, evade, hedge, eschew
ant. confront, encounter, face

doleful
syn. dolorous, mournful, plaintive, rueful, grievous, regrettable
ant. gleeful, joyous, elated

doodle
syn. fool, putter, mess around, fiddle, tinker, scribble
ant. labour, toil, work

doughty
syn. intrepid, plucky, gallant, audacious, mettlesome, courageous
ant. timid, meek, reticent

dowdy
syn. frumpish, antique, outdated, outmoded, dated, old-fashioned
ant. chic, modern, fashionable

dupable

syn. gullible, credulous, naive, susceptible, easy, exploitable
ant. skeptical, suspecting, untrusting

duress

syn. coercions, compulsion, constraint, pressure, force, violence
ant. independence, freedom, liberty

Exercise

Choose the word which is CLOSEST in meaning to the given word.

1. Dither
   (a) evade (b) coerce (c) hesitate (d) dispute

2. Duress
   (a) liberty (b) constraint (c) credulity (d) delay

Choose the word which is MOST SIMILAR in meaning to the underlined word in the given sentence.

3. One must not treat the poor with disdain.
   (a) scorn (b) respect (c) severity (d) gifts

4. The stories in Panchtantra are didactic.
   (a) amoral (b) messy (c) confusing (d) instructive

5. Babbu dodged to her right to avoid the bullet.
   (a) ducked (b) tottered (c) tinkered (d) fiddled

Choose the word which is OPPOSITE in meaning to the given word.

6. Dastardly
   (a) cruel (b) soft (c) kind (d) opportunistic

7. Doodle
   (a) play (b) toil (c) dupe (d) revere

Choose the word which is MOST OPPOSITE in meaning to the underlined word in the given sentence.

8. Revellers desecrated the streets on New Year's eve.
   (a) tainted (b) sullied
   (c) sanctified (d) innovated

9. Wasn't that a daft decision?
   (a) original (b) chaste
   (c) sane (d) proficient

10. Tapan was used as a decoy to stop him.
   (a) aid (b) reveller (c) bluff (d) protestor

E

ebullient
syn. effervescent, exuberant, sparkling, buoyant, effusive, exhilarated
ant. depressed, apathetic, disinterested

eclectic
syn. diverse, broad, heterogeneous, multifarious, varied, assorted
ant. specific, particular, narrow

edacious
syn. greedy, ravenous, gluttonous, hoggish, voracious, rapacious
ant. generous, liberal, quenched

effete
syn. debased, decadent, dissipated, vitiated, feeble, drained
ant. benevolent, moral, tireless

effrontery
syn. audacity, brashness, brazenness, overconfidence, nerve, rudeness
ant. modesty, shyness, humility

effulgent
syn. incandescent, lucent, luminous, lustrous, radiant, brilliant
ant. dark, dim, unpolished

egregious
syn. arrant, flagrant, glaring, nefarious, rank, atrocious
ant. concealed, hidden, inoffensive

embellish
syn. adorn, bedeck, garnish, beautify, enhance, trim
ant. deface, mar, disfigure

emollient
syn. palliative, relieving, remedial, softening, healing, demulcent
ant. rigorous, severe, intolerant

enamored
syn. infatuated, smitten, attracted, influenced, afflicted, lured
ant. unaffected, disinclined, unwilling

encomium
syn. acclaim, applause, celebration, compliment, eulogy, plaudit
ant. demerit, criticism, jeering

ensue
syn. attend, follow, result, succeed, supervene, occur
ant. antecede, precede, forerun

enunciate
syn. articulate, pronounce, say, utter, vocalise, state
ant. muffle, mumble, bumble

entail
syn. carry, involve, demand, necessitate, require
ant. exclude, free, remove

envisage
syn. conceive, envision, fantasise, imagine, visualise, think
ant. ignore, know, experience

equanimity
syn. aplomb, composure, nonchalance, poise, sangfroid, unflappability
ant. anxiety, worry, alarm

erudite
syn. learned, scholarly, wise, lettered, savvy, scholastic
ant. uncultured, ignorant, common

esoteric
syn. abstruse, profound, deep, recondite, arcane, cryptic
ant. familiar, public, obvious

espouse
syn. adopt, embrace, take on, uphold, champion, approve
ant. forsake, reject, renounce

estrange
syn. alienate, disaffect, disunite, antagonise, split, sunder
ant. engage, marry, unite

evanescent
syn. fleeting, momentary, passing, temporal, transient, transitory
ant. encountering, enticing, facing

exacting
syn. demanding, stern, tough, unyielding, fastidious, arduous
ant. trivial, facile, unchallenging

execrable
syn. bloody, confounded, cursed, damn, infernal, blasted
ant. nice, pleasant, blessed

exiguous
syn. meager, scant, puny, skimpy, sparse, stingy
ant. plenty, abundant, ample

expedient
syn. appropriate, befitting, convenient, proper, suitable, useful
ant. inappropriate, improper, unsuitable

expeditious
syn. breakneck, fast, rapid, swift, hasty, hurried
ant. retarded, slow, sluggish

extant
syn. actual, existent, around, contemporary, subsisting, real
ant. dead, extinct, gone

extenuate
syn. excuse, justify, rationalise, palliate, gloss over, sleek over
ant. impugn, intensify, criticise

exuberance
syn. ebullient, opulent, prodigal, effervescent, profuse, luxuriant
ant. lifeless, depressed, wanting

exult
syn. jubilate, triumph, delight, rejoice, crow, celebrate
ant. grieve, mourn, bewail

Exercise

Choose the word which is CLOSEST in meaning to the given word.

1. Espouse
(a) alienate (b) antagonise (c) exterminate (d) embrace
2. Evanescent
(a) environmental (b) momentary (c) monumental (d) vacillating
3. Execrable
(a) fastidious (b) cursed (c) enticing (d) demanding

Choose the word which is MOST SIMILAR in meaning to the underlined word in the given sentence.

4. It seemed that the arrangements were made in an <u>expeditious</u> manner.
(a) contemporary (b) effective (c) swift (d) surreal
5. Federer <u>exulted</u> after winning the Grand Slam.
(a) rejoiced (b) grieved (c) slogged (d) rampaged

Choose the word which is OPPOSITE in meaning to the given word.

6. Estrange
(a) uphold (b) unite (c) renounce (d) split
7. Encomiums
(a) intolerance (b) anxiety (c) ignorance (d) criticism
8. Effrontery
(a) modesty (b) rigour (c) nerve (d) audacity

Choose the word which is MOST OPPOSITE in meaning to the underlined word in the given sentence.

9. We are living in an <u>egalitarian</u> society.
(a) feminist (b) equal (c) elitist (d) cosmopolitan
10. White-washing the house will <u>entail</u> a lot of money.
(a) require (b) antecede (c) engulf (d) include

F

facetious
syn. comedic, funny, humorous, jocose, jocular, witty
ant. formal, grave, serious

factitious
syn. artificial, pretentious, unnatural, false, sham, specious
ant. real, genuine, natural

fag
syn. drudge, grub, plodder, moil, toil, travail
ant. animate, refresh, invigorate

fatuous
syn. foolish, senseless, absurd, imbecile, moronic, puerile
ant. bright, sensible, smart

fawn
syn. cringe, kowtow, grovel, slaver, toady, truckle
ant. bully, force, repel

faze
syn. abash, chagrin, confound, embarrass, mortify, discomfit
ant. reassure, encourage, comfort

feckless
syn. irresponsible, reckless, heedless, unconcerned, unmindful, inattentive
ant. effectual, competent, responsible

fecund
syn. fertile, fruitful, productive, prolific, rich, fructiferous
ant. impotent, infertile, sterile

felicitous
syn. appropriate, befitting, proper, apt, suitable, becoming
ant. inopportune, improper, infelicitous

felony
syn. crime, illegality, misdeed, offence, violation, foul play
ant. kindness, goodness, defence

feral
syn. savage, barbarous, bestial, ferocious, truculent, vicious
ant. civilized, cultured, refined

fetid
syn. foul, malodorous, noisome, stinking, mephitic, putrid
ant. aromatic, fragrant, fresh

fetter
syn. chain, hamper, hobble, leash, manacle, shackle
ant. free, loosen, release

fib
syn. canard, falsehood, falsity, fiction, lie, inveracity
ant. truth, veracity, certainty

fizzle
syn. decline, degenerate, deteriorate, fade, flag, languish
ant. build, develop, progress

flabbergast
syn. boggle, dumbfound, floor, stagger, amaze, daze
ant. expect, assure, repose

flaccid
syn. flabby, floppy, limp, sapped, emasculated, slack
ant. firm, taut, tight

fluster
syn. agitate, bother, ruffle, perturb, rock, flurry
ant. comfort, reassure, smoothen

foible
syn. failing, frailty, infirmity, shortcoming, weakness, fault
ant. strength, firmness, advantage

foment
syn. goad, impel, incite, instigate, prod, prick
ant. halt, prevent, hinder

forbearance
syn. patience, tolerance, refraining, abstinence, leniency, moderation
ant. continuation, involvement, indulgence

forlorn
syn. desolate, lonely, deserted, forsaken, desperate, despondent
ant. cheerful, consolable, pleased

fortuitous
syn. accidental, unexpected, casual, contingent, fluky, inadvertent
ant. deliberate, designed, intentional

frenetic
syn. delirious, frantic, frenzied, mad, wild, agitated
ant. calm, quiet, assured

furtive
syn. feline, slinky, sneaking, stealthy, secretive, sly
ant. aboveboard, forthright, truthful

Exercise

Choose the word which is CLOSEST in meaning to the given word.

1. Feral
   (a) civilized (b) ferocious
   (c) cultured (d) pretentious

2. Fetid
   (a) vicious (b) inopportune
   (c) pleasant (d) putrid

Choose the word which is MOST SIMILAR in meaning to the underlined word in the given sentence.

3. Varnika has a very fecund imagination.
   (a) befitting (b) reckless
   (c) prolific (d) limited

4. Pankaj's facetious remarks were not appreciated.
   (a) jocular (b) pretentious
   (c) senseless (d) grave

5. That was a fatuous idea.
   (a) bright (b) sensible
   (c) moronic (d) awesome

Choose the word which is OPPOSITE in meaning to the given word.

6. Fizzle
   (a) progress (b) release
   (c) defend (d) deteriorate

7. Forlorn
   (a) desperate (b) dazed
   (c) cheerful (d) rigid

Choose the word which is MOST OPPOSITE in meaning to the underlined word in the given sentence.

8. She glanced furtively at her fiancee.
   (a) shyly (b) excitedly
   (c) continuously (d) forthrightly

9. Padmavat's release was postponed on the grounds that it may foment tension in some states.
   (a) increase (b) hinder
   (c) abstain (d) instigate

10. Jayanti was in a fluster when so many guests arrived at her home.
   (a) meeting (b) ruffle
   (c) comfort (d) dizzy

G-H

gag
syn. burke, choke, muffle, quench, repress, smother
ant. release, permit, unblock

gaffe
syn. blooper, blunder, faux pas, boo-boo, impropriety, howler
ant. correction, fix, restitution

garish
syn. flashy, gaudy, chintzy, glaring, loud, tawdry
ant. discreet, modest, tasteful

gauche
syn. brash, clumsy, tactless, awkward, bumbling, inept
ant. elegant, tactful, refined

gaunt
syn. bony, lanky, skinny, slender, worn, emaciated
ant. plump, beefy, overweight

germane
syn. applicable, apposite, apropos, pertinent, relevant, related
ant. inappropriate, irrelevant, unsuitable

glower
syn. glare, scowl, frown, stare, sulk, watch
ant. grin, smile, ignore

glum
syn. morose, saturnine, sulky, sullen, desolate, dreary
ant. joyous, upbeat, cheerful

gnarled
syn. twisted, bent, curved, rough, deformed, curled
ant. straight, uncurled, untwisted

gorge
syn. cloy, glut, pall, stuff, satiate, surfeit
ant. abstain, forgo, constrain

gouge
syn. fleece, overcharge, exploit, con, defraud, circumvent, swindle
ant. be honest, be faithful, protect

grabby
syn. acquisitive, avaricious, avid, covetous, greedy, hungry
ant. benevolent, generous, abstemious

grandiloquent
syn. aureate, declamatory, orotund, sonorous, rhetorical, magniloquent
ant. unadorned, unpretentious, simple

gripe
syn. complain, grouch, grump, whine, crab, grieve
ant. compliment, flatter, praise

grisly
syn. ghastly, grim, gruesome, hideous, horrible, horrid
ant. pleasant, pretty, joyous

grotesque
syn. freaky, monstrous, antic, bizarre, fantastic, far-fetched
ant. shapely, logical, rational

halcyon
syn. calm, placid, serene, still, tranquil, untroubled
ant. inauspicious, inopportune, ominous

haggle
syn. bargain, dicker, argue, huckster, negotiate, palter
ant. agree, concur, harmonise

hallowed
syn. consecrated, sacred, blessed, holy, sacrosanct, devoted
ant. desecrated, profane, unsanctified

hangdog
syn. ashamed, browbeaten, cowering, downcast, sheepish, wretched
ant. commendable, exalted, noble

hanker
syn. ache, covet, desire, pant, pine, yearn
ant. dislike, hate, abhor

harangue
syn. diatribe, fulmination, jeremiad, exhortation, tirade, censure
ant. panegyric, praise, recommendation

hauteur
syn. arrogance, insolence, loftiness, presumption, pride, superciliousness
ant. humility, modesty, politeness

hedonist
syn. epicure, sensualist, sybarite, voluptuary, libertine, lecher
ant. ascetic, puritan, chaste

hegemony
syn. authority, command, leadership, power, predominance, domination
ant. subservience, yielding, surrender

heresy

syn. atheism, blasphemy, dissidence, infidelity, nonconformity, disbelief
ant. orthodoxy, conservatism, agreement

hiatus

syn. interim, lacuna, void, aperture, chasm, rift
ant. continuity, occupied, homogeneous

hodgepodge

syn. assortment, conglomeration, jumble, medley, potpourri, patchwork
ant. singular, lone, order

hovel

syn. hole, hut, shanty, shack, shed, cabin, burrow
ant. closure, solid, cover

hullabaloo

syn. outcry, rumpus, pandemonium, clamour, vociferation, din
ant. truce, calm, peace

Exercise

Choose the word which is CLOSEST in meaning to the given word.

1. Gouge
   (a) cloy (b) deform
   (c) fleece (d) glare
2. Harangue
   (a) tirade (b) presumption
   (c) acclaim (d) endorsement
3. Hovel
   (a) advance (b) religious
   (c) intern (d) burrow

Choose the word which is MOST SIMILAR in meaning to the underlined word in the given sentence.

4. She is slim like a <u>gaunt</u>.
   (a) bony (b) radical
   (c) suffuse (d) precise
5. I wish I could visit the <u>hallowed</u> halls of my school.
   (a) serene (b) logical
   (c) gruesome (d) respected
6. It seems that the media was <u>gagged</u> as nothing was reported about the incident.
   (a) bribed (b) helped (c) muffled (d) rebuked

7. Why are you glowering at me like this?
   (a) smiling
   (b) laughing
   (c) scowling
   (d) jostling

Choose the word which is OPPOSITE in meaning to the given word.

8. Grotesque
   (a) bizarre
   (b) normal
   (c) hideous
   (d) sonorous

9. Hegemony
   (a) libertine
   (b) subservience
   (c) dissidence
   (d) insolence

10. Germane
   (a) relevant
   (b) irrelevant
   (c) shameful
   (d) detain

Choose the word which is MOST OPPOSITE in meaning to the underlined word in the given sentence.

11. The whole room is in a hodgepodge way.
   (a) order
   (b) noble
   (c) drain
   (d) enclose

12. Do you like hedonists?
   (a) socialists
   (b) sensualists
   (c) puritans
   (d) feminists

13. The gnarled frame looked awful to me.
   (a) decorated
   (b) curred
   (c) clumsy
   (d) straightened

14. Why are they hankering for it?
   (a) yearning
   (b) ducking
   (c) colluding
   (d) moving

I - K

iconoclastic

syn. dissident, individualistic, irreverent, nonconforming, radical, unorthodox

ant. religious, conformist, conventional

idolatry

syn. adoration, worship, idolism, devotion, infatuation, reverence

ant. dishonour, disrespect, hate

ignoble

syn. mean, sordid, base, vile, plebeian, vulgar

ant. dignified, noble, worthy

ignominious

syn. disgraceful, dishonourable, opprobrious, shameful, disreputable, shameful

ant. admirable, worthy, respectful

imbue

syn. freight, impregnate, permeate, pervade, saturate, suffuse

ant. drain, withdraw, empty

immure

syn. cage, enclose, confine, detain, imprison, intern

ant. free, release, let go

impassive

syn. apathetic, detached, listless, stolid, phlegmatic, insusceptible

ant. passionate, responsive, sensitive

impeccable

syn. absolute, consummate, flawless, indefectible, precise, infallible

ant. blemished, defective, flawed

impecunious

syn. destitute, impoverished, penurious, indigent, needy, broke

ant. affluent, opulent, prosperous

impede

syn. encumber, hinder, bog down, obstruct, block, bar

ant. advance, facilitate, forward

imperious
syn. authoritarian, dictatorial, domineering, overbearing, peremptory, dogmatic
ant. fawning, servile, subservient

impervious
syn. immune, resistant, unapproachable, impassive, sealed, hermetic
ant. exposed, penetrable, sensitive

impetuous
syn. brash, foolhardy, improvident, reckless, slapdash, temerarious
ant. cautious, circumspect, considerate

impinge
syn. encroach, entrench, intrude, obtrude, trespass, infringe
ant. avoid, dodge, withdraw

implacable
syn. adamant, grim, intransigent, obdurate, relentless, glum
ant. merciful, sunny, nice

implausible
syn. flimsy, improbable, incredible, unsubstantial, unconvincing, shaky
ant. reasonable, believable, likely

implore
syn. supplicate, sue, beseech, crave, entreat, plead
ant. abjure, spurn, dislike

importune
syn. badger, beleaguer, beset, besiege, hound, pester
ant. disclaim, retract, renounce

impregnable
syn. indomitable, invincible, unconquerable, indestructible, fortified, secure
ant. conquerable, destructible, beatable

improbity
syn. corruption, dishonesty, decadence, perversion, profligacy, turpitude
ant. honesty, decency, probity

impugn
syn. assail, attack, shred, contravene, negate, disaffirm
ant. flatter, praise, shield

impute
syn. assign, accredit, ascribe, attribute, fix, charge
ant. disapprove, exculpate, exonerate

inane
syn. blank, empty, vacuous, void, bare, lacking
ant. filled, occupied, full

incendiary
syn. dissentious, inflammatory, provocative, seditious, demagogic, dangerous
ant. mitigating, placating, tranquilising

inchoate
syn. amorphous, formless, shapeless, unformed, unshaped, indeterminate
ant. definite, distinctive, shapely

incongruous
syn. discordant, incompatible, inconsistent, inapt, malapropos, unbecoming
ant. compatible, harmonious, corresponding

indigent
syn. destitute, impecunious, impoverished, penurious, necessitous, beggarly
ant. wealthy, prosperous, opulent

ingratiate
syn. please, insinuate, flatter, blandish, captivate, grovel
ant. deter, disgust, repel

interdict
syn. debar, enjoin, forbid, inhibit, proscribe, taboo
ant. permit, allow, authorise

intractable
syn. fractious, indocile, recalcitrant, unruly, untoward, obstreperous
ant. amenable, manageable, facile

intransigence
syn. grimness, implacability, incompliance, obduracy, remorselessness, rigidity
ant. compliance, cooperation, submission

inundate
syn. deluge, engulf, overwhelm, swamp, drown, flush
ant. underwhelm, pass up, float

inured
syn. accustom, condition, habituate, disarrange, acclimatise, adjust
ant. ignore, neglect, upset

invective
syn. abuse, obloquy, revilement, railing, scurrility, vituperation
ant. compliment, flattery, praise

inveigle
syn. allure, beguile, entice, seduce, tempt, lure
ant. disenchant, disgust, turn off

invidious
syn. calumnious, defamatory, detractive, scandalous, slanderous, covetous
ant. delightful, likeable, lovable

invigorating
syn. bracing, exhilarant, intoxicating, reviving, stimulating, restorative
ant. debilitative, boring, uninspiring

irascible
syn. cantankerous, crabbed, cranky, grumpy, surly, waspish
ant. cheerful, pleasant, amiable

jaunty
syn. breezy, buoyant, debonair, dashing, animated, frolicsome
ant. depressed, lethargic, lifeless

jejune
syn. bland, innocuous, insipid, vapid, washy, dull
ant. exciting, original, lively

jinx
syn. curse, hex, hoodoo, nemesis, plague, voodoo
ant. boon, luck, blessing

jocose
syn. comedic, facetious, funny, humorous, jocular, witty
ant. formal, grave, serious

jocund
syn. blithe, convivial, gay, gleeful, mirthful, merry
ant. morose, sad, depression

ken
syn. apprehend, grasp, perceive, conceive, fathom, behold
ant. overlook, misinterpret, misunderstand

kibitz
syn. instruct, opine, suggest, direct, counsel, commend
ant. delude, pretend, trick

Exercise

Choose the word which is CLOSEST in meaning to the given word.

1. Jinx
   (a) boon (b) glee
   (c) nemesis (d) vituperation

2. Jaunty
   (a) amiable (b) lethargic
   (c) comic (d) bouncy

Choose the word which is MOST SIMILAR in meaning to the underlined word in the given sentence.

3. Ravana was an ignoble creature.
   (a) vile (b) dignified
   (c) radical (d) conformist

4. The plot impinges on the defence land.
   (a) dodges (b) trespasses
   (c) obstructs (d) facilitates

5. The CFO was shielded from importunate visitors by her secretary.
   (a) retracing (b) surging
   (c) pleasant (d) dogged

Choose the word which is OPPOSITE in meaning to the given word.

6. Jejune
   (a) calumnious (b) mature
   (c) exciting (d) pathetic

7. Kerfuffle
   (a) commotion (b) calm
   (c) debate (d) ceremony

Choose the word which is MOST OPPOSITE in meaning to the underlined word in the given sentence.

8. Shruti was given the invidious task of judging her classmates.
   (a) extraneous (b) debilitating
   (c) delightful (d) covetous

9. The columnist's article was incendiary.
   (a) dissentious (b) amorphous
   (c) tertiary (d) mitigating

10. Army's efforts to interdict the terrorists convoy were successful.
    (a) inhibit (b) proscribe
    (c) allow (d) placate

L - M

labyrinth

syn. entanglement, knot, maze, morass, snarl, tangle
ant. clue, solution, elimination

laconic

syn. compendious, concise, lean, succinct, summary, terse
ant. loquacious, prosy, wordy

lassitude

syn. languor, lethargy, listlessness, stupor, phlegm, stolidity
ant. revival, relaxation, cheer

leash

syn. chain, fetter, hamper, hobble, manacle, shackle
ant. discharge, liberate, release

leery

syn. distrustful, doubting, mistrustful, suspicious, untrusting, precarious
ant. secure, assured, trustworthy

legerdemain

syn. chicanery, magic, deception, sleight, trick, sorcery
ant. disenchantment, exorcism, dispossession

legion

syn. cloud, crowd, horde, multitude, ruck, swarm
ant. handful, single, individual

limber

syn. agile, alert, deft, nimble, brisk, sprightly
ant. rigid, stiff, brittle

limn

syn. portray, depict, delineate, render, represent, express
ant. distort, confuse, misrepresent

lissome

syn. agile, flexible, athletic, pliant, lithe, graceful
ant. portly, awkward, stiff

lopsided

syn. asymmetrical, cockeyed, disproportionate, uneven, crooked, askew
ant. even, straight, balanced

loquacious
syn. chatty, conversational, garrulous, talkative, voluble, jabbering
ant. restrained, silent, subdued

loutish
syn. boorish, bungling, cantankerous, cloddish, uncouth, churlish
ant. polite, refined, sophisticated

ludicrous
syn. comic, farcical, laughable, ridiculous, absurd, bizarre
ant. logical, reasonable, sensible

luminary
syn. celebrity, dignitary, star, personality, cynosure, heavyweight
ant. nobody, commoner, unknown

lurid
syn. ghastly, grim, macabre, horrid, bloody, gory
ant. clean, modest, pleasing

macabre
syn. morbid, sick, unhealthy, gruesome, hideous, unwholesome
ant. calming, pleasant, comforting

malediction
syn. anathema, curse, damnation, imprecation, execration, jinx
ant. blessing, pleasantry, liking

malingerer
syn. slacker, dodger, idler, loafer, shirker, lazy
ant. active, alert, diligent

malleable
syn. ductile, flexible, pliable, adaptable, supple, pliant
ant. intractable, rigid, stiff

malodorous
syn. fetid, foul, mephitic, noisome, reeky, stinking
ant. aromatic, flagrant, perfumed

maneuver
syn. remove, shift, navigate, exploit, manipulate, guide
ant. operate, wield, use

mangy
syn. decaying, decrepit, dingy, dilapidated, shabby, tattered
ant. kempt, neat, maintained

maven
syn. connoisseur, expert, adept, buff, aficionado, freak
ant. amateur, clumsy, inept

medley
syn. assortment, conglomeration, hodgepodge, jumble, mishmash, potpourri
ant. order, organisation, separate

miff
syn. dudgeon, huff, offence, displeasure, resentment, umbrage
ant. appeasement, pleasure, happiness

minatory
syn. threatening, alarming, cautionary, impending, grim, dire
ant. aiding, assisting, helping

mirth
syn. blitheness, glee, jocularity, hilarity, gaiety, merriment
ant. blues, depression, distress

mordant
syn. acerbic, acrid, caustic, pungent, scathing, trenchant
ant. nice, pleasant, soothing

moribund
syn. dying, declining, doomed, fated, perishing, expiring
ant. blessed, hopeful, vibrant

mulish
syn. dogged, bullheaded, obstinate, pertinacious, perverse, tenacious
ant. willing, yielding, amenable

multifarious
syn. diverse, heterogeneous, motley, sundry, varied, various
ant. homogeneous, singular, individual

munificence
syn. generosity, lavishness, liberality, magnanimity, bounteousness, unselfishness
ant. meanness, stinginess, selfishness

murky
syn. dark, dim, dusky, muddy, hazy, turbid
ant. luminous, sparkling, bright

mutable
syn. alterable, uncertain, unstable, variable, unsteady
ant. constant, invariable, steady

Exercise

Choose the word which is CLOSEST in meaning to the given word.

1. Limn
   (a) depict (b) distort (c) hobble (d) manacle

2. Labyrinth
   (a) clue (b) sleight (c) cynosure (d) morass

Choose the word which is MOST CLOSEST in meaning to the underlined word in the given sentence.

3. I do not approve of his <u>loutish</u> behaviour.
   (a) jabbering (b) cantankerous
   (c) askew (d) blithe

4. The auto expo was attended by many bike <u>mavens</u>.
   (a) inepts (b) haters
   (c) riders (d) aficionados

5. There was a <u>malodorous</u> smell coming from the inn.
   (a) morbid (b) pleasant
   (c) stinking (d) flagrant

Choose the word which is OPPOSITE in meaning to the given word.

6. Moribund
   (a) fated (b) vibrant
   (c) perished (d) dying

7. Miff
   (a) appeasement (b) dudgeon
   (c) hilarity (d) distress

8. Lissome
   (a) pliant (b) awkward
   (c) cockeyed (d) balanced

Choose the word which is MOST OPPOSITE in meaning to the underlined word in the given sentence.

9. She was a <u>luminary</u> in her heydays.
   (a) sophisticated (b) awkward
   (c) commoner (d) pedantic

10. Emperor Akbar was known for his <u>munificence</u>.
    (a) deception (b) kindness
    (c) aggressiveness (d) meanness

N - O

naive

syn. guileless, unsophisticated, credulous, dupable, gullible, susceptible

ant. skeptical, wise, experienced

nascence

syn. beginning, commencement, dawn, inception, onset, outset

ant. conclusion, end, finish

natty

syn. elegant, fashionable, stylish, swanky, dashing, neat

ant. dull, old-fashioned, out-moded

naysayer

syn. cynic, gloomy, defeatist, downer, killjoy, complainer

ant. optimist, hoper, idealist

niggard

syn. mean, miserly, parsimonious, penurious, stingy, tightfisted

ant. generous, unselfish, kind

nimble

syn. agile, brisk, facile, adroit, deft, dexterous

ant. awkward, clumsy, lumbering

nonchalance

syn. composure, equanimity, poise, sangfroid, imperturbability, unflappability

ant. agitation, discomposure, excitement

nondescript

syn. ordinary, unclassified, featureless, uninspiring, unremarkable, dull

ant. illustrative, remarkable, distinguished

nonentity

syn. insignificant, nebbish, nobody, nothing, cipher, upstart

ant. somebody, important, significant

nonplus

syn. confound, baffle, flummox, stump, boggle, faze

ant. enlighten, explain, clarify

nugatory

syn. negligible, niggling, paltry, trifling, petty, piddling

ant. abundant, copious, productive

obeisance
syn. bow, curtsy, genuflection, kowtow, nod, deference
ant. disobedience, disregard, disrespect

obfuscate
syn. blur, eclipse, obscure, befog, blear, overshadow
ant. uncover, unveil, unfog

obloquy
syn. abuse, invective, disgrace, humiliation, ignominy, opprobrium
ant. acclamation, plaudit, adulation

obsequious
syn. menial, servile, slavish, subservient, cringing, beggarly
ant. assertive, brazen, presumptuous

obstreperous
syn. intractable, docile, fractious, recalcitrant, unruly, boisterous
ant. orderly, compliant, quiet

obviate
syn. avert, forestall, forefend, preclude, prevent, stave off
ant. allow, permit, facilitate

occlude
syn. choke, clog, congest, throttle, plug, impede
ant. clear, free, release

odious
syn. abominable, filthy, loathsome, obnoxious, repugnant, vile
ant. agreeable, loveable, delightful

ogreish
syn. devilish, fiendish, diabolic, hellish, satanic, wicked
ant. decent, moral, nice

onerous
syn. exacting, formidable, demanding, rigorous, taxing, laborious
ant. easy, facile, trivial

opprobrium
syn. disgrace, discredit, humiliation, ignominy, obloquy, odium
ant. acclamation, adulation, commendation

otiose
syn. empty, hollow, idle, vacant, vain, indolent
ant. lively, energetic, attentive

outlandish
syn. eccentric, freakish, idiosyncratic, quirky, unusual, weird
ant. familiar, ordinary, usual

overwrought
syn. affected, distracted, agitated, nervous, neurotic, frantic
ant. unruffled, calm, cool

Exercise

Choose the word which is CLOSEST in meaning to the given word.

1. Obviate
(a) throttle (b) bear
(c) preclude (d) unveil

2. Obfuscate
(a) unveil (b) enlighten
(c) blur (d) boggle

3. Nonplus
(a) eclipse (b) confound
(c) disregard (d) obviate

Choose the word which is MOST SIMILAR in meaning to the underlined word in the given sentence.

4. My friend lives in a natty bungalow in Cuffe Parade.
(a) swanky (b) small
(c) oblivious (d) deserted

5. Namrata fell in the trap as she was naive.
(a) new (b) penurious
(c) kind (d) credulous

Choose the word which is OPPOSITE in meaning to the given word.

6. Obloquy
(a) disgrace (b) plaudit
(c) invective (d) discomposure

7. Nugatory
(a) valuable (b) paltry
(c) cringing (d) flowing

8. Onerous
(a) trivial (b) moral
(c) subservient (d) confound

Choose the word which is MOST OPPOSITE in meaning to the underlined word in the given sentence.

9. I can't bear the odious smell any more.
(a) pleasant (b) decent
(c) facile (d) stinking

10. Roopali's nonchalant attitude did not help her in succeeding in her life.
(a) conformist (b) enthusiastic
(c) bad (d) noble

P - Q

palter

syn. equivocate, prevaricate, bargain, dicker, haggle, negotiate
ant. agree, comply, concur

pejorative

syn. deprecatory, derogatory, disparaging, depreciatory, low, slighting
ant. complimentary, positive, flattering

pellucid

syn. limpid, lucid, crystalline, transparent, see-through, clear
ant. dreary, dusky, cloudy

penitent

syn. contrite, regretful, remorseful, repentant, apologetic, sorry
ant. content, satisfied, defiant

perfidious

syn. disloyal, faithless, recreant, traitorous, treacherous, untrue
ant. faithful, trustworthy, principled

perfunctory

syn. automatic, mechanical, careless, routine, indifferent, casual
ant. caring, concerned, involved

pernicious

syn. baneful, malignant, noxious, pestilent, virulent, destructive
ant. innocuous, loving, kind

perspicacity

syn. acumen, astuteness, discernment, keenness, sagacity, shrewdness
ant. ineptness, stupidity, ignorance

pertinacious

syn. dogged, hardheaded, mulish, obstinate, persistent, stubborn
ant. irresolute, tentative, flexible

petulant

syn. cantankerous, cranky, grouchy, grumpy, irascible, peevish
ant. happy, pleasant, amiable

pique
syn. affront, miff, offend, foment, incite, propel
ant. hinder, hold, please

plaudits
syn. acclaim, applause, celebration, compliment, kudos, laudation
ant. criticism, disapproval, vituperation

postulant
syn. appellant, claimant, aspirant, petitioner, seeker, suitor
ant. boss, manager, judge

precocious
syn. premature, untimely, advanced, forward, progressive, early
ant. delayed, mature, overdue

predilection
syn. disposition, leaning, partiality, penchant, propensity, tendency
ant. antipathy, dislike, hatred

prefatory
syn. inductive, preliminary, preparatory, introductory, prolegomenous, initial
ant. secondary, complex, intricate

presage
syn. augur, bode, forecast, foretell, portend, prognosticate
ant. withhold, hide, be quiet

prevaricate
syn. equivocate, palter, shuffle, falsify, fib, forswear
ant. clarify, agree, tell truth

prissy
syn. bluenosed, genteel, priggish, puritanical, prim, prudish
ant. informal, casual, unconcerned

proffer
syn. extend, offer, present, volunteer, propose, submit
ant. discourage, dissuade, take back

prowl
syn. creep, glide, lurk, sneak, skulk, slink
ant. rush, expose, divulge

pry
syn. poke, snoop, nose, meddle, gape, intrude
ant. leave, withdraw, dodge

puckish
syn. devilish, naughty, mischievous, prankish, whimsical, playful
ant. subdued, behaved, decent

pugnacious

syn. bellicose, belligerent, combative, contentious, quarrelsome, truculent

ant. tender, cooperative, agreeable

puissance

syn. potency, strength, power, might, peppiness

ant. idleness, lethargy, inactivity

pulverise

syn. crush, grind, raze, destroy, dismantle, wreck

ant. construct, create, build

pusillanimous

syn. chickenhearted, craven, dastardly, coward, timorous, gutless

ant. undaunted, daring, courageous

putrid

syn. rotten, rancid, frowsy, fusty, moldy, rank

ant. fresh, sweet, perfumed

quagmire

syn. mire, swamp, dilemma, plight, predicament, soup

ant. blessing, solution, success

qualm

syn. compunction, misgiving, scruple, mistrust, apprehension, foreboding

ant. approval, comfort, contentment

quell

syn. crush, extinguish, quash, quench, squelch, suppress

ant. succeed, win, release

querulous

syn. cantankerous, crabbed, cross, fretful, grouchy, irascible

ant. cheerful, relaxed, pleased

quibble

syn. niggle, bicker, nitpick, spat, squabble, tiff

ant. approve, concur, agree

quiescent

syn. abeyant, dormant, inactive, lament, slumbering, inert

ant. active, progressive, operative

quotidian

syn. commonplace, everyday, common, usual, daily, trivial

ant. extraordinary, exceptional, peculiar

Exercise

Choose the word which is CLOSEST in meaning to the given word.

1. Pejorative
(a) complementary (b) deprecatory
(c) crystalline (d) pellucid

2. Quagmire
(a) apprehension (b) muddle
(c) squabble (d) huddle

3. Penitent
(a) content (b) limpid
(c) virulent (d) repentant

Choose the word which is MOST SIMILAR in meaning to the underlined word in the given sentence.

4. Isn't Rishabh <u>petulant</u>?
(a) irascible (b) tentative
(c) amiable (d) obstinate

5. Sedentary lifestyle often has a <u>pernicious</u> effect in one's life.
(a) innocuous (b) sagacious
(c) malignant (d) devious

Choose the word which is OPPOSITE in meaning to the given word.

6. Presage
(a) withhold (b) augur
(c) portend (d) bode

7. Puckish
(a) abstract (b) subdued
(c) aggressive (d) simple

8. Pusillanimous
(a) prankish (b) undaunted
(c) piggish (d) chickenhearted

Choose the word which is MOST OPPOSITE in meaning to the underlined word in the given sentence.

9. Navita has a <u>predilection</u> for attending parties.
(a) penchant (b) antipathy
(c) fondness (d) premonition

10. The only <u>quibble</u> about my office is that it is too far from my home.
(a) grouse (b) point
(c) praise (d) complaint

R

rabble
syn. dreg, riffraff, trash, herd, drove, masses, commoners
ant. special, gentry, unusual

rabid
syn. ardent, fervent, zealous, radical, irate, wrathful
ant. dispirited, delighted, apathetic

rambunctious
syn. boisterous, raucous, rowdy, tumultuous, turbulent, unruly
ant. introvert, meek, quiet

rancour
syn. acrimony, bitterness, animosity, resentment, virulence, aversion
ant. kindness, sympathy, love

rapacious
syn. avid, edacious, greedy, omnivorous, ravenous, voracious
ant. dispassionate, content, indifferent

rapt
syn. deep, intent, absorbed, preoccupied, earnest, engrossed
ant. distracted, flippant, unenthusiastic

raucous
syn. hoarse, jarring, raspy, scratchy, grating, strident
ant. quiet, soft, subdued

rebut
syn. belie, confute, discredit, disprove, refute, negate
ant. concede, agree, approve

recant
syn. abjure, retract, recall, withdraw, annul, backtrack
ant. confirm, recapitulate, advance

recluse
syn. secluded, ascetic, monk, solitary, anchorite, hermit
ant. extrovert, social, gregarious

recondite
syn. abstruse, deep, esoteric, profound, cryptic, arcane
ant. obvious, plain, straightforward

rectitude
syn. morality, probity, righteousness, uprightness, virtue, goodness
ant. dishonesty, infamy, vice

repartee
syn. retort, riposte, comeback, quip, banter, rejoinder
ant. request, question, compliment

reprehensible
syn. blameworthy, culpable, censurable, guilty, amiss, ignoble
ant. creditable, respectable, kind

reprobate
syn. evil, immoral, iniquitous, peccant, sinful, vicious
ant. virtuous, just, true

reproach
syn. admonish, castigate, chastise, chide, reprimand, reprove
ant. approve, praise, respect

repudiate
syn. deny, disavow, disclaim, disown, reject, renounce
ant. admit, approve, vouch

repugnance
syn. abhorrence, abomination, antipathy, aversion, loathing, revulsion
ant. esteem, regard, appreciation

rescind
syn. remove, lift, recall, repeal, reverse, revoke
ant. enact, validate, sanction

resilient
syn. elastic, flexible, buoyant, supple, expansive, pliant
ant. rigid, inflexible, stiff

resplendent
syn. brilliant, gorgeous, magnificent, glorious, splendid, proud
ant. gloomy, withering, dull

resuscitate
syn. restore, revive, reactivate, rekindle, resurrect, revitalise
ant. bury, suppress, smother

reticent
syn. incommunicable, taciturn, aloof, solitary, standoffish, withdrawn
ant. communicative, unrestrained, forward

reverberate
syn. echo, rebound, reflect, recoil, re-echo, resound
ant. quieten, hush, lull

revile
syn. abuse, assail, vituperate, censure, denigrate, disparage
ant. acclaim, adulate, commend

rhapsodise
syn. harangue, jabber, perorate, prate, prattle, rage
ant. denounce, discourage, pacify

ribald
syn. bawdy, filthy, profane, foul, scurrilous, smutty
ant. chaste, decent, clean

rife
syn. current, predominant, prevailing, regnant, widespread, replete
ant. low, scarce, wanting

rigour
syn. austerity, harshness, rigidity, asperity, stringency, vicissitude
ant. leniency, pliability, ease

righteous
syn. honourable, incorruptible, upright, ethical, oral, virtuous
ant. corrupt, unfair, immoral

rile
syn. aggravate, annoy, chafe, exasperate, fret, peeve
ant. please, placate, soothe

roiled
syn. cloudy, muddy, murky, tumultuous, rugged, tempestuous
ant. bright, luminous, orderly

rue
syn. deplore, regret, repent, deplore, grieve, lament
ant. laud, commend, celebrate

ruminate
syn. cogitate, contemplate, excogitate, mull, muse, ponder
ant. ignore, discard, scorn

ruse
syn. artifice, deception, dodge, maneuver, sleight, wile
ant. candour, frankness, ingenuousness

Exercise

Choose the word which is CLOSEST in meaning to the given word.

1. Rescind
   (a) repeal (b) enact
   (c) esteem (d) renounce
2. Reprobate
   (a) virtuous (b) culpable
   (c) strident (d) principled
3. Repudiate
   (a) chastise (b) ratify
   (c) vouch (d) repeal

Choose the word which is MOST SIMILAR in meaning to the underlined word in the given sentence :

4. The company was <u>resuscitated</u> after it received a grant from the government.
   (a) revived (b) smothered
   (c) recoiled (d) criticised
5. India must keep the <u>rigour</u> to win every match in the tournament.
   (a) prate (b) chafe
   (c) diligence (d) fret

Choose the word which is OPPOSITE in meaning to the given word.

6. Ruse
   (a) inquitous (b) vicious
   (c) candour (d) placate
7. Raucous
   (a) subdued (b) raspy
   (c) content (d) pliant
8. Rancour
   (a) virulence (b) sympathy
   (c) turbulence (d) joy

Choose the word which is MOST OPPOSITE in meaning to the underlined word in the given sentence.

9. MF Hussain was a <u>recluse</u>.
   (a) ascetic (b) esoteric
   (c) profound (d) gregarious
10. Kavita was <u>reproached</u> for taking a stand for him.
    (a) praised (b) disowned
    (c) criticised (d) validated

S

sacrosanct
syn. blessed, hallowed, pious, sacred, inviolable, consecrated
ant. condemned, profane, unsanctified

salubrious
syn. healthsome, hygienic, salutary, wholesome, invigorating, benign
ant. hurting, rotten, noxious

sanctimonious
syn. hypocritical, pharisaical, smug, unctuous, canting, inordinate
ant. reasonable, forthright, righteous

sapient
syn. sagacious, levelheaded, sage, reasonable, sound, well-grounded
ant. idiotic, reckless, stupid

sardonic
syn. cynic, ironic, wry, derisive, taunting, sneering
ant. genial, considerate, deferential

scorn
syn. despise, disdain, scout, deride, spurn, trash
ant. admire, adore, sanction

scurrilous
syn. abusive, invective, vituperative, ribald, smutty, foul
ant. upright, chaste, decent

sedate
syn. demure, placid, serene, unflappable, inscrutable, reticent
ant. aggressive, agitated, chatty

serendipity
syn. blessing, fortune, certainty, destiny, chance, prospect
ant. choice, volition, misfortune

serried
syn. brimful, compact, bundled, loaded, seething, stuffed
ant. deserted, empty, smooth

servile
syn. menial, obsequious, slavish, subservient, despicable, ignoble
ant. aggressive, dormant, brazen

shove
syn. drive, propel, push, ram, thrust, poke
ant. pull, hold, keep

skittish
syn. edgy, fidgety, jittery, restive, tense, twitchy
ant. calm, collected, unworried

slake
syn. appease, assuage, gratify, satiate, captivate, conciliate
ant. dissatisfy, upset, disappoint

slighting
syn. deprecatory, derogatory, detractive, disparaging, pejorative, low
ant. appreciative, flattering, complementary

sluggard
syn. idle, indolent, lazy, shiftless, slothful, sluggish
ant. overachiever, workaholic, active

slumberous
syn. dozy, drowsy, nodding, somnolent, soporific, sleepy
ant. restless, awake, attentive

smug
syn. complacent, conceited, snobbish, priggish, vainglorious, pompous
ant. modest, unsure, benevolent

sobriety
syn. graveness, sedateness, solemnity, staidness, abstinence, soberness
ant. drunkenness, inebriety, intoxication

somnolent
syn. sleepy, slumberous, soporific, hypnotic, opiate, sleepy
ant. attentive, awake, conscious

sophomoric
syn. brash, foolish, naive, reckless, young, headlong
ant. experienced, professional, expert

sordid
syn. base, ignoble, men, squalid, abject
ant. honourable, reputable, wonderful

spartan
syn. austere, doughty, frugal, rigorous, laconic, undaunted
ant. luxuriant, opulent, generous

sprightly

syn. brisk, dynamic, strenuous, vigorous, spry, zippy

ant. sluggish, indifferent, lethargic

stentorian

syn. blaring, deafening, earsplitting, roaring, resounding, sonorous

ant. inaudible, subdued, soft

stolid

syn. apathetic, detached, impassive, listless, phlegmatic, unresponsive

ant. aware, interested, enthusiastic

strut

syn. flounce, prance, swagger, swank, swash, flaunt

ant. be modest, be humble, be meek

subterfuge

syn. artifice, deception, feint, gimmick, maneuver, ruse

ant. honesty, frankness, uprightness

subvert

syn. overthrow, overturn, topple, tumble, sabotage, undermine

ant. comply, obey, uphold

succinct

syn. brief, compendious, concise, laconic, summary, terse

ant. lengthy, wordy, elaborate

sunder

syn. fracture, rift, rive, shatter, smash, splinter

ant. reconcile, mend, fix

supine

syn. flat, horizontal, prostrate, reclining, recumbent, even

ant. elevated, uneven, rugged

surfeit

syn. excess, overindulgence, repletion, exorbitance, plethora, superfluity

ant. lack, want, base

surreptitious

syn. furtive, secretive, sly, sneaky, clandestine, covert

ant. aboveboard, authorised, honest

sweltering

syn. ardent, blistering, broiling, scalding, searing, sizzling

ant. freezing, soothing, cold

Exercise

Choose the word which is CLOSEST in meaning to the given word.

1. Skittish
   (a) restive (b) loathsome
   (c) slothful (d) drowsy
2. Sardonic
   (a) wry (b) genuine
   (c) vituperative (d) snotty
3. Scurrilous
   (a) chaste (b) vituperative
   (c) unflappable (d) serene

Choose the word which is MOST SIMILAR is meaning to the underlined word in the given sentence.

4. The monk sold the Ferrari and led a spartan life.
   (a) austere (b) pompous
   (c) opulent (d) brash
5. Freedom of the press is sacrosanct.
   (a) impeachable (b) inviolable
   (c) temporary (d) dependent

Choose the word which is OPPOSITE in meaning to the given word.

6. Subterfuge
   (a) feint (b) honesty
   (c) serenity (d) plethora
7. Sordid
   (a) abject (b) honourable
   (c) naive (d) laconic

Choose the word which is MOST OPPOSITE in meaning to the underlined word in the given sentence.

8. The article is written in a succinct way.
   (a) terse (b) wily
   (c) elaborate (d) plain
9. There is a surfeit of community halls in our locality.
   (a) excess (b) want
   (c) grant (d) slowing
10. The thief gained access to his details surreptitiously.
    (a) openly (b) secretly
    (c) ruggedly (d) knowingly

T - U

tangential
syn. digressive, discursive, excursive, parenthetic, rambling, extraneous
ant. central, crucial, internal

tantamount
syn. equal, equivalent, identical, commensurate, synonymous
ant. different, polar, reverse

tatty
syn. bedraggled, faded, mangy, scrubby, scruffy, tattered
ant. priceless, superior, valuable

tawdry
syn. chintzy, garish, gaudy, glaring, tinsel, meretricious
ant. tasteful, sophisticated, decent

tedium
syn. banality, boredom, drabness, dreariness, ennui, routine
ant. entertainment, excitement, pleasure

temerity
syn. brashness, foolhardiness, incautiousness, rashness, recklessness, carelessness
ant. caution, care, hesitation

temperance
syn. moderation, abstinence, sobriety, reasonableness, balance, control
ant. excess, wildness, outrageousness

tendentious
syn. biased, partial, partisan, prejudiced, one-sided, prepossessed
ant. impartial, genuine, truthful

timorous
syn. apprehensive, fainthearted, hesitant, shuddering, tentative, timid
ant. bold, brazen, forthcoming

torpor
syn. dullness, languor, lassitude, lethargy, listlessness, stupor
ant. alertness, wakefulness, vigour

tractable
syn. amenable, biddable, compliant, docile, submissive, supple
ant. balking, stubborn, refractory

transcend
syn. exceed, overrun, surpass, better, outdo, outshine
ant. fail, lose, lag

transgress
syn. defy, disobey, flout, violate, offend, infringe
ant. behave, obey, follow

transmute
syn. convert, metamorphose, mutate, transform, transpose, transfigure
ant. maintain, preserve, sustain

tremulous
syn. aquiver, shaky, quaky, shivery, trembling, twittery
ant. stable, steady, unwavering

trenchant
syn. incisive, penetrating, probing, acerbic, corrosive, scathing
ant. frivolous, gentle, impotent

trepidation
syn. alarm, apprehension, dread, fear, funk, panic
ant. calm, contentment, peace

truculent
syn. bellicose, combative, pugnacious, mordant, vitriolic, ferocious
ant. gentle, cooperative, tame

truncate
syn. chop, clip, prune, shear, slash, trim
ant. elongate, expand, stretch

turbid
syn. muddy, murky, roiled, hazy, smoggy, confounded
ant. clear, sunny, bright

turgid
syn. flatulent, inflated, overblown, tumescent, tumid, windy
ant. modest, self-effacing, underrated

turncoat
syn. apostate, defector, deserter, recreant, renegade, runagate
ant. adherent, faithful, loyalist

twit
syn. deride, gibe, jeer, mock, ridicule, scoff
ant. commend, praise, revere

ubiquitous
syn. omnipresent, universal, pervasive, everywhere, all-over, wall-to-wall
ant. rare, scarce, confined

umbrage
syn. dudgeon, huff, miff, offence, pique, umbra
ant. happiness, love, pleasure

unflappable
syn. composed, detached, imperturbable, nonchalant, possessed, unruffled
ant. nervous, upset, disconcerted

unkempt
syn. disheveled, messy, slipshod, sloppy, slovenly, untidy
ant. neat, tidy, trim

unctuous
syn. fulsome, sleek, oleaginous, adipose, greedy, fatty
ant. genuine, sincere, reasonable

untenable
syn. flawed, illogical, unsound, unsupportable, invalid, unjustifiable
ant. defensible, excusable, justifiable

untoward
syn. adverse, hapless, unfortunate, intractable, indecorous, unbecoming
ant. auspicious, lucky, happy

unwitting
syn. oblivious, unacquainted, unconscious, inadvertent, unintended, unmeant
ant. conscious, intentional, realising

unwonted
syn. atypical, unconventional, awesome, bizarre, conspicuous, abnormal
ant. customary, familiar, usual

upbraid
syn. admonish, castigate, chide, reprimand, reproach, reprove
ant. acclaim, adulate, approve

upheaval
syn. convulsion, revolution, eruption, catastrophe, outburst, clamour
ant. stagnation, harmony, submission

usurp
syn. appropriate, arrogate, assume, commandeer, preempt, seize
ant. relinquish, surrender, give in

Exercise

Choose the word which is CLOSEST in meaning to the given word.

1. Trenchant
(a) incisive (b) frivolous
(c) unwavering (d) impotent

2. Timorous
(a) forthcoming (b) vigorous
(c) fainthearted (d) shivery

Choose the word which is MOST SIMILAR in meaning to the underlined word in the given sentence.

3. Mobile phones are <u>ubiquitous</u> these days.
(a) costly (b) uncommon
(c) smart (d) pervasive

4. Rupin had the <u>temerity</u> to call his boss dishonest.
(a) recklessness (b) drabness
(c) hesitation (d) sobriety

5. The doctor's resignation was <u>tantamount</u> to his admission of guilt.
(a) polar (b) extraneous
(c) resultant (d) commensurate

Choose the word which is OPPOSITE in meaning to the given word.

6. Torpor
(a) alertness (b) langour
(c) lassitude (d) listlessness

7. Trepidation
(a) apprehension (b) contentment
(c) ridicule (d) realisation

Choose the word which is MOST OPPOSITE in meaning to the underlined word in the given sentence.

8. The King <u>usurped</u> the land of the poor.
(a) arrogated (b) assumed
(c) relinquished (d) preempted

9. He went to the office carrying an <u>unkempt</u> look.
(a) messy (b) tidy
(c) slovenly (d) sleek

10. I hope that nothing <u>untoward</u> happens now.
(a) inadvertent (b) hapless
(c) auspicious (d) averse

V - Z

vacuous
syn. bare, blank, clear, empty, vacant, void
ant. full, filled, intelligent

vapid
syn. bland, innocuous, insipid, jejune, washy, watery
ant. lively, pungent, spicy

variegated
syn. motley, assorted, diverse, heterogeneous, mixed, varied
ant. homogeneous, uniform, similar

vaunting
syn. arrogant, cocky, conceited, egotistic, exultant, pretentious
ant. deprecating, modest, humble

veer
syn. chop, skew, swerve, digress, stray, deflect
ant. stay, straighten, maintain

venal
syn. buyable, corrupt, mercenary, praetorian, crooked, dishonest
ant. honourable, principled, trustworthy

veneer
syn. cloak, disguise, façade, front, guise, pretense
ant. reality, entity, authenticity

venial
syn. excusable, forgivable, pardonable, defensible, justifiable
ant. unjustifiable, invalid, indefensible

veracious
syn. accurate, correct, truthful, precise, rigorous, veridical
ant. false, untrue, genuine

verity
syn. accuracy, exactitude, fidelity, veracity, exactness, veridicality
ant. falseness, inaccuracy, erroneous

verve
syn. animation, bounce, spirit, vigour, vim, vivacity
ant. discouragement, dullness, inactivity

vilify
syn. asperse, backbite, calumniate, defame, malign, slander
ant. compliment, praise, glorify

vim
syn. bounce, dash, spirit, verve, vigour, vivacity
ant. languor, lifelessness, dullness

virility
syn. machismo, manhood, muscularity, potency, ruggedness, vigour
ant. idleness, lethargy, tiredness

vituperative
syn. abusive, opprobrious, invective, scurrilous, castigating, censorious
ant. complimentary, respectful, flattering

voluptuous
syn. epicurean, hedonic, sybaritic, voluptuary, sensual, suggestive
ant. flat, underdeveloped, ascetic

vulpine
syn. crafty, cunning, foxy, shrewd, sly, wily
ant. naive, simpleton, credulous

wacky
syn. absurd, idiotic, imbecilic, insane, moronic, demented
ant. rational, sane, balanced

waffle
syn. equivocate, euphemise, hedge, shuffle, tergiversate, weasel
ant. conceal, mask, repudiate

wallop
syn. bash, clout, smash, knock, smite, whack
ant. aid, solace, comfort

wallow
syn. bask, indulge, luxuriate, revel, roll, rollick
ant. distress, hurt, dislike

wan
syn. careworn, drawn, gaunt, haggard, ashen, livid
ant. flushed, strong, vibrant

wanting
syn. lacking, deficient, barren, devoid, void, scarce
ant. ample, flawless, superfluous

wanton

syn. dissolute, licentious, rakish, unbridled, libertine, gratuitous
ant. moral, righteous, clean

warp

syn. brutalise, canker, debauch, debase, belie, pervert
ant. straighten, upgrade, elevate

waver

syn. sway, vacillate, wobble, stagger, dither, swing
ant. stay, steady, repose

welter

syn. flounder, wallow, jumble, toss, tumble, roll
ant. succeed, do well, manage

wheedle

syn. blandish, cajole, coax, banter, persuade, finagle
ant. bully, force, repel

whet

syn. acuminate, edge, hone, sharpen, grind, finish
ant. blunt, make dull, thicken

wield

syn. manipulate, ply, exert, exercise, command, maneuver
ant. shun, abandon, disuse

wilt

syn. droop, flag, sag, lop, loll
ant. neglect, strengthen, rise

wince

syn. blench, cringe, flinch, recoil, shrink, shy
ant. confront, face, meet

wizened

syn. dry, shriveled, withered, thin, lean, parched
ant. damp, moist, soggy

wonted

syn. accustomed, customary, habitual, regular, usual, conventional
ant. unusual, irregular, occasional

wry

syn. cynic, ironic, sardonic, derisive, sneering, taunting
ant. genial, respectful, polite

Exercise

Choose the word which is CLOSEST in meaning to the given word.

1. Wry
(a) accustomed (b) general
(c) derisive (d) soggy

2. Wanton
(a) flawless (b) licentious
(c) debauched (d) derisive

Choose the word which is MOST SIMILAR in meaning to the underlined word in the given sentence.

3. The leaves of the plant <u>wilted</u> in the sun.
(a) neglected (b) flinched
(c) cringed (d) withered

4. Nafisa has a <u>voluptuous</u> figure.
(a) curvaceous (b) simple
(c) great (d) sober

5. The President has been <u>vilified</u> in the press.
(a) glorified (b) denigrated
(c) shuffled (d) highlighted

Choose the word which is OPPOSITE in meaning to the given word.

6. Verve
(a) vim (b) guise
(c) dullness (d) compliment

7. Variegated
(a) assorted (b) uniform
(c) crooked (d) verdant

8. Vaunting
(a) varied (b) deprecating
(c) motley (d) exultant

Choose the word which is MOST OPPOSITE in meaning to the underlined word in the given sentence.

9. He wasn't going to tell me but I <u>wheedled</u> it out of him.
(a) bullied (b) praised
(c) coaxed (d) stunned

10. The saint was able to fool the public with his <u>veneer</u> of respectability.
(a) authenticity (b) cloak
(c) front (d) pretense

ANSWERS
to all the
Super Nuts Exercises

A	1 (a)	2 (c)	3 (d)	4 (a)	5 (a)	6 (a)	7 (b)	8 (c)	9 (d)	10 (c)
B	1 (b)	2 (b)	3 (c)	4 (d)	5 (c)	6 (a)	7 (a)	8 (c)	9 (b)	10 (c)
C	1 (a)	2 (d)	3 (c)	4 (a)	5 (a)	6 (b)	7 (d)	8 (c)	9 (a)	10 (c)
	11 (b)	12 (b)	13 (d)	14 (b)						
D	1 (c)	2 (b)	3 (a)	4 (d)	5 (a)	6 (c)	7 (b)	8 (c)	9 (c)	10 (a)
E	1 (d)	2 (b)	3 (b)	4 (c)	5 (a)	6 (b)	7 (d)	8 (a)	9 (c)	10 (a)
F	1 (b)	2 (d)	3 (c)	4 (a)	5 (b)	6 (a)	7 (c)	8 (d)	9 (b)	10 (c)
G - H	1 (c)	2 (a)	3 (d)	4 (a)	5 (d)	6 (c)	7 (c)	8 (b)	9 (b)	10 (b)
	11 (a)	12 (c)	13 (d)	14 (b)						
I - K	1 (c)	2 (d)	3 (a)	4 (b)	5 (d)	6 (b)	7 (b)	8 (c)	9 (d)	10 (c)
L - M	1 (a)	2 (d)	3 (b)	4 (d)	5 (c)	6 (b)	7 (a)	8 (b)	9 (c)	10 (d)
N - O	1 (c)	2 (c)	3 (b)	4 (a)	5 (d)	6 (b)	7 (a)	8 (a)	9 (a)	10 (b)
P - Q	1 (b)	2 (b)	3 (d)	4 (a)	5 (c)	6 (a)	7 (b)	8 (b)	9 (b)	10 (c)
R	1 (a)	2 (d)	3 (b)	4 (a)	5 (c)	6 (c)	7 (a)	8 (b)	9 (d)	10 (a)
S	1 (a)	2 (a)	3 (b)	4 (a)	5 (b)	6 (b)	7 (b)	8 (c)	9 (b)	10 (a)
T - U	1 (a)	2 (c)	3 (d)	4 (a)	5 (d)	6 (a)	7 (b)	8 (c)	9 (b)	10 (c)
V - Z	1 (c)	2 (b)	3 (d)	4 (a)	5 (b)	6 (c)	7 (b)	8 (b)	9 (a)	10 (a)

PREVIOUS YEARS' QUESTIONS

PREVIOUS YEARS' QUESTIONS

Based on Synonyms

Type A (Word Type)

Exercise 1

Choose the word which is CLOSEST in meaning to the given word.

1. Hiatus **[NDA 2008]**
(a) uphill task (b) distant place (c) fading memory (d) gap

2. Obscure **[CDS 2012]**
(a) unknown (b) neglectful (c) occasional (d) old

3. Spawn **[UBI PO 2010]**
(a) create (b) counterfeit (c) fake (d) falsify
(e) copy

4. Shocked **[OBC PO 2011]**
(a) alarmed (b) annoyed (c) pleased (d) coloured
(e) electrocuted

5. Deduced **[Bank Clerk 2011]**
(a) predicted (b) presented (c) inferred (d) confirmed
(e) targeted

6. Grumble **[SSC FCI 2012]**
(a) scold (b) complain (c) sheer (d) fight

7. Dangerous **[SSC CISF 2010]**
(a) safe (b) hazardous (c) strong (d) secure

8. Brisk **[SSC LDC 2012]**
(a) puzzled (b) active (c) quick (d) bright

9. Fuel **[IB PO 2010]**
(a) petrol (b) stimulate (c) sustain (d) heat
(e) charge

10. Consensus **[SSC DEO 2009]**
(a) unanimity (b) equanimity (c) magnanimity (d) proximity

Exercise 2

Choose the word which is CLOSEST in meaning to the given word.

1. Want **[OBC PO 2011]**
(a) love (b) importance (c) need (d) dreams

2. Sage **[Delhi Police SI 2010]**
(a) wiseman (b) tale (c) era (d) fool

3. Plump **[CBI Clerk 2011]**
(a) desired (b) beautiful (c) delicate (d) expensive
(e) fat

4. Desert **[SSC MTS 2011]**
(a) wasteland (b) abandon (c) sweet-dish (d) broth

5. Crude **[SSC FCI 2012]**
(a) unrefined (b) cruel (c) rude (d) savage

6. Reluctant **[CDS 2010]**
(a) averse (b) forego (c) redundant (d) amenable

7. Decimate **[UBI PO 2010]**
(a) destroy (b) divide (c) augment (d) vacate
(e) equalise

8. Pensive **[SSC SI 2010]**
(a) successful (b) soothing (c) annoying (d) distressing

9. Ruse **[SSC TA 2007]**
(a) break (b) stratagem (c) mandlin (d) guru

10. Delectation **[NDA 2008]**
(a) envy (b) inspiration (c) astuteness (d) enjoyment

Exercise 3

Choose the word which is CLOSEST in meaning to the given word.

1. Evident **[NDA 2009]**
(a) prominent (b) seen (c) observed (d) quiet clear

2. Obscene **[SSC CISF 2011]**
(a) beautiful (b) unhealthy
(c) unwanted (d) indecent

3. Coarse **[SSC LDC 2012]**
(a) smooth (b) refined (c) stiff (d) rough

4. Spotted **[P and S Bank Clerk 2010]**
(a) patched (b) supplied (c) spoiled (d) noticed
(e) provided

5. Condemn [CDS 2011]
(a) censure (b) despair (c) kill (d) hit

6. Lucidity [SSC CGL PT 2011]
(a) Fluidity (b) politeness (c) clarity (d) fluency

7. Gratify [UBI Clerk 2011]
(a) indulge (b) cease (c) submit (d) satisfy
(e) quiet

8. Summoned [UCO Bank Clerk 2010]
(a) called (b) scolded (c) approached (d) consoled
(e) assembled

9. Callous [SSC ESIC 2012]
(a) liberal (b) ignorant (c) irresponsible (d) insensitive

10. Censure [SSC CISF 2010]
(a) unlawful (b) disgraceful (c) improper (d) infamous

Exercise 4

Choose the word which is CLOSEST in meaning to the given word.

1. Proposal [UBI Clerk 2011]
(a) fact (b) application (c) suggestion (d) routine
(e) wish

2. Grant [P and S Bank Clerk 2010]
(a) assign (b) reward (c) give (d) generate
(e) request

3. Effect [SSC CISF 2011]
(a) result (b) warning (c) chance (d) purpose

4. Jealous [CDS 2011]
(a) envious (b) unhappy (c) regretful (d) remorse

5. Absurd [NDA 2009]
(a) senseless (b) clean (c) abrupt (d) candid

6. Fetid [Delhi Police 2009]
(a) comical (b) ornamental (c) stinking (d) regular

7. Impromptu [SSC Steno. 2010]
(a) unrehearsed (b) uninfluenced (c) unconvincing (d) improbable

8. Innocuous [SSC LDC 2012]
(a) malicious (b) offensive (c) harmless (d) faultless

9. Propitious [SSC ESIC 2012]
(a) favourable (b) similar (c) humble (d) versatile

10. Indict [SSC CGL PT 2011]
(a) implicate (b) elude (c) charge (d) manifest

Exercise 5

Choose the word which is CLOSEST in meaning to the given word.

1. Dilemma **[LIC ADO 2010]**
(a) fear (b) price (c) condition (d) fix

2. Arduous **[NABARD PO 2010]**
(a) pleasurable (b) different (c) difficult (d) shrewd
(e) legal

3. Solitary **[SSC 2013]**
(a) solid (b) solicitous (c) lonely (d) voluntary

4. Engross **[SSC 2013]**
(a) dismiss (b) oppress (c) absorb (d) endanger

5. Kiosk **[SSC FCI 2013]**
(a) store (b) shop (c) booth (d) mall

6. Absolve **[SSC FCI 2013]**
(a) consume (b) punish (c) acquit (d) withhold

7. Fortitude **[CDS 2011]**
(a) fortune (b) fortification (c) bravery (d) breakthrough

8. Judicious **[IOB PO 2012]**
(a) hardworking (b) thoughtful (c) legal (d) shrewd
(e) difficult

9. Parsimony **[SSC 2013]**
(a) expenditure (b) bankruptcy (c) bribery (d) miserliness

10. Rampart **[SSC 2013]**
(a) ropeway (b) staircase (c) parapet (d) scaffold

Exercise 6

Choose the word which is CLOSEST in meaning to the given word.

1. Content **[IOB PO 2011]**
(a) unhappy (b) matter (c) closure (d) satisfied
(e) substance

2. Blunder **[SSC LDC 2011]**
(a) blemish (b) danger (c) worry (d) mistake

3. Humorous **[SSC Cons. 2013]**
(a) witty (b) innovative (c) fashionable (d) timid

4. Gather **[SSC Cons. 2013]**
(a) scatter (b) disperse (c) congregate (d) separate

5. Fruition [SSC ESIC 2012]
   (a) gamble
   (b) establishment
   (c) balance
   (d) realisation of hopes
6. Reticent [CDS 2011]
   (a) sensitive
   (b) secretive
   (c) not feeling well
   (d) not saying much
7. Canny [SSC CGL 2014]
   (a) obstinate (b) proud (c) stout (d) clever
8. Impeccable [SSC CGL 2014]
   (a) remarkable (b) unbelieving (c) flawless (d) displeasing
9. Erudite [SSC TA 2011]
   (a) snobbish (b) scholarly (c) saintly (d) secretive
10. Incredible [NDA 2009]
   (a) hard to believe (b) considerable (c) inconsistent (d) unsatisfactory

Exercise 7

Choose the word which is CLOSEST in meaning to the given word.

1. Mimic [SSC FCI 2013]
   (a) tease (b) refresh (c) greet (d) copy
2. Obstinate [SSC CISF 2013]
   (a) antagonistic (b) abstruse (c) intrinsic (d) stubborn
3. Laud [SSC Steno. 2011]
   (a) live (b) acknowledge (c) praise (d) record
4. Toil [SSC FCI 2013]
   (a) test (b) spoil (c) work hard (d) tell
5. Formulate [NABARD PO 2010]
   (a) regularise (b) contemplate (c) apply (d) frame
   (e) fix
6. Fiscal [Delhi Metro 2012, 08]
   (a) concerning hospital service
   (b) concerning physics
   (c) concerning human body
   (d) concerning government tax revenue
7. Deluge [SSC CGL PT 2011]
   (a) confusion (b) deception (c) flood (d) weapon
8. Hallucination [SSC 2013]
   (a) delusion (b) habitat (c) dress (d) deception
9. Inadvertent [SSC CPO 2016]
   (a) insignificant (b) careless (c) unintentional (d) difficult
10. Pandemonium [SSC CPO 2016]
   (a) pander (b) chaos (c) gratify (d) panic

Exercise 8

Choose the word which is CLOSEST in meaning to the given word.

1. Recollect **[SSC 2017]**
(a) return (b) remember (c) unite (d) assemble

2. Adapt **[SSC CGL 2016]**
(a) bring up (b) adjust (c) encourage (d) serve

3. Drenched **[UCO Clerk 2010]**
(a) tortured (b) visible (c) soaked (d) exposed

4. Promptly **[UCO Bank Clerk 2010]**
(a) obediently (b) quickly (c) successively (d) cleverly

5. Ingenuous **[SSC Graduate Level 2013]**
(a) innocent (b) clever (c) cunning (d) artful

6. Mundane **[SSC Multitasking Staff 2013]**
(a) musical (b) ordinary (c) mortal (d) mandatory

7. Genre **[SSC CHSL 2017]**
(a) celebrity (b) category (c) common man (d) pleasant

8. Apposite **[SSC Tier-II 2017]**
(a) kind (b) favourable (c) eloquent (d) appropriate

9. Consternation **[SSC CGL Tier-I 2016]**
(a) dismay (b) anxiety (c) hatred (d) ignorance

10. Lassitude **[SSC ASI 2016]**
(a) delicacy (b) stagnation (c) depression (d) sluggishness

Exercise 9

Choose the word which is CLOSEST in meaning to the given word.

1. Catastrophe **[SSC Cons. GD 2013]**
(a) clumsy (b) disease (c) rustic (d) calamity

2. Derive **[SSC Graduate Level Tier-I 2010]**
(a) contain (b) attain (c) sustain (d) obtain

3. Confidential **[SSC CISF 2010]**
(a) obvious (b) honest (c) secret (d) accurate

4. Negligent **[SSC Steno. 2011]**
(a) ignorant (b) unimportant (c) careless (d) cheat

5. Hospitable **[NDA 2008]**
(a) convivial (b) liberal (c) congenial (d) welcoming

6. Flung **[SSC Multitasking Staff 2014]**
(a) threw (b) caught (c) cast (d) spat

7. Tepid [SSC CGL 2014]
(a) hot (b) warm (c) cold (d) boiling

8. Salacious [SSC Graduate Level Tier-I 2013]
(a) angry (b) unhappy (c) satisfied (d) lustful

9. Vexation [CDS 2013]
(a) comfort (b) slyness (c) fright (d) annoyance

10. Connote [SSC CPO 2016]
(a) pay (b) convey (c) conspire (d) print

Exercise 10

Choose the word which is CLOSEST in meaning to the given word.

1. Greet [SSC Cons. GD 2013]
(a) welcome (b) hostile (c) unsociable (d) aloof

2. Advance [SSC Multitasking Staff 2017]
(a) bend (b) give (c) change (d) move forward

3. Rational [SSC CGL Tier-I 2016]
(a) tidy (b) agreeable (c) landable (d) logical

4. Indifferent [CDS 2011]
(a) dissimilar (b) various (c) interference (d) unconcerned

5. Finicky [SSC ESIC 2012]
(a) manual (b) expression (c) tropical (d) fastidious

6. Exaggerate [NDA 2009]
(a) bluff (b) overstate (c) explain (d) underestimate

7. Pragmatic [SSC CGL Tier-I 2017]
(a) theoretical (b) realistic (c) perfect (d) simple

8. Hoodwink [SSC CGL Tier-I 2016]
(a) deceive (b) negate (c) upset (d) cover

9. Masticate [SSC CGL 2016]
(a) chew (b) choke (c) bite (d) swallow

10. Obdurate [SSC CAPF SI 2016]
(a) careless (b) contrary (c) callous (d) stubborn

Exercise 11

Choose the word which is CLOSEST in meaning to the given word.

1. Bliss [SSC LDC 2012]
(a) pleasure (b) fantasy (c) happiness (d) laughter

2. Humble **[SBI Clerk 2009]**
(a) elegant (b) polite (c) modest (d) real
(e) vast

3. Spirited **[SSC FCI 2012]**
(a) heated (b) drunk (c) enthusiastic (d) possessed

4. Indolent **[SSC CGL Tier-I 2016]**
(a) lazy (b) expensive (c) active (d) happy

5. Negotiation **[SSC CGL 2016]**
(a) bargaining (b) in-between (c) slackness (d) carelessness

6. Sycophant **[SSC CGL Tier-I 2016]**
(a) psyche (b) flatterer (c) critic (d) slave

7. Peruse **[SSC CGL Tier-I 2014]**
(a) overuse (b) examine (c) abuse (d) defuse

8. Catankerous **[SSC CGL Tier-I 2014]**
(a) noisy (b) quarrelsome (c) rash (d) disrespectful

9. Rapacity **[NDA 2008]**
(a) anger (b) cruelty (c) pride (d) greed

10. Fatuous **[SSC SASA 2010]**
(a) fastidious (b) fantastic (c) funny (d) silly

Exercise 12

Choose the word which is CLOSEST in meaning to the given word.

1. Firmly **[Allahabad Bank Clerk 2011]**
(a) unevenly (b) drastically (c) tightly (d) steadily
(e) gracefully

2. Gloomy **[SSC FCI 2012]**
(a) misty (b) obscure (c) murky (d) shadowy

3. August **[SSC CAPF 2014]**
(a) common (b) ridiculous (c) dignified (d) petty

4. Grave **[SSC 2017]**
(a) dead (b) still (c) serious (d) sad

5. Copious **[SSC ASI 2016]**
(a) vast (b) identical (c) plentiful (d) messy

6. Podium **[SSC CAPF 2015]**
(a) arena (b) tripod (c) stand (d) dais

7. Surveillance **[Corp Bank PO 2011]**
(a) spying (b) cameras (c) security (d) observation
(e) alertness

8. Imbecile [NDA 2009]
(a) astute (b) cunning (c) stupid (d) ludicrous

9. Congruent [SSC CPO SI/ASI 2016]
(a) different (b) identical (c) parallel (d) unfit

10. Labyrinth [SSC CGL 2016]
(a) maze (b) rotating (c) pacing (d) wriggling

Exercise 13

Choose the word which is CLOSEST in meaning to the given word.

1. Erroneous [SSC CGL Tier-II 2015]
(a) inaccurate (b) unfair (c) wrong (d) false

2. Maestro [SSC CHSL LDC 2015]
(a) genius (b) admirer (c) employee (d) novice

3. Weary [CDS 2011]
(a) careless (b) shivering (c) troubled (d) weak

4. Caricature [SSC Steno. 2011]
(a) biographical sketch (b) grotesque likeness
(c) eccentricity (d) personality trait

5. Affliate [SSC MTS 2011]
(a) control (b) associate (c) copy (d) discriminate

6. Supercede [SSC DEO 2009]
(a) suspend (b) enforce (c) repeal (d) set aside

7. Odium [CDS 2013]
(a) illness (b) hatred (c) oddity (d) devious

8. Obstreperous [SSC CGL 2014]
(a) sullen (b) unruly (c) complicate (d) lazy

9. Antagonist [SSC Multitasking Staff 2013]
(a) non-believer (b) trouble-maker (c) trouble-shooter (d) opponent

10. Defiance [CDS-I 2015]
(a) insult (b) denial (c) degradation (d) resistance

Exercise 14

Choose the word which is CLOSEST in meaning to the given word.

1. Tinsel [SSC Graduate Level Tier-I 2013]
(a) tinkle (b) decoration (c) tin (d) colourful

2. Taciturn [SSC Multitasking 2014]
(a) gloomy (b) sarcastic (c) upset (d) silent

3. Motivation **[CDS-I 2015]**
(a) inducement (b) emotion (c) ambition (d) incitement

4. Residue **[CDS-I 2015]**
(a) remainder (b) nothing (c) recede (d) little

5. Profligate **[SSC CGL Tier-I 2016]**
(a) talkative (b) intelligent (c) unconventional (d) wasteful

6. Dessicated **[SSC CAPF SI/ASI 2016]**
(a) dry (b) drain (c) clear (d) fade

7. Receptacle **[SSC CGL Tier-I 2016]**
(a) compartment (b) hole (c) container (d) funnel

8. Affectation **[CDS 2013]**
(a) adoration (b) artificiality (c) appreciation (d) proficiency

9. Stifle **[CDS 2013]**
(a) starve (b) stumble (c) smother (d) stagger

10. Reproof **[SSC CGL Tier-I 2016]**
(a) warning (b) ridicule (c) rebuke (d) threat

Exercise 15

Choose the word which is CLOSEST in meaning to the given word.

1. Eulogy **[SSC CGL Tier-II 2016]**
(a) praise (b) harmony (c) euphoria (d) homily

2. Insolent **[SSC CGL Tier-I 2016]**
(a) distasteful (b) impatient (c) diabolic (d) rude

3. Epidemic **[SSC LDC 2014]**
(a) endemic (b) local (c) widespread (d) natural

4. Mocked **[IBPS Clerk 2013]**
(a) faked (b) pretended (c) teased (d) helped
(e) begged

5. Painstaking **[CDS 2013]**
(a) feeling panic (b) thorough and rigorous
(c) taking risk (d) painful and sorrowful

6. Headway **[Postal Asst. 2014]**
(a) progress (b) thinking (c) efforts (d) start

7. Convalesce **[SSC CGL 2014]**
(a) diminish (b) admonish (c) recover (d) convey

8. Vehemently **[CDS 2013]**
(a) devoutly (b) serenely (c) hysterically (d) forcefully

9. Pallid [SSC CGL Tier-I 2016]
(a) friendly (b) pale
(c) worthless (d) comforting

10. Conscript [SSC CHSL 2016]
(a) draftee (b) draw
(c) encircle (d) subscribe

Exercise 16

Choose the word which is CLOSEST in meaning to the given word.

1. Constrain [SSC CGL Tier-I 2016]
(a) stress (b) contradict (c) restrict (d) obstruct

2. Assent [CDS-I 2015]
(a) climb (b) confirm
(c) answer (d) agree

3. Emancipate [CDS-I 2015]
(a) liberate (b) release (c) acquit (d) unchain

4. Brutalise [SSC CGL 2014]
(a) stir (b) ill-treat
(c) devise (d) strike

5. Penury [CDS 2013]
(a) poverty (b) petty (c) phony (d) pathetic

6. Artifact [Postal Asst. 2014]
(a) synthetic (b) man-made
(c) natural (d) exact-copy

7. Perchance [DMRC 2014]
(a) prerogative (b) fluke
(c) debauched (d) sordid

8. Sheath [SSC CHSL 2017]
(a) weapon (b) hide
(c) encourage (d) coat

9. Obsequious [SSC CGL Tier-I 2016]
(a) defiant (b) dishonest
(c) servile (d) honest

10. Contraband [SSC CGL Tier-I 2016]
(a) burgled (b) smuggled
(c) baffled (d) juggled

Exercise 17

Choose the word which is CLOSEST in meaning to the given word.

1. Perpetual **[CDS-I 2015]**
(a) perfect (b) confused (c) never ending (d) seasonal

2. Deplore **[CDS-I 2015]**
(a) lose heart (b) entreat (c) regret (d) malign

3. Credulous **[SSC CGL 2015]**
(a) funny (b) silly (c) innocent (d) gullible

4. Uncouth **[PA and SA 2014]**
(a) unmannerly (b) untoward (c) unwanted (d) unwilling

5. Impetus **[Central TET 2014]**
(a) welfare (b) trend (c) catalyst (d) reality

6. Flout **[SSC GL 2014]**
(a) condemn (b) disregard (c) respect (d) refuse

7. Spine **[SSC CHSL Tier-I 2017]**
(a) supple (b) vertebrae (c) rotund (d) grime

8. Nonplussed **[SSC CGL Tier-I 2016]**
(a) injurious (b) abusive (c) puzzled (d) enormous

9. Proselytise **[AMU Medical 2008]**
(a) convert (b) translate (c) attack (d) hypnotise

10. Punctilious **[CDS 2013]**
(a) serious (b) careful (c) punctual (d) hardworking

Exercise 18

Choose the word which is CLOSEST in meaning to the given word.

1. Zenith **[IBPS PO 2014]**
(a) bottom (b) periphery (c) peak (d) surrounding
(e) roof

2. Jeopardy **[Postal Asst. 2014]**
(a) magic (b) adventure (c) safety (d) danger

3. Prognosis **[NICL AO 2013]**
(a) diagnosis (b) forecast (c) preface (d) identity

4. Stalemate **[CDS 2013]**
(a) degeneration (b) deadlock (c) exhaustion (d) settlement

5. Beseech **[SSC LDC 2014]**
(a) crave (b) praise (c) bless (d) beg

Previous Years' Questions

6. Hostility [CDS-I 2015]
   (a) hospitality (b) jealously (c) enmity (d) envy

7. Espionage [SSC CGL Tier-II 2016]
   (a) hypnotism (b) spying (c) perception (d) detente

8. Scandalised [SSC CGL Tier-I 2016]
   (a) irritated (b) scared (c) worried (d) shocked

9. Gourmet [SSC CHSL 2015]
   (a) fussy (b) praise (c) gastronome (d) constant

10. Acquiescent [SSC CGL CBE 2016]
    (a) tractable (b) insurgent (c) obstreperous (d) recalcitrant

Exercise 19

Choose the word which is CLOSEST in meaning to the given word.

1. Stroll [SSC Steno. 2016]
   (a) trot (b) gallop (c) walk (d) jog

2. Cupidity [SSC CGL Tier-I 2016]
   (a) fear (b) friendship (c) greed (d) love

3. Bifurcated [SSC DEO 2009]
   (a) dissected into pieces (b) divided into two
   (c) thoroughly evaluated (d) verbally abused

4. Prerequisite [Corp Bank PO 2010]
   (a) result (b) association (c) necessity (d) factor
   (e) mystery

5. Grandiose [Delhi Police SI 2009]
   (a) imposing (b) unpretentious (c) boring (d) lanky

6. Inscrutable [NDA 2009]
   (a) strange (b) mysterious (c) marvellous (d) sublime

7. Repugnance [SSC Steno. 2014]
   (a) fragmentation (b) aversion (c) absorption (d) repression

8. Commensurate [Corp Bank 2010]
   (a) match (b) extracting (c) contemplating (d) request
   (e) employing

9. Pernicious (SSC CGL Tier-II 2016)
   (a) fithy (b) foul (c) continuous (d) injurious

10. Moribund (SSC CGL Tier-I 2016)
    (a) stagnant (b) gloomy (c) dying (d) superfluous

Exercise 20

Choose the word which is CLOSEST in meaning to the given word.

1. **Nap** [SSC CGL Tier-I 2016]
(a) nape (b) sneeze (c) siesta (d) snore

2. **Swap** [SSC FCI 2012]
(a) snap (b) exchange (c) break (d) exclude

3. **Entail** [SBI PO 2014]
(a) limit (b) occasion (c) involve (d) subject
(e) end

4. **Petition** [SSC LDC 2014]
(a) rotation (b) administration (c) appeal (d) vocation

5. **Meadow** [NICL Asst. 2015]
(a) enmity (b) conflict (c) grassland (d) friendship
(e) cow shed

6. **Porous** [SSC CGL 2014]
(a) adventurous (b) permeable (c) pungent (d) concrete

7. **Supercilious** [Haryana TET 2014]
(a) proud and haughty (b) unfriendly
(c) barbaric (d) intriguing

8. **Portent** [CDS 2013]
(a) profess (b) portray (c) think (d) foreshadow

9. **Discreet** [CDS 2013]
(a) mature (b) intelligent (c) clever (d) prudent

10. **Panacea** [NDA 2011]
(a) praise (b) cure-all (c) poison (d) ambrosia

ANSWERS

Exercise 1

1. *(d)* **2.** *(a)* **3.** *(a)* **4.** *(a)* **5.** *(c)* **6.** *(b)* **7.** *(b)* **8.** *(c)* **9.** *(b)* **10.** *(a)*

Exercise 2

1. *(c)* **2.** *(a)* **3.** *(e)* **4.** *(a)* **5.** *(a)* **6.** *(a)* **7.** *(a)* **8.** *(b)* **9.** *(b)* **10.** *(d)*

Exercise 3

1. *(d)* **2.** *(d)* **3.** *(d)* **4.** *(d)* **5.** *(a)* **6.** *(c)* **7.** *(d)* **8.** *(a)* **9.** *(d)* **10.** *(a)*

Exercise 4

1. *(c)* **2.** *(c)* **3.** *(a)* **4.** *(a)* **5.** *(a)* **6.** *(c)* **7.** *(a)* **8.** *(c)* **9.** *(a)* **10.** *(c)*

Exercise 5

1. *(d)* **2.** *(c)* **3.** *(c)* **4.** *(c)* **5.** *(c)* **6.** *(c)* **7.** *(c)* **8.** *(b)* **9.** *(d)* **10.** *(c)*

Exercise 6

1. *(d)* **2.** *(d)* **3.** *(a)* **4.** *(c)* **5.** *(d)* **6.** *(d)* **7.** *(d)* **8.** *(c)* **9.** *(b)* **10.** *(a)*

Exercise 7

1. *(d)* **2.** *(d)* **3.** *(c)* **4.** *(c)* **5.** *(d)* **6.** *(d)* **7.** *(c)* **8.** *(a)* **9.** *(c)* **10.** *(b)*

Exercise 8

1. *(b)* **2.** *(b)* **3.** *(c)* **4.** *(b)* **5.** *(a)* **6.** *(b)* **7.** *(b)* **8.** *(d)* **9.** *(a)* **10.** *(d)*

Exercise 9

1. *(d)* **2.** *(d)* **3.** *(c)* **4.** *(b)* **5.** *(d)* **6.** *(a)* **7.** *(b)* **8.** *(d)* **9.** *(d)* **10.** *(b)*

Exercise 10

1. *(a)* **2.** *(d)* **3.** *(d)* **4.** *(d)* **5.** *(d)* **6.** *(b)* **7.** *(b)* **8.** *(a)* **9.** *(a)* **10.** *(d)*

Exercise 11

1. *(c)* **2.** *(c)* **3.** *(c)* **4.** *(a)* **5.** *(a)* **6.** *(b)* **7.** *(b)* **8.** *(b)* **9.** *(d)* **10.** *(d)*

Exercise 12

1. *(c)* **2.** *(c)* **3.** *(c)* **4.** *(c)* **5.** *(c)* **6.** *(d)* **7.** *(d)* **8.** *(c)* **9.** *(b)* **10.** *(a)*

Exercise 13

1. *(d)* **2.** *(a)* **3.** *(d)* **4.** *(b)* **5.** *(b)* **6.** *(d)* **7.** *(b)* **8.** *(b)* **9.** *(d)* **10.** *(d)*

Exercise 14

1. *(b)* **2.** *(d)* **3.** *(a)* **4.** *(a)* **5.** *(d)* **6.** *(a)* **7.** *(c)* **8.** *(b)* **9.** *(c)* **10.** *(c)*

Exercise 15

1. *(a)* **2.** *(d)* **3.** *(c)* **4.** *(c)* **5.** *(b)* **6.** *(a)* **7.** *(c)* **8.** *(d)* **9.** *(b)* **10.** *(a)*

Exercise 16

1. *(c)* **2.** *(a)* **3.** *(a)* **4.** *(b)* **5.** *(a)* **6.** *(b)* **7.** *(b)* **8.** *(b)* **9.** *(c)* **10.** *(b)*

Exercise 17

1. *(c)* **2.** *(a)* **3.** *(d)* **4.** *(a)* **5.** *(c)* **6.** *(b)* **7.** *(b)* **8.** *(c)* **9.** *(a)* **10.** *(b)*

Exercise 18

1. *(c)* **2.** *(d)* **3.** *(b)* **4.** *(b)* **5.** *(d)* **6.** *(c)* **7.** *(b)* **8.** *(d)* **9.** *(c)* **10.** *(a)*

Exercise 19

1. *(c)* **2.** *(d)* **3.** *(b)* **4.** *(c)* **5.** *(a)* **6.** *(b)* **7.** *(b)* **8.** *(a)* **9.** *(d)* **10.** *(c)*

Exercise 20

1. *(c)* **2.** *(b)* **3.** *(c)* **4.** *(c)* **5.** *(c)* **6.** *(b)* **7.** *(a)* **8.** *(d)* **9.** *(d)* **10.** *(b)*

Type B (Sentence Type)

Exercise 1

Choose the word which is MOST SIMILAR in meaning to the underlined word in the given sentence.

1. Please do not interfere with my work. **[CDS 2012]**
(a) meddle (b) help
(c) object (d) copy

2. I possess a new red bicycle. **[PA/SA 2014]**
(a) want (b) own
(c) find (d) take

3. Strive for excellence. **[SCRA 2013]**
(a) cooperate with others (b) be patient
(c) pay well (d) make efforts

4. His efforts at helping the poor are laudable. **[NDA 2016]**
(a) praiseworthy (b) welcome
(c) sincere (d) good

5. He is very impulsive in everything he does. **[NICL AO 2013]**
(a) deliberate (b) wary
(c) rash (d) impressive

6. He is employed in an ordnance factory. **[CDS 2014]**
(a) orthodox (b) arms and ammunition
(c) electrical and electronics (d) ordinary and common

7. Drink only tepid liquids. **[SCRA 2013]**
(a) lukewarm (b) slightly cold
(c) very hot (d) very cold

8. Although the boys in his class were naughty, he never resorted to corporal punishment. **[CDS 2014]**
(a) harsh (b) physical
(c) unjust (d) general

9. She adjusted quite well with her husband's idiosyncrasies. **[CDS 2014]**
(a) peculiar habits (b) bad habits
(c) weakness (d) stupid manners

10. He is quite parsimonious by nature. **[Navy MB 2008]**
(a) cruel (b) spendthrift
(c) haughty (d) miserly

Previous Years' Questions

Exercise 2

Choose the word which is MOST SIMILAR in meaning to the underlined word in the given sentence.

1. The audience thoroughly enjoyed the hilarious drama. **[CDS 2017]**
(a) amusing (b) delightful (c) serious (d) momentous

2. Hospitality is a virtue for which the natives of the East in general are highly admired. **[NDA 2016]**
(a) duty of a doctor (b) generosity shown to guests
(c) cleanliness in hospitals (d) kindness

3. Most of the decisions taken by officers were unjust. **[NDA 2017]**
(a) serious (b) lenient (c) correct (d) unfair

4. His candid opinions have won him many friends. **[NDA 2017]**
(a) kind (b) courteous (c) generous (d) frank

5. The entrance exam will begin precisely at eight thirty. **[SCRA 2013]**
(a) usually (b) occasionally (c) definitely (d) exactly

6. It is mandatory for all the workers to come on time. **[ESIC LDC 2013]**
(a) regular (b) obligatory (c) dutiful (d) necessary

7. After he came back from his evening walk, he felt famished. **[NDA 2007]**
(a) exhausted (b) hungry (c) peevish (d) relaxed

8. I cannot stand his supercilious manner. **[Central TET 2014]**
(a) proud and haughty (b) unfriendly
(c) barbaric (d) intriguing

9. She has unquenchable curiosity about natural phenomena. **[SSC IB 2014]**
(a) thirsty (b) hunger (c) very high (d) insatiable

10. The boy thought it would be churlish to take the last slice of cake and offered it to me. **[SSC IB 2014]**
(a) impolite (b) courteous (c) irritable (d) grumpy

Exercise 3

Choose the word which is MOST SIMILAR in meaning to the underlined word in the given sentence.

1. The Finance Minister said that he would work for the impartial distribution of wealth. **[NICL AO 2013]**
(a) equitable (b) just (c) fair (d) none of these

2. It is difficult to deal with a stubborn child. **[SCRA 2013]**
(a) obstinate (b) indignant (c) object (d) depressed

3. At the end of the marathon everybody was exhausted. [NDA 2017]
(a) weakened (b) honoured (c) satisfied (d) tired

4. Appropriate technology holds the key to a nation's development. [NDA 2016]
(a) modern (b) suitable (c) effective (d) growing

5. This job is very tedious. [CDS 2012]
(a) tiresome (b) dull (c) interesting (d) exciting

6. People thronged to pay homage to the departed leader. [CDS 2012]
(a) humility (b) tribute (c) obedience (d) allegiance

7. The batsman's debut performance was appreciated by the public. [SSC IB 2014]
(a) starting (b) inauguration (c) outstanding (d) first

8. He tried to coax her to sing, but she refused. [SSC IB 2014]
(a) motivate (b) coerce (c) force (d) cajole

9. The police fired indiscriminately at the crowd, killing many innocent women and children. [NDA 2017]
(a) continuously (b) without distinguishing
(c) foolishly (d) rapidly

10. Businessmen who lack acumen cannot be expected to be very successful. [NDA 2017]
(a) fairness (b) sharpness (c) boldness (d) righteousness

Exercise 4

Choose the word which is MOST SIMILAR in meaning to the underlined word in the given sentence.

1. He is extremely meticulous in his approach. [NDA 2017]
(a) simple (b) careful (c) fair (d) reasonable

2. Bad tendencies are to be countered by good ones until all that is evil disappears. [NDA 2017]
(a) opposed (b) balanced (c) reduced (d) bypassed

3. In a hole below a mango tree, a snake was staying. [Dena Bank Clerk 2007]
(a) halting (b) stopping (c) living (d) sitting
(e) creeping

4. We must realise the futility of wars. [RRB Kolkata 2002]
(a) value (b) usefulness (c) importance (d) uselessness

5. Due to extreme pressure, underwater drivers are often sluggish. [SCRA 2013]
(a) hurt (b) careful (c) worried (d) slow

6. There is no dearth of talent in this country. [NDA 2016]
(a) scarcity (b) availability (c) plenty (d) absence

Previous Years' Questions

7. I cannot believe in the veracity of his statement. **[CDS 2014]**
(a) truth (b) usefulness (c) sincerity (d) falsity

8. The young man is quite sanguine about the result of his competitive examination. **[Navy MB 2007]**
(a) depressed (b) pessimistic (c) anxious (d) optimistic

9. Temperance in eating is conducive to health. **[CDS 2008]**
(a) discipline (b) caution (c) moderation (d) care

10. A scientist generally carries out his investigations empirically. **[CDS 2014]**
(a) intuitively (b) verbally
(c) through written communication (d) by observation and experiment

Exercise 5

Choose the word which is MOST SIMILAR in meaning to the underlined word in the given sentence.

1. The police officer tried to intimidate the witness but in vain. **[NDA 2017]**
(a) inform (b) reward (c) frighten (d) persuade

2. He gave me a counterfeit coin. **[NDA 2017]**
(a) rare (b) fake (c) unmatured (d) inferior

3. She is a woman of sterling qualities. **[CDS 2014]**
(a) interesting (b) genuine (c) irritating (d) exciting

4. What a tedious lecture we had yesterday! **[SCRA 2012]**
(a) outstanding (b) exciting (c) ordinary (d) boring

5. After his father's death he became insolvent. **[NDA 2012]**
(a) rich (b) poor (c) bankrupt (d) nonchalant

6. Their common interest cemented their relationship. **[SSC IB 2014]**
(a) strengthened (b) covered (c) smoothened (d) fixed

7. He is a sycophant who tries to win over politicians. **[CDS 2014]**
(a) psychologist (b) opportunist
(c) unscrupulous man (d) flatterer

8. The work needs to be expediated if it has to meet the deadline. **[SSC IB 2014]**
(a) done well (b) accelerated (c) experimented (d) postponed

9. Sin is the sole calamity that a wise man should apprehend. **[NDA 2012]**
(a) give up (b) discourage (c) comprehend (d) fear

10. Sagacity increases with age. **[RRB 2008]**
(a) kindness (b) maturity (c) wisdom (d) love

Exercise 6

Choose the word which is MOST SIMILAR in meaning to the underlined word in the given sentence.

1. He was fired for negligence on duty. **[NDA 2015]**
(a) relieved of his job (b) scolded
(c) rebuked (d) attacked

2. The committee conducted an exhaustive inquiry. **[CDS 2015]**
(a) time-consuming (b) complicated
(c) renewed (d) thorough

3. Mountaineering in bad weather is dangerous. **[CDS 2015]**
(a) threatening (b) shaky (c) perilous (d) slippery

4. Graduation day is a momentous day for most students. **[CDS 2015]**
(a) memorable (b) melancholy (c) important (d) hectic

5. The work in my factory is extremely monotonous. **[SSC IB 2014]**
(a) interesting (b) unattractive (c) repetitive (d) irritating

6. Picasso's painting can inspire a pensive mood. **[SCRA 2015]**
(a) cheerful (b) thoughtful (c) depressed (d) confused

7. He is notorious for his voracious appetite. **[Navy MB 2008]**
(a) strong (b) gluttonous (c) acute (d) explosive

8. The government did all it could to bring the recalcitrant opposition round to its views. **[Haryana TET 2013]**
(a) reproaching (b) conciliatory
(c) accommodating (d) obstinate in opposition

9. He is just laying up a lot of trouble for himself. **[CDS 2015]**
(a) clearing (b) accumulating (c) accepting (d) removing

10. The attitude of the western countries towards the third-world countries is rather callous to say the least. **[NDA 2014]**
(a) passive (b) unkind (c) cursed (d) unfeeling

Exercise 7

Choose the word which is MOST SIMILAR in meaning to the underlined word in the given sentence.

1. The Delhi Airport Authorities have confiscated a large consignment of illegal weapons. **[SCRA 2013]**
(a) seized (b) discarded (c) concealed (d) destroyed

2. Proximity to the court house makes an office building more valuable. **[CDS 2014]**
(a) distance (b) similarity (c) nearness (d) usefulness

Previous Years' Questions

3. It is compulsory for all the students to join this year. **[SCRA 2013]**
   (a) regular (b) obligatory (c) dutiful (d) necessary

4. The radio apprised the public of the safe return of the first space pilot. **[SCRA 2012]**
   (a) advised (b) informed (c) instructed (d) revealed

5. The boy gave a vivid description of all that happened. **[ESIC LDC 2013]**
   (a) brilliant (b) picturesque (c) explanatory (d) necessary

6. The sage did not want to be bothered with mundane concerns. **[CDS 2015]**
   (a) worldly (b) meaningless (c) trivial (d) superfluous

7. One who rules with unlimited power is called a dictator. **[CDS 2015]**
   (a) anarchist (b) autocrat (c) egoist (d) sycophant

8. The decision of the Union Government to repeal the Urban Land Ceiling Act has been welcomed by all. **[NDA 2017]**
   (a) suppress (b) amend (c) cancel (d) withhold

9. It is exasperating to listen to the suggestions of the minister about the educational reforms of which he knows nothing. **[CDS 2009]**
   (a) irritating (b) amusing (c) disappointing (d) boring

10. The police had to bear the opprobrium generated by their blatant partisan conduct. **[CAT 2010]**
    (a) harsh criticism (b) acute distrust
    (c) bitter enmity (d) stark oppressiveness

Exercise 8

Choose the word which is MOST SIMILAR in meaning to the underlined word in the given sentence.

1. The story is too fantastic to be credible. **[NDA 2014]**
   (a) believable (b) false (c) readable (d) praiseworthy

2. He fought the demon with all his might. **[CDS 2015]**
   (a) heaviness (b) strength (c) density (d) popularity

3. The decision to drop the atom bomb on Hiroshima was a grave one. **[CDS 2014]**
   (a) serious (b) momentous (c) instinctive (d) impulsive

4. He spent most of his years debunking politicians. **[MAT 2009]**
   (a) exposing (b) cheating (c) threatening (d) pacifying

5. Officers responsible for the abortive coup were punished. **[NDA 2007]**
   (a) unsatisfying (b) bloodless (c) unsuccessful (d) chaotic

6. The convict's ingenuous explanation brought tears in every eye. **[NDA 2012]**
   (a) candid (b) secret (c) insincere (d) consistent

7. The rebels returned home under an amnesty. **[Navy MB 2007]**
(a) general pardon (b) judicial trial
(c) police security (d) financial assistance

8. Ram is very careful and particular about everything he writes. **[RRB 2008]**
(a) precise (b) careful (c) meticulous (d) scrupulous

9. The disgruntled members of a party are a constant source of tension to the party leader. **[CDS 2011]**
(a) disloyal (b) dishonest (c) discontented (d) dispirited

10. Some journalists are guilty of indulging in yellow journalism. **[NDA 2016]**
(a) misrepresentation (b) vulgarisation
(c) sensational reporting (d) loud gestures

Exercise 9

Choose the word which is MOST SIMILAR in meaning to the underlined word in the given sentence.

1. The servants retired to their quarters. **[NDA 2016]**
(a) entered (b) went away (c) ran away (d) mobilised

2. A genius tends to deviate from the routine way of thinking. **[NDA 2016]**
(a) dispute (b) disagree (c) distinguish (d) differ

3. There was a mammoth gathering to listen to the leader. **[CDS 2017]**
(a) negligible (b) tiny (c) poor (d) large

4. There was a devastating attack on his work. **[CDS 2015]**
(a) terrible (b) casual (c) unethical (d) motivated

5. Devotees believe that God dwells in their heart. **[CDS 2015]**
(a) lives (b) insists (c) travels (d) enters

6. He did not succeed in his endeavour. **[RRB 2013]**
(a) effort (b) plan (c) enterprise (d) trick (e) none of these

7. The courage shown by the soldiers at this moment of crisis is exemplary. **[RRB 2012]**
(a) suitable (b) clear (c) elementary (d) admirable

8. We should emulate the examples of our teachers. **[CDS 2007]**
(a) study (b) admire (c) follow (d) imitate

9. The question is not whether the court vindicates him with regard to his involvement in the case, but how he feels about it. **[CDS 2017]**
(a) reprieves (b) absolves (c) indicts (d) summons

10. House rent in cities like Mumbai or Delhi has risen to astronomical figures beyond the reach of even high-salaried people. **[NDA 2016]**
(a) exorbitant (b) commercial (c) planetary (d) illogical

Previous Years' Questions

Exercise 10

Choose the word which is MOST SIMILAR in meaning to the underlined word in the given sentence.

1. A busy person cannot waste his time on trivial issues. **[CDS 2015]**
(a) unimportant (b) rude (c) crude (d) tribal

2. Stellar groupings tend to be unlimited. **[CDS 2015]**
(a) lengthy (b) heavenly (c) huge (d) infinite

3. The discussion was wound up after a long and fruitful exchange of views. **[NDA 2017]**
(a) postponed (b) cut short (c) interrupted (d) concluded

4. He was fully alive to the need for making adjustments. **[NDA 2017]**
(a) concerned about (b) worried about
(c) aware of (d) indifferent about

5. It is possible that printed books will soon become obsolete. **[NDA 2017]**
(a) boring (b) inaccessible (c) unfashionable (d) out of date

6. I am filled with remorse for my failure to help the young man. **[IBPS Clerk 2011]**
(a) despair (b) regret (c) anger (d) hatred

7. A posthumous award was given to the poet. **[Navy MB 2007]**
(a) postal (b) after death (c) literary (d) creditable

8. It is unwise to sever diplomatic relations with a neighbouring country over small matters. **[NDA 2017]**
(a) engage (b) estrange (c) cut off (d) twist

9. All these items have been marked down. **[CDS 2015]**
(a) reserved (b) packed up (c) reduced in price (d) entered

10. Since our plans are amorphous, we shall send you the detail. **[NDA 2015]**
(a) impractical (b) prohibitive (c) inimical (d) formless

Exercise 11

Choose the word which is MOST SIMILAR in meaning to the underlined word in the given sentence.

1. We should always try to maintain and promote communal amity. **[NDA 2014]**
(a) bondage (b) contention (c) friendship (d) understanding

2. Many species of animals have become extinct during the last hundred years. **[NDA 2014]**
(a) aggressive (b) non-existent (c) scattered (d) feeble

3. Not everyone can respond to a difficult question quickly. **[CDS 2015]**
(a) discuss (b) argue (c) answer (d) deny

4. He was not ready with his annual accounts. **[CDS 2015]**
(a) yearly (b) important (c) monthly (d) permanent

5. The spectators looked at the batsman in amazement when he hit six after six. **[CDS 2012]**
(a) shock (b) hatred (c) surprise (d) suspicion

6. Please do not wreck the flower bed. **[PA/SA 2014]**
(a) help (b) water (c) ruin (d) track

7. He was not at all abashed by her open admiration. **[NDA 2013]**
(a) delighted (b) piqued (c) embarrassed (d) livid

8. He has been very feeble since his illness. **[Haryana TET 2013]**
(a) thin (b) unwell (c) foolish (d) weak

9. How can you have the effrontery to ask for another loan? **[CDS 2015]**
(a) right (b) impudence (c) heart (d) courage

10. He was enamoured of his own golden voice. **[NDA 2016]**
(a) very fond of (b) concerned with (c) obsessed with (d) imbued with

Exercise 12

Choose the word which is MOST SIMILAR in meaning to the underlined word in the given sentence.

1. We must adapt drastic measures to control population growth. **[NDA 2017]**
(a) simple (b) dramatic (c) realistic (d) severe

2. He wanted to mitigate his burdens. **[CDS 2014]**
(a) lessen (b) increase (c) postpone (d) leave

3. If the client insists upon being stubborn, I will also have to be tough. **[SSC CGL Tier-I 2009]**
(a) disagrees (b) consists (c) persists (d) declines

4. The advertisement assured the public that the medicine would give back to users their youthful vigour and appearance. **[RRB 2008]**
(a) replenish (b) rejuvenate (c) restore (d) render

5. It is said that travel broadens one's outlook. **[RRB 2008]**
(a) narrows (b) enhances (c) shrinks (d) restricts
(e) none of these

6. This is his maiden appearance on the screen. **[NDA 2017]**
(a) first (b) last (c) girlish (d) shy

7. I was discomfited to find the boss in the disco. **[MAT 2008]**
(a) irritated (b) uncomfortable (c) embarrassed (d) displeased

8. Her <u>ostensible</u> calm makes a deep seated fear. **[MAT 2010]**
(a) illusory (b) apparent (c) dubious (d) visible

9. His conduct brought him <u>reproach</u> from all quarters. **[NDA 2016]**
(a) rebuke (b) sympathy (c) indifference (d) remorse

10. Society cannot depend upon a <u>fanatic</u> for guidance. **[CDS 2015]**
(a) optimist (b) martyr (c) bigot (d) anarchist

Exercise 13

Choose the word which is MOST SIMILAR in meaning to the underlined word in the given sentence.

1. The experts' <u>minute</u> examination brought to light some important clues. **[NDA 2017]**
(a) quick (b) detailed (c) superficial (d) prolonged

2. His efforts at helping the poor are <u>laudable.</u> **[NDA 2016]**
(a) welcome (b) sincere (c) good (d) praiseworthy

3. Suddenly there was a bright flash, followed by a <u>deafening</u> explosion. **[NDA 2016]**
(a) dangerous (b) terrifying (c) mild (d) very loud

4. He gave a <u>fictitious</u> address. **[RRB 2010]**
(a) urban (b) fake (c) rural (d) wrong (e) unknown

5. The individual's freedom is <u>circumscribed</u> by his responsibility to others. **[MAT 2008]**
(a) limited (b) entangled (c) destroyed (d) eroded

6. The judge asked the contending parties to state their position <u>unequivocally.</u> **[CDS 2009]**
(a) adequately (b) completely (c) effectively (d) plainly

7. Indians are likely to be <u>parochial.</u> **[MAT 2007]**
(a) generous (b) narrow-minded (c) brave (d) short-sighted

8. The navy gave <u>tactical</u> support to the marines. **[NDA 2016]**
(a) sensitive (b) strategic (c) immediate (d) expert

9. Divine grace is truly <u>ineffable.</u> **[NDA 2015]**
(a) that which cannot be rubbed out
(b) incapable of being understood
(c) that which is too great to be expressed in words
(d) too powerful to be defeated

10. After the announcement of the election results the party workers were in a state of <u>euphoria.</u> **[B.Ed IGNOU 2009]**
(a) utter depression (b) disorder
(c) rapturous excitement (d) great anger

Exercise 14

Choose the word which is MOST SIMILAR in meaning to the underlined word in the given sentence.

1. His performance in the examination stunned his friends. **[NDA 2007]**
(a) apathetic (b) stupefied (c) angered (d) subdued

2. He was confident that his plan would work out well. **[Dena Bank 2007]**
(a) doubtful (b) careful (c) sure (d) upset
(e) determined

3. He never recovered from the loss of his wife. **[RRB 2008]**
(a) got by (b) got over (c) got aside (d) got rid

4. He is a docile person. **[B.Ed IGNOU 2007]**
(a) excitable (b) confused
(c) an easily manageable soul (d) easily irritable

5. One evening two female camels belonging to two different men strayed away from their houses. **[RRB 2009]**
(a) escaped (b) walked (c) moved (d) wandered

6. His convocation address was very edifying. **[NDA 2015]**
(a) tedious (b) in need of editing
(c) instructive (d) exciting

7. He gave his tacit approval to the proposition. **[NDA 2015]**
(a) full (b) loud (c) clean (d) implied

8. He corroborated the statement of his brother. **[NDA 2014]**
(a) confirmed (b) disproved (c) condemned (d) seconded

9. That the plan is both inhuman and preposterous needs no further proof. **[NDA 2014]**
(a) heartless (b) impractical (c) absurd (d) abnormal

10. He ended his speech on a supercilious note which was quite unexpected. **[IES 2008]**
(a) defamatory (b) contemptuous (c) superfluous (d) irrelevant

Exercise 15

Choose the word which is MOST SIMILAR in meaning to the underlined word in the given sentence.

1. He was exhilarated at the outcome of the election results. **[NDA 2015]**
(a) satisfied (b) surprised (c) disappointed (d) overjoyed

2. In spite of hard work, the farmers could only get a meagre yield. **[NDA 2015]**
(a) satisfactory (b) scanty (c) plenty (d) normal

3. Whatever opinion he gives is sane. [NDA 2014]
(a) rational (b) obscure (c) wild (d) arrogant

4. Whatever the verdict of history may be, Chaplin will occupy a unique place in its pages. [NDA 2014]
(a) judgement (b) voice (c) outcome (d) prediction

5. A truly respectable old man is a ripe person. [CDS 2018]
(a) senior (b) mature (c) perfect (d) seasoned

6. Vendors must have license. [CDS 2018]
(a) one who drives a car
(b) one who works in a hospital
(c) one who is employed in food serving
(d) one engaged in selling

7. The jewels have been stolen from her bedroom. [CDS 2018)
(a) embezzled (b) asserted (c) yielded (d) abdicated

8. True religion does not require one to proselytise through guile or force. [NDA 2014]
(a) translate (b) hypnotise (c) attack (d) convert

9. Democracy is not the standardising of everyone so as to obliterate all peculiarity. [NDA 2015]
(a) demolish (b) extinguish (c) erase (d) change

10. He bore the pain with great fortitude. [NDA 2015]
(a) resignation (b) defiance (c) indifference (d) forbearance

ANSWERS

Exercise 1

1. *(a)* **2.** *(b)* **3.** *(d)* **4.** *(a)* **5.** *(c)* **6.** *(b)* **7.** *(a)* **8.** *(b)* **9.** *(a)* **10.** *(d)*

Exercise 2

1 *(a)* **2.** *(b)* **3.** *(d)* **4.** *(d)* **5.** *(c)* **6.** *(b)* **7.** *(a)* **8.** *(a)* **9.** *(d)* **10.** *(a)*

Exercise 3

1 *(a)* **2.** *(a)* **3.** *(d)* **4.** *(b)* **5.** *(a)* **6.** *(b)* **7.** *(d)* **8.** *(d)* **9.** *(b)* **10.** *(b)*

Exercise 4

1. *(b)* **2.** *(a)* **3.** *(c)* **4.** *(d)* **5.** *(d)* **6.** *(a)* **7.** *(a)* **8.** *(d)* **9.** *(c)* **10.** *(d)*

Exercise 5

1. *(c)* **2.** *(b)* **3.** *(b)* **4.** *(d)* **5.** *(c)* **6.** *(a)* **7.** *(d)* **8.** *(b)* **9.** *(d)* **10.** *(c)*

Exercise 6

1. *(a)* **2.** *(d)* **3.** *(c)* **4.** *(c)* **5.** *(c)* **6.** *(b)* **7.** *(b)* **8.** *(d)* **9.** *(b)* **10.** *(d)*

Exercise 7

1. *(a)* **2.** *(c)* **3.** *(b)* **4.** *(b)* **5.** *(b)* **6.** *(a)* **7.** *(b)* **8.** *(c)* **9.** *(a)* **10.** *(a)*

Exercise 8

1. *(a)* **2.** *(b)* **3.** *(a)* **4.** *(a)* **5.** *(c)* **6.** *(a)* **7.** *(a)* **8.** *(c)* **9.** *(c)* **10.** *(c)*

Exercise 9

1. *(b)* **2.** *(d)* **3.** *(d)* **4.** *(a)* **5.** *(a)* **6.** *(a)* **7.** *(d)* **8.** *(c)* **9.** *(b)* **10.** *(a)*

Exercise 10

1. *(a)* **2.** *(d)* **3.** *(d)* **4.** *(c)* **5.** *(d)* **6.** *(b)* **7.** *(b)* **8.** *(c)* **9.** *(c)* **10.** *(d)*

Exercise 11

1. *(c)* **2.** *(b)* **3.** *(c)* **4.** *(a)* **5.** *(c)* **6.** *(c)* **7.** *(c)* **8.** *(d)* **9.** *(b)* **10.** *(a)*

Exercise 12

1. *(d)* **2.** *(a)* **3.** *(c)* **4.** *(c)* **5.** *(b)* **6.** *(a)* **7.** *(c)* **8.** *(b)* **9.** **(a)** **10.** *(c)*

Exercise 13

1. *(b)* **2.** *(d)* **3.** *(d)* **4.** *(b)* **5.** *(a)* **6.** *(d)* **7.** *(b)* **8.** *(b)* **9.** *(c)* **10.** *(c)*

Exercise 14

1. *(b)* **2.** *(c)* **3.** *(b)* **4.** *(c)* **5.** *(d)* **6.** *(c)* **7.** *(d)* **8.** *(a)* **9.** *(c)* **10.** *(b)*

Exercise 15

1. *(d)* **2.** *(b)* **3.** *(a)* **4.** *(a)* **5.** *(b)* **6.** *(d)* **7.** *(a)* **8.** *(d)* **9.** *(c)* **10.** *(d)*

PREVIOUS YEARS' QUESTIONS

PREVIOUS YEARS' QUESTIONS

Based on Antonyms

Type A (Word Type)

Exercise 1

Choose the word which is OPPOSITE in meaning to the given word.

1. Intricate **[NDA 2009]**
(a) complicated (b) simple (c) colourful (d) good

2. Salient **[SSC DEO 2009]**
(a) correct (b) insignificant (c) central (d) convenient

3. Thrifty **[SSC MTS 2011]**
(a) clean (b) royal (c) wasteful (d) reverent

4. Affluence **[CDS 2014]**
(a) continuance (b) poverty (c) diffidence (d) insurance

5. Compulsion **[DMRC 2014]**
(a) constraint (b) choice (c) skill (d) spontaneity

6. Taint **[SSC LDC 2014]**
(a) construct (b) clear (c) purify (d) repair

7. Ungainly **[CDS 2013]**
(a) quick (b) short
(c) awkward (d) graceful

8. Retrench **[SSC Graduate Level 2013]**
(a) revamp (b) belie
(c) deviate (d) recruit

9. Vacillation **[SSC CGL Tier-I 2015]**
(a) steadfastness (b) relief
(c) inoculation (d) morose

10. Quiescent **[SSC CGL Tier-I 2016]**
(a) active (b) rough (c) quaint (d) queer

Exercise 2

Choose the word which is OPPOSITE in meaning to the given word.

1. Brutal **[SSC Multitasking Staff 2013]**
(a) humane (b) fearless (c) criminal (d) adamant

2. Inhale **[SSC FCI Asst. Grade 3 2013]**
(a) insert (b) extricate (c) hate (d) exhale

3. Handsomely **[SBI Clerk 2009]**
(a) meagerly (b) tidily (c) ugly (d) ruggedly
(e) plenty

4. Deficit **[CDS 2011]**
(a) surplus (b) sufficiency (c) luxury (d) explicit

5. Shimmering **[SSC TA 2009]**
(a) gloomy (b) glimmering (c) refreshing (d) ripening

6. Jittery **[Delhi Metro 2009]**
(a) bold (b) shaky (c) profuse (d) tense

7. Amnesty **[Delhi Police SI 2009]**
(a) loyalty (b) punishment (c) depth (d) dearth

8. Scrupulous **[SSC CGL Mains 2012]**
(a) careless (b) wise (c) caring (d) careful

9. Ebullient **[SSC CGL 2014]**
(a) spiritless (b) soulless (c) mindless (d) heartless

10. Genteel **[SSC CHSL Tier-I 2017]**
(a) uncivilised (b) stuffy (c) urbane (d) prim

Exercise 3

Choose the word which is OPPOSITE in meaning to the given word.

1. Flood **[SSC Constable 2015]**
(a) drought (b) dry (c) cyclone (d) desert

2. Overt **[SSC Graduate Level 2013]**
(a) open (b) complete (c) hidden (d) culvert

3. Modesty **[SSC LDC 2013]**
(a) vanity (b) honesty (c) originality (d) variety

4. Docile **[SSC CGL 2013]**
(a) good (b) static (c) stupid (d) stubborn

5. Denounce **[SSC CGL 2014]**
(a) signify (b) confirm (c) grant (d) praise

6. Senility [CDS 2013]
   (a) virility (b) laziness (c) maturity (d) exhaustion
7. Amalgamate [PA 2014]
   (a) generate (b) repair (c) materialise (d) separate
8. Extemporaneous [SSC Steno. 2014]
   (a) planned (b) skilful (c) confined (d) calm
9. Defile [CDS 2013]
   (a) purify (b) pollute (c) disturb (d) glorify
10. Scrimp [DMRC 2014]
   (a) lavish (b) parsimonious (c) meticulous (d) polite

Exercise 4

Choose the word which is OPPOSITE in meaning to the given word.

1. Comrade [SSC Multitasking Staff 2013]
   (a) friend (b) associate (c) follower (d) enemy
2. Harmony [Delhi Metro 2008]
   (a) agreement (b) melody (c) confusion (d) discord
3. Incessant [SSC LDC 2012]
   (a) continuous (b) intermittent (c) unceasing (d) constant
4. Retreat [Delhi Police 2009]
   (a) haven (b) shelter (c) advance (d) egress
5. Fickle [CDS 2011]
   (a) constant (b) convenient (c) questionable (d) faithful
6. Dilate [SSC LDC 2012]
   (a) expand (b) rotate (c) frustrate (d) contract
7. Imperious [CDS 2013]
   (a) characterless (b) impermanent (c) imperfect (d) submissive
8. Cogent [SSC CGL 2014]
   (a) logical (b) weighty (c) dissuasive (d) persuasive
9. Primed [SSC CHSL 2017]
   (a) fit (b) able (c) unready (d) prepped
10. Flippant [SSC Multitasking Staff 2017]
   (a) earnest (b) warm (c) urgent (d) busy

Exercise 5

Choose the word which is OPPOSITE in meaning to the given word.

1. Genial **[SSC Multitasking Staff 2013]**
(a) stupid (b) intelligent (c) hostile (d) affable

2. Compatible **[SCRA 2014]**
(a) quite similar (b) expressing admiration
(c) showing compassion (d) unable to exist together

3. Absolve **[ESIC LDC 2013]**
(a) bless (b) blame (c) discern (d) ascent

4. Indispensable **[CDS 2013]**
(a) tolerable (b) superfluous (c) expensive (d) hostile

5. Doleful **[CDS 2013]**
(a) aggressive (b) cheerful (c) tired (d) involved

6. Feigned **[SSC Steno. 2014]**
(a) spurious (b) genuine (c) strong (d) dishonest

7. Fortuitous **[CDS 2013]**
(a) unfortunate (b) accidental (c) planned (d) ludicrous

8. Irascible **[SSC CGL Tier-I 2016]**
(a) cranky (b) choleric (c) amiable (d) waspish

9. Disapproval **[SSC CGL Tier-I 2016]**
(a) rebuttal (b) repeal (c) approval (d) appeal

10. Debauched **[SSC CGL Tier-I 2016]**
(a) dissipated (b) depraved (c) honourable (d) unrestrained

Exercise 6

Choose the word which is OPPOSITE in meaning to the given word.

1. Egoist **[SSC Cons. 2013]**
(a) spiritless (b) selfless (c) senseless (d) soulless

2. Lunacy **[SSC Graduate Level I 2013]**
(a) sanity (b) stupidity (c) sensibility (d) insanity

3. Sterile **[SCRA 2014]**
(a) barren (b) productive (c) without germs (d) infectious

4. Preferential **[YES Bank Officer Scale 2014]**
(a) unconventional (b) insignificant
(c) influential (d) standard
(e) meticulous

5. Indigenous **[NDA 2014]**
(a) genuine (b) foreign (c) indigent (d) indignant

6. Menial **[LIC ADO 2010]**
(a) feminine (b) physical (c) dignified (d) artificial

7. Differential **[Corp. Bank PO 2010]**
(a) solitude (b) homogeneous (c) synonymous (d) unique
(e) different

8. Demure **[SSC CHSL Tier-I 2010]**
(a) humble (b) bold (c) coy (d) sober

9. Intangible **[SSC CGL Tier-I 2016]**
(a) ethereal (b) concrete (c) insubstantial (d) abstract

10. Levity **[SSC CPO ASI 2016]**
(a) gravity (b) jocularity (c) bounce (d) frivolity

Exercise 7

Choose the word which is OPPOSITE in meaning to the given word.

1. Querulous **[SSC CGL Tier-I 2016]**
(a) strange (b) uncomplaining (c) answerable (d) stranger

2. Meandering **[SSC CGL 2014]**
(a) sliding (b) sloping (c) strained (d) straight

3. Antidote **[Delhi Police SI 2009]**
(a) medicine (b) poison (c) anodyne (d) amity

4. Innovate **[SSC MTS 2011]**
(a) sell (b) buy (c) choose (d) copy

5. Latent **[SSC DEO 2009]**
(a) primitive (b) evident (c) potent (d) talented

6. Detraction **[PA/SA 2014]**
(a) contraction (b) flattery (c) cannery (d) deacon

7. Contentious **[SSC CAPFs 2016]**
(a) precious (b) controversial (c) benevolent (d) extravagant

8. Ostracise **[SSC CAPFs 2016]**
(a) crucify (b) shun (c) discard (d) patronise

9. Impediment **[SBI PO 2014]**
(a) freedom (b) advantage (c) extravagance (d) luxury
(e) autonomy

10. Laudatory **[CDS 2013]**
(a) laughable (b) derogatory (c) abusive (d) detriment

Exercise 8

Choose the word which is OPPOSITE in meaning to the given word.

1. Devout **[SSC CGL 2016]**
(a) pious (b) pure (c) ardent (d) treacherous

2. Amorphous **[SSC CAPFs 2013]**
(a) amoral (b) definite (c) perfect (d) irregular

3. Yield **[SSC GL 2014]**
(a) respond (b) survive (c) attack (d) resist

4. Disjointed **[SSC CGL 2014]**
(a) united (b) connected (c) solid (d) smooth

5. Spite **[SSC LDC 2013]**
(a) spleen (b) venom (c) spirit (d) affection

6. Orderly **[SSB SI 2014]**
(a) extravagant (b) stingy (c) chaotic (d) benevolent

7. Pertinent **[CDS 2013]**
(a) eloquent (b) distant (c) relevant (d) irrelevant

8. Novel **[SSC CHSL 2014]**
(a) naughty (b) novelist (c) banal (d) nasty

9. Disconsolate **[SSC CGL Tier-I 2015]**
(a) prominent (b) joyous (c) thankful (d) unprejudiced

10. Misanthropist **[SSC CAPFs 2016]**
(a) pedant (b) pragmatist (c) zealot (d) philanthropist

Exercise 9

Choose the word which is OPPOSITE in meaning to the given word.

1. Stingy **[SSC MTS 2014]**
(a) extravagant (b) self-sufficient (c) spiteful (d) broadminded

2. Reconciliation **[NIACL Asst. 2015]**
(a) agreement (b) recognition (c) disagreement (d) recitation
(e) recollection

3. Frugal **[NICL AO 2013]**
(a) miserly (b) gluttonous (c) plentiful (d) extravagant

4. Vigorous **[SSC CGL 2014]**
(a) rough (b) rare (c) feeble (d) artful

5. Sporadic **[CDS 2013]**
(a) rare (b) frequent (c) sharp (d) coordinated

Previous Years' Questions

6. Equivocal **[SSC SASA 2010]**
   (a) logical (b) diplomatic (c) clear (d) perfidious
7. Desecration **[SSC TA 2009]**
   (a) consecration (b) discouragement (c) despondency (d) expectation
8. Redundant **[SSC CAPFs 2016]**
   (a) wordy (b) concise (c) surplus (d) repetitive
9. Gumption **[SSC CGL Tier-I 2016]**
   (a) ingenuity (b) stupidity (c) sagacity (d) acumen
10. Malleable **[SSC CGL Tier-I 2016]**
    (a) teachable (b) intractable (c) manageable (d) pliable

Exercise 10

Choose the word which is OPPOSITE in meaning to the given word.

1. Mammoth **[SSC CGL PT 2011]**
   (a) quiet (b) significant (c) huge (d) small
2. Delectable **[SSC ESIC 2012]**
   (a) agonising (b) appetising (c) distasteful (d) laborious
3. Artful **[SSC UPC 2010]**
   (a) artistic (b) cunning (c) intelligent (d) naive
4. Clamp down **[SSC SASA 2010]**
   (a) move up (b) let off (c) ease off (d) ease up
5. Insolent **[SSC Delhi Metro 2009]**
   (a) magnificent (b) innocent (c) rude (d) courteous
6. Aggravated **[CDS 2011]**
   (a) increased (b) mitigated (c) aggregated (d) magnified
7. Traditional **[SSC LDC 2014]**
   (a) avant-garde (b) present (c) unusual (d) fresh
8. Extraneous **[SSC CGL Tier-I 2016]**
   (a) unusual (b) dispirited (c) relevant (d) intrusive
9. Diffident **[SSC CGL Tier-II 2016]**
   (a) reserved (b) happy (c) confident (d) strong
10. Ingenious **[SSC CGL Tier-I 2016]**
    (a) brilliant (b) foolish (c) crafty (d) original

Exercise 11

Choose the word which is OPPOSITE in meaning to the given word.

1. Alcoholic **[PA/SA 2014]**
(a) drunk (b) addict (c) teetotaler (d) venom

2. Initiative **[Central TET 2014]**
(a) advance (b) enterprise (c) idleness (d) indifference

3. Aberration **[SSC SI 2010]**
(a) regularity (b) commonality (c) particularity (d) normality

4. Publicise **[SSC LDC 2012]**
(a) promulgate (b) withhold (c) silence (d) disseminate

5. Viable **[NABARD PO 2010]**
(a) impossible (b) negative (c) deadly (d) practical
(e) rudimentary

6. Burgeoning **[IOB PO 2011]**
(a) minimising (b) growing (c) escalating (d) dwindling (e) easing

7. Gullible **[SSC SASA 2010]**
(a) susceptible (b) cynical (c) severe (d) sceptical

8. Plummet **[SSC CGL 2014]**
(a) stagnate (b) fall (c) soar (d) equate

9. Profound **[SSC CAPFs 2016]**
(a) superficial (b) obscure (c) intense (d) hidden

10. Epitome **[SSC CHSL (10+2) LDC & DEO, DP SI 2013]**
(a) quintessence (b) paragon (c) enlargement (d) incarnation

Exercise 12

Choose the word which is OPPOSITE in meaning to the given word.

1. Inertia **[SSC CGL Tier-I 2016]**
(a) stupor (b) vigour (c) langour (d) inertness

2. Penurious **[SSC CGL Tier-I 2016]**
(a) destitute (b) impoverished (c) impecunious (d) opulent

3. Forbearance **[CDS 2004]**
(a) patience (b) self-control (c) intolerance (d) preference

4. Ruefully **[SSC SI 2010]**
(a) defunct (b) cheerfully (c) daring (d) deceptive

5. Inevitably **[NABARD PO 2010]**
(a) avoidably (b) mostly (c) certainly (d) expectedly (e) predictably

6. Unitary [SSC CPO 2013]
   (a) single (b) triple (c) multiple (d) double
7. Acquitted [SSB SI 2014]
   (a) convicted (b) suspected (c) argued (d) pleaded
8. Wholesome [NDA 2014]
   (a) complete (b) unhealthy
   (c) incomprehensible (d) few
9. Indomitable [SSC LDC 2013]
   (a) arrogant (b) cowardly (c) adamant (d) certain
10. Consanguinity [NACL AO 2014]
   (a) affinity (b) corpulent (c) estrangement (d) anarchy

Exercise 13

Choose the word which is OPPOSITE in meaning to the given word.

1. Spiritual [DMRC 2014]
   (a) earthly (b) superior (c) material (d) real
2. Controversy [SCRA 2014]
   (a) debate (b) agreement (c) discussion (d) contradiction
3. Nonconformist [SSC CGL Tier-I 2016]
   (a) conventional (b) practical (c) fashionable (d) nomad
4. Visionary [SSC CGL Tier-I 2016]
   (a) realist (b) artist (c) idealist (d) socialist
5. Gregarious [SSC CGL Tier-I 2016]
   (a) unsociable (b) unsympathetic (c) ungrateful (d) unattractive
6. Industrious [SCRA 2012]
   (a) indolent (b) mercenary (c) fortunate (d) factious
7. Recession [SCRA 2013]
   (a) inflation (b) deflation (c) jubilation (d) boom
8. Dissent [SSC CGL 2014]
   (a) agreement (b) discord (c) disagreement (d) unacceptable
9. Particularly [NICL PO 2013]
   (a) elaborately (b) generally
   (c) comprehensively (d) entirely
10. Vindictive [CDS 2013]
   (a) forgiving (b) humane
   (c) polite (d) liberal

Exercise 14

Choose the word which is OPPOSITE in meaning to the given word.

1. Fierce **[IOB PO 2011]**
(a) strong (b) weak (c) tame (d) bold (e) Timid

2. Camouflage **[SSC DEO 2009]**
(a) hide (b) reveal (c) disguise (d) pretend

3. Anxious **[SSC MTS 2011]**
(a) crafty (b) light (c) carefree (d) careless

4. Snare **[SBI Clerk 2011]**
(a) plan (b) alarm (c) protection (d) arrangement

5. Prolific **[Central TET 2013]**
(a) Barren (b) backward (c) reckless (d) profound

6. Advanced **[SSC TA 2011]**
(a) progressed (b) outpaced (c) receded (d) retarded

7. Prospects **[Corp. Bank PO 2010]**
(a) assimilation (b) demand (c) brochure (d) hopelessness
(e) diagnostic

8. Maverick **[SSC CHSL 2014]**
(a) dependable (b) conventional (c) redundant (d) old

9. Urbane **[SSC CGL Tier-I 2015]**
(a) loud (b) native (c) crude (d) rural

10. Mediocre **[IOB PO 2011]**
(a) superlative (b) middle (c) overage (d) pleasant
(e) ordinary

Exercise 15

Choose the word which is OPPOSITE in meaning to the given word.

1. Carnal **[SSC CHSL 2014]**
(a) civilised (b) spiritual (c) brave (d) friendly

2. Effeminacy **[SSC CGL Tier-I 2015]**
(a) aggressiveness (b) attractiveness (c) manliness (d) boorishness

3. Tremulous **[SSC CGL Tier-I 2015]**
(a) healthy (b) steady (c) obese (d) young

4. Affirmed **[SSC CGL Tier-I 2015]**
(a) contradicted (b) opposed
(c) disputed (d) denied

5. Alacrity **[SSC CPO SI 2016]**
(a) liveliness (b) indifference (c) promptness (d) doubt

6. Evasive **[SSC Steno. 2016]**
(a) indefinite (b) explicit (c) unclear (d) categorical

7. Accidentally **[SBI Clerk 2011]**
(a) deliberately (b) mistakenly (c) erroneously (d) cautiously
(e) hastily

8. Boisterous **[SSC ESIC 2012]**
(a) serene (b) tumultous (c) brazen (d) opaque

9. Detrimental **[NDA 2009]**
(a) demolition (b) aversion (c) beneficial (d) bad

10. Adulteration **[SSC CPO 2014]**
(a) purification (b) normalisation (c) rejuvenation (d) consternation

Exercise 16

Choose the word which is OPPOSITE in meaning to the given word.

1. Squander **[SSC CGL Tier-I 2016]**
(a) spend (b) reduce (c) slander (d) skimp

2. Terminate **[SSC CGL Tier-I 2016]**
(a) confine (b) repeal (c) commence (d) progress

3. Veteran **[SSC LDC 2014]**
(a) activist (b) enthusiast (c) novice (d) master

4. Economical **[SSC MTS 2014]**
(a) extravagant (b) stingy (c) prosperous (d) benevolent

5. Seamy **[SSC CGL 2014]**
(a) honest (b) pure (c) unpleasant (d) sincere

6. Despondent **[SSB SI 2014]**
(a) grim (b) pessimistic (c) cheerful (d) divided

7. Exceptionally **[Central TET 2014]**
(a) easily (b) extraordinarily (c) generally (d) markedly

8. Grating **[SSC Graduate Level Tier-I 2013]**
(a) musical (b) unmusical (c) hoarse (d) strident

9. Capricious **[SSC Graduate Level Tier-I 2013]**
(a) fanciful (b) reasonable (c) intolerant (d) indifferent

10. Predilection **[SSC CGL Tier-I 2014]**
(a) predicament (b) afterthought (c) aversion (d) postponement

Exercise 17

Choose the word which is OPPOSITE in meaning to the given word.

1. Marvellous **[CDS 2013]**
(a) awful (b) mechanical (c) meaningless (d) unsentimental

2. Audacious **[SSC Steno. 2014]**
(a) cultivated (b) timid (c) mute (d) visible

3. Immortal **[SSC LDC 2014]**
(a) eternal (b) permanent (c) deadly (d) temporary

4. Indulge **[PA/SA 2014]**
(a) regress (b) abstain (c) deter (d) imbibe

5. Tacit **[SSC SASA 2010]**
(a) implied (b) wise (c) expressed (d) tactful

6. Exodus **[SSC SO 2013]**
(a) influx (b) home-coming (c) return (d) restoration

7. Perspicuity **[SSC CGL Tier-I 2010]**
(a) vagueness (b) dullness (c) unfairness (d) unwillingness

8. Benevolent **[SSC CAPFs 2015]**
(a) malignant (b) malevolent (c) equivalent (d) prevalent

9. Autonomy **[SSC CAPFs 2015]**
(a) subordination (b) dependence (c) slavery (d) conformity

10. Enduring **[SSC CHSL 2015]**
(a) abiding (b) unwavering (c) transient (d) transitory

Exercise 18

Choose the word which is OPPOSITE in meaning to the given word.

1. Bizarre **[SSC CHSL 2015]**
(a) droll (b) ridiculous (c) ordinary (d) comical

2. Thorough **[SSC Steno. 2016]**
(a) cursory (b) detailed (c) intensive (d) utter

3. Notorious **[SSC CHSL 2015]**
(a) infamous (b) honourable (c) prominent (d) reputed

4. Recoiled **[SCRA 2013]**
(a) shrank (b) moved forward
(c) pushed backward (d) expanded

5. Successor **[DMRC 2014]**
(a) follower (b) predecessor (c) guide (d) processor

Previous Years' Questions

6. Vocal **[SSC CGL 2014]**
(a) voluble (b) calm (c) quite (d) silent

7. Lethal **[SCRA 2013]**
(a) injurious (b) innocent (c) dangerous (d) harmless

8. Elation **[SSC MTS 2014]**
(a) depression (b) pride (c) animation (d) bliss

9. Mitigating **[SBI PO 2014]**
(a) aggravating (b) irritating (c) annoying (d) frustrating
(e) infuriating

10. Protract **[CDS 2004]**
(a) defy (b) supplement (c) postpone (d) expedite

Exercise 19

Choose the word which is OPPOSITE in meaning to the given word.

1. Flawless **[SSC CHSL 2015]**
(a) deficient (b) defective (c) seconds (d) sick

2. Ignite **[SSC CPO 2016]**
(a) light (b) rekindle (c) extinguish (d) genuine

3. Arid **[SSC CGL Tier-I 2016]**
(a) dry (b) fertile (c) barren (d) fallow

4. Rugged **[SSC CGL Tier-I 2016]**
(a) hard (b) sturdy (c) smooth (d) rough

5. Cautious **[SSC Multitasking Staff 2015]**
(a) daring (b) inviting (c) careful (d) exude

6. Apprised **[RRB 2008]**
(a) informed (b) declared (c) summoned (d) concealed

7. Ostensible **[NDA 2010]**
(a) illusory (b) apparent (c) genuine (d) visible

8. Squalid **[SBI Clerk 2016]**
(a) poor (b) bright (c) filthy (d) muddy
(e) fetid

9. Equilibrium **[SSC LDC 2014]**
(a) composure (b) imbalance (c) stability (d) inequality

10. Adjunct **[NDA 2011]**
(a) joined (b) prosperous (c) nefarious (d) separated

Exercise 20

Choose the word which is OPPOSITE in meaning to the given word.

1. Virtue **[SSC TA 2010]**
(a) truth (b) vice (c) wisdom (d) idiocy
2. Accordance **[NABARD PO 2010]**
(a) division (b) quarrel (c) tune (d) enmity (e) conflict
3. Waste **[Delhi Metro 2008]**
(a) gain (b) profit (c) nourish (d) loss
4. Tame **[SSC CISF 2011]**
(a) wild (b) savage (c) domesticated (d) temporary
5. Robust **[SSC Steno. 2011]**
(a) lean (b) strong (c) flexible (d) feeble
6. Adept **[SSC CAPFs 2014]**
(a) ignorant (b) inept (c) lacunae (d) inexperienced
7. Fluent **[SSC CHSL 2014]**
(a) inappropriate (b) halting (c) degrading (d) insensitive
8. Sweltering **[SSC CAPFs 2015]**
(a) smelly (b) clammy (c) freesing (d) cozy
9. Accentuate **[SSC CGL Tier-I 2016]**
(a) disparage (b) enunciate (c) aggrandise (d) mask
10. Insular **[SSC CGL Tier-I 2016]**
(a) cosmopolitan (b) isolated (c) narrow (d) parochial

ANSWERS

Exercise 1

1. *(b)* **2.** *(b)* **3.** *(c)* **4.** *(b)* **5.** *(b)* **6.** *(c)* **7.** *(d)* **8.** *(d)* **9.** *(a)* **10.** *(a)*

Exercise 2

1. *(a)* **2.** *(d)* **3.** *(a)* **4.** *(a)* **5.** *(a)* **6.** *(a)* **7.** *(b)* **8.** *(a)* **9.** *(a)* **10.** *(c)*

Exercise 3

1. *(a)* **2.** *(c)* **3.** *(a)* **4.** *(d)* **5.** *(d)* **6.** *(a)* **7.** *(d)* **8.** *(a)* **9.** *(a)* **10.** *(a)*

Exercise 4

1. *(d)* **2.** *(d)* **3.** *(b)* **4.** *(c)* **5.** *(a)* **6.** *(d)* **7.** *(d)* **8.** *(c)* **9.** *(c)* **10.** *(a)*

Exercise 5

1. *(c)* **2.** *(d)* **3.** *(b)* **4.** *(b)* **5.** *(b)* **6.** *(b)* **7.** *(c)* **8.** *(c)* **9.** *(c)* **10.** *(c)*

Previous Years' Questions

Exercise 6

1. *(b)* **2.** *(a)* **3.** *(b)* **4.** *(b)* **5.** *(b)* **6.** *(c)* **7.** *(b)* **8.** *(b)* **9.** *(b)* **10.** *(a)*

Exercise 7

1. *(b)* **2.** *(d)* **3.** *(b)* **4.** *(d)* **5.** *(b)* **6.** *(b)* **7.** *(c)* **8.** *(d)* **9.** *(a)* **10.** *(b)*

Exercise 8

1. *(d)* **2.** *(b)* **3.** *(d)* **4.** *(b)* **5.** *(d)* **6.** *(c)* **7.** *(d)* **8.** *(c)* **9.** *(b)* **10.** *(d)*

Exercise 9

1. *(a)* **2.** *(c)* **3.** *(c)* **4.** *(c)* **5.** *(b)* **6.** *(c)* **7.** *(a)* **8.** *(b)* **9.** *(b)* **10.** *(b)*

Exercise 10

1. *(d)* **2.** *(c)* **3.** *(d)* **4.** *(b)* **5.** *(d)* **6.** *(b)* **7.** *(c)* **8.** *(c)* **9.** *(c)* **10.** *(b)*

Exercise 11

1. *(c)* **2.** *(d)* **3.** *(d)* **4.** *(b)* **5.** *(a)* **6.** *(d)* **7.** *(d)* **8.** *(c)* **9.** *(a)* **10.** *(c)*

Exercise 12

1. *(b)* **2.** *(d)* **3.** *(c)* **4.** *(b)* **5.** *(a)* **6.** *(c)* **7.** *(a)* **8.** *(b)* **9.** *(b)* **10.** *(c)*

Exercise 13

1. *(c)* **2.** *(b)* **3.** *(a)* **4.** *(a)* **5.** *(a)* **6.** *(a)* **7.** *(d)* **8.** *(a)* **9.** *(b)* **10.** *(a)*

Exercise 14

1. *(b)* **2.** *(b)* **3.** *(c)* **4.** *(c)* **5.** *(a)* **6.** *(c)* **7.** *(d)* **8.** *(b)* **9.** *(c)* **10.** *(a)*

Exercise 15

1. *(a)* **2.** *(b)* **3.** *(b)* **4.** *(d)* **5.** *(b)* **6.** *(b)* **7.** *(a)* **8.** *(a)* **9.** *(c)* **10.** *(a)*

Exercise 16

1. *(b)* **2.** *(c)* **3.** *(c)* **4.** *(a)* **5.** *(a)* **6.** *(c)* **7.** *(c)* **8.** *(a)* **9.** *(b)* **10.** *(c)*

Exercise 17

1. *(a)* **2.** *(b)* **3.** *(d)* **4.** *(b)* **5.** *(c)* **6.** *(b)* **7.** *(a)* **8.** *(b)* **9.** *(b)* **10.** *(d)*

Exercise 18

1. *(c)* **2.** *(a)* **3.** *(b)* **4.** *(b)* **5.** *(b)* **6.** *(d)* **7.** *(d)* **8.** *(a)* **9.** *(a)* **10.** *(d)*

Exercise 19

1. *(b)* **2.** *(c)* **3.** *(b)* **4.** *(c)* **5.** *(a)* **6.** *(d)* **7.** *(c)* **8.** *(b)* **9.** *(b)* **10.** *(d)*

Exercise 20

1. *(b)* **2.** *(e)* **3.** *(c)* **4.** *(a)* **5.** *(d)* **6.** *(d)* **7.** *(b)* **8.** *(c)* **9.** *(d)* **10.** *(a)*

Type B (Sentence Type)

Exercise 1

Choose the word which is MOST OPPOSITE in meaning to the underlined word in the given sentence.

1. In ancient India, scholars had no interest in political power or material growth. **[NDA 2014]**
   (a) internal (b) spiritual
   (c) psychic (d) celestial
2. The land is fertile. **[SCRA 2012]**
   (a) poor (b) barren
   (c) deserted (d) fruitless
3. The confrontation between the two parties could not be averted. **[SCRA 2012]**
   (a) friendship (b) angry disagreement
   (c) reconstitution (d) agreement
4. His short but pointed speech was applauded by all sections of the audience. **[NDA 2014]**
   (a) disapproved (b) misunderstood
   (c) praised (d) welcomed
5. Adversity teaches man to be humble and self-reliant. **[NDA 2014]**
   (a) sincerity (b) animosity
   (c) curiosity (d) prosperity
6. The students expected an eminent scientist to inaugurate the programme. **[CDS 2012]**
   (a) illustrious (b) notorious
   (c) intelligent (d) unknown
7. My mother has been working hard for the last two weeks and she feels run down. **[NDA 2017]**
   (a) morbid (b) energetic
   (c) exhausted (d) emotional
8. Spurious drugs can prove to be fatal. **[CDS 2015]**
   (a) virtuous (b) inferior (c) genuine (d) contemptuous
9. Mala is always defiant in her behaviour. **[CDS 2014]**
   (a) obedient (b) rebellious (c) meek (d) friendly
10. The question is not whether the court vindicates him with regard to his involvement in the case, but how he feels about it. **[CDS 2017]**
    (a) reprieves (b) absolves (c) indicts (d) summons

Previous Years' Questions

Exercise 2

Choose the word which is MOST OPPOSITE in meaning to the underlined word in the given sentence.

1. The students made a <u>generous</u> contribution to the flood relief fund. **[NDA 2017]**

(a) niggard (b) selfish (c) spendthrift (d) indecent

2. Wars leave behind a large number of <u>emaciated</u> soldiers in the camps of both the victorious and the vanquished. **[CDS 2017]**

(a) hefty (b) thin (c) disillusioned (d) determined

3. The students' council was <u>dissolved</u> as the university closed for vacation. **[SCRA 2013]**

(a) rejected (b) continued (c) allowed (d) disbanned

4. History <u>abounds</u> in instances of courage. **[NDA 2014]**

(a) shines (b) lacks (c) suffices (d) fails

5. You may not <u>violate</u> the rules and regulations of the college. **[SCRA 2012]**

(a) respect (b) study (c) comply with (d) adopt

6. He is <u>frugal</u> in his spending. **[CDS 2012]**

(a) economical (b) extravagant (c) misery (d) greedy

7. A new court has been established to try <u>juvenile</u> offenders. **[SCRA 2012]**

(a) young (b) female (c) aged (d) male

8. Not taking medicines regularly turned out to be <u>hazardous</u> for him. **[SCRA 2013]**

(a) grouchy (b) grotesque (c) safe (d) perilous

9. In those days many monarchs enjoyed <u>ecclesiastical</u> powers. **[CDS 2017]**

(a) permanent (b) temporal (c) contemporary (d) constitutional

10. The TV has many <u>indigenous</u> components. **[NDA 2017]**

(a) Indian (b) foreign (c) unnatural (d) genuine

Exercise 3

Choose the word which is MOST OPPOSITE in meaning to the underlined word in the given sentence.

1. Kapil's bowling yesterday proved very <u>costly</u>. **[CDS 2014]**

(a) economical (b) frugal
(c) thrifty (d) expensive

2. The older ways of thrashing wheat have become <u>obsolete</u>. **[SCRA 2013]**

(a) extinct (b) outdated
(c) fashionable (d) modern

3. The criminal was <u>detained</u> by the local police. **[RRB 2007]**
(a) arrested (b) released (c) dismissed (d) challenged
(e) None of these

4. The music was <u>soft</u> on the ears. **[B.Ed. IGNOU 2008]**
(a) gentle (b) low (c) harsh (d) loud

5. There are no permanent <u>adversaries</u> in politics. **[IES 2008]**
(a) associates (b) allies (c) collaborators (d) partners

6. The students stood in an <u>orderly</u> line. **[SSB SI 2013]**
(a) methodical (b) confused (c) neat (d) chaotic

7. <u>Reckless</u> driving causes accidents. **[CDS 2012]**
(a) careful (b) slow (c) good (d) correct

8. It was indeed <u>arduous</u> to cross streets in New York. **[NDA 2017]**
(a) pleasant (b) effortless (c) interesting (d) risky

9. The audience thoroughly enjoyed the <u>hilarious</u> drama. **[CDS 2017]**
(a) amusing (b) delightful (c) serious (d) momentous

10. The officer <u>exaggerated</u> the damage caused by the rowdies. **[CDS 2015]**
(a) underwrote (b) condemned (c) ignored (d) underestimated

Exercise 4

Choose the word which is MOST OPPOSITE in meaning to the underlined word in the given sentence.

1. There was a <u>mammoth</u> gathering to listen to the leader. **[CDS 2017]**
(a) negligible (b) tiny (c) poor (d) large

2. Unlike his brother, he is <u>affable</u>. **[NDA 2017]**
(a) reserved (b) gullible (c) irritable (d) lovable

3. He is disliked by all his colleagues for his <u>arrogance</u>. **[SCRA 2012]**
(a) humility (b) generosity (c) joviality (d) decency

4. The developed countries should stop selling <u>lethal</u> weapons. **[SCRA 2013]**
(a) injurious (b) innocent (c) dangerous (d) harmless

5. His success is a <u>tribute</u> to his mother. **[SCRA 2012]**
(a) criticism (b) honour (c) praise (d) admiration

6. His lawyer got him <u>acquitted</u> in the case. **[SSB SI 2014]**
(a) convicted (b) suspected (c) argued (d) pleaded

7. He has a <u>delicate</u> constitution. **[NIFT 2013]**
(a) fit (b) ungainly (c) strong (d) rugged

8. The witness <u>corroborated</u> word for word statement of the victim. **[NDA 2017]**
   (a) accepted (b) confirmed
   (c) denied (d) repeated
9. <u>Servitude</u> is not helpful for mental growth. **[CDS 2015]**
   (a) disserrice (b) retirement
   (c) freedom (d) termination
10. I find his views <u>repugnant</u>. **[CDS 2014]**
    (a) amiable (b) repulsive
    (c) amoral (d) apolitical

Exercise 5

Choose the word which is MOST OPPOSITE in meaning to the underlined word in the given sentence.

1. The birth of his child decidedly proved to be an <u>auspicious</u> event in his life. **[NDA 2017]**
   (a) precious (b) ominous (c) useless (d) unforgettable
2. He <u>yielded</u> to temptation. **[CDS 2008]**
   (a) succumbed (b) rescinded (c) skirted (d) resisted
3. Old people are generally more <u>conservative</u> than young people. **[B.Ed. IGNOU 2007]**
   (a) modern (b) traditional (c) dynamic (d) liberal
4. Never adopt a <u>callous</u> attitude towards your duties. **[RRB (Kolkata) 2009]**
   (a) cooperative (b) considerate (c) courteous (d) cautious
5. The long sickness has turned the boy <u>flimsy</u>. **[RRB (Kolkata) 2010]**
   (a) strong (b) healthy (c) agile (d) wholesome
6. He got <u>voluntary</u> retirement on account of his failing health. **[SCRA 2012]**
   (a) urgent (b) compulsory (c) premature (d) undesirable
7. Repeated failure left him <u>despondent.</u> **[SSB SI 2013]**
   (a) grim (b) pessimistic (c) cheerful (d) divided
8. My first lecture in the classroom was a <u>fiasco</u>. **[NDA 2017]**
   (a) success (b) joy (c) fun (d) disaster
9. <u>Cumulatively</u>, the effect of these drugs is quite bad. **[NDA 2016]**
   (a) individually (b) obviously (c) clearly (d) collectively
10. The writer's <u>erudition</u> in science is revealed in every page of his book. **[CDS 2017]**
    (a) unlightened (b) ignorance (c) intelligence (d) hollowness

Exercise 6

Choose the word which is MOST OPPOSITE in meaning to the underlined word in the given sentence.

1. The young leader was reluctant to shoulder the responsibilities of the ministerial office. **[NDA 2014]**
(a) wanting (b) willing (c) anxious (d) eager

2. John is always shabbily dressed. **[NDA 2015]**
(a) decently (b) beautifully (c) extravagantly (d) scantily

3. He is a loving father and takes great delight in his children. **[NDA 2017]**
(a) revolt (b) dissatisfaction (c) enjoyment (d) disgust

4. We must realise the futility of wars. **[RRB 2009]**
(a) value (b) usefulness (c) importance (d) urgency
(e) none of these

5. He has a weakness for foreign goods. **[RRB 2008]**
(a) fashionable (b) exotic (c) exported (d) indigenous

6. He is suffering from a severe cough. **[NDA 2016]**
(a) violent (b) mild (c) bad (d) continuous

7. Many people suffer because of pride. **[NDA 2015]**
(a) lowliness (b) submission (c) humility (d) obedience

8. He hates these continual arguments with his friend. **[NDA 2016]**
(a) repeated (b) irrational (c) occasional (d) regular

9. Rakesh is vulnerable to political pressure. **[CDS 2018]**
(a) weak (b) unguarded (c) exposed (d) resilient

10. Terrorists profess fanatical ideology. **[CDS 2018]**
(a) bigoted (b) militant (c) moderate (d) fervid

Exercise 7

Choose the word which is MOST OPPOSITE in meaning to the underlined word in the given sentence.

1. His timidity proved costly. **[NDA 2016]**
(a) arrogance (b) boldness (c) skilfulness (d) cunning

2. Real happiness does not lie in material possessions alone. **[CDS 2014]**
(a) physical (b) essential (c) spiritual (d) manual

3. He is quite optimistic about the new measures he has introduced to alleviate poverty. **[RRB 2010]**
(a) pessimistic (b) cynical (c) doubtful (d) unsure

Previous Years' Questions

4. He gave the reply in a terse style. **[CDS 2009]**
(a) pleasant (b) verbose (c) rude (d) concise

5. He showed a marked antipathy to foreigners. **[NDA 2008]**
(a) profundity (b) fondness (c) objection (d) willingness

6. He walked in ungainly strides. **[RRB 2009]**
(a) quick (b) short (c) awkward (d) graceful

7. The consultant analysed the proposal carefully before he decided to jettison it. **[NDA 2010]**
(a) abandon (b) strengthen (c) accept (d) modify

8. He likes all the games but he has a predilection for football. **[CDS 2011]**
(a) partiality (b) preference (c) love (d) antipathy

9. Arrangements were made to handle the mammoth gathering tactfully. **[NDA 2016]**
(a) significant (b) small (c) unruly (d) noisy

10. He abandoned his family. **[NDA 2014]**
(a) supported (b) encouraged (c) pleased (d) saved

Exercise 8

Choose the word which is MOST OPPOSITE in meaning to the underlined word in the given sentence.

1. His officer was a very strict person. **[CDS 2015]**
(a) pleasant (b) open-hearted (c) lenient (d) indifferent

2. The speaker was unable to pacify the crowd. **[CDS 2015]**
(a) excite (b) antagonise (c) threaten (d) challenge

3. The President condemned the act of violence during the celebration of the festival. **[NDA 2017]**
(a) reason (b) instigation (c) restraint (d) sob

4. He was just idle by temperament. **[NDA 2017]**
(a) employed (b) occupied (c) industrious (d) happy

5. The new officer is a brash young man. **[B.Ed. IGNOU 2008]**
(a) handsome (b) kind (c) arrogant (d) polite

6. The old man asserted that the whole art of medicine lay in Judicious planning. **[RRB 2009]**
(a) curious (b) unreasonable (c) clever (d) cautious

7. The speaker recalled the deceased leader's benevolent deeds. **[CDS 2010]**
(a) unpopular (b) unkind (c) unbecoming (d) unplanned

8. When I suggested that war is a method of controlling population, my father remarked that I was being facetious. **[CAT 2009]**
(a) serious (b) jovial (c) jocular (d) joking

9. Whether the rewards are in commensurate with the efforts or not, a society will always have workaholics and the shirk works group. **[CDS 2017]**
(a) disproportionate (b) equal to
(c) matched (d) unparalled

10. I was prepared to show my hand provided he agreed to do the same. **[NDA 2016]**
(a) to yield (b) to shake hands
(c) to conceal my plan (d) to lose my ground

Exercise 9

Choose the word which is MOST OPPOSITE in meaning to the underlined word in the given sentence.

1. The seminar which Ravi organised proved to be a momentous event. **[CDS 2017]**
(a) trivial (b) futile (c) vain (d) useless

2. Don't you think his account of things was monotonous? **[CDS 2015]**
(a) agreeable (b) acceptable (c) varied (d) indecent

3. The sergeant was heartily welcomed for his deeds for the people. **[RRB 2007]**
(a) disregarded (b) fight (c) criticised (d) abused

4. The complainant was not supportive of providing all the facts in the court. **[NDA 2012]**
(a) defendant (b) advocate (c) indulgence (d) servant

5. My friend dissuaded me from giving up the lucrative business. **[SCRA 2013]**
(a) persuaded (b) prevented (c) disagreed (d) agreed

6. My son is gifted with an extraordinary inquisitive mind. **[SCRA 2012]**
(a) dull (b) unattractive (c) capable (d) curious

7. His sudden appearance on the scene was fortuitous. **[NDA 2007]**
(a) circumstantial (b) unfortunate (c) sudden (d) calculated

8. Self-reproach is not always a very good thing. **[NDA 2008]**
(a) self-esteem (b) self-assurance (c) self-justification (d) self-satisfaction

9. I am still dubious about that plan. **[CDS 2014]**
(a) certain (b) doubtful (c) docile (d) faithful

10. It was no altruistic motive that prompted him to help her. **[NDA 2015]**
(a) selfish (b) inhuman (c) brutal (d) wicked

Previous Years' Questions

Exercise 10

Choose the word which is MOST OPPOSITE in meaning to the underlined word in the given sentence.

1. He concealed his thoughts very easily. **[NDA 2015]**
   (a) emphasised (b) expressed (c) affirmed (d) revealed

2. He is extremely intelligent but proud. **[NDA 2014]**
   (a) dull (b) weak (c) ignorant (d) arrogant

3. A friendly dog met us at the farm gate. **[NDA 2014]**
   (a) helpful (b) understanding (c) quiet (d) hostile

4. He has an aversion to milk. **[CDS 2015]**
   (a) dear (b) loving (c) liking (d) pet

5. He made several attempts to placate his opponents. **[IES 2009]**
   (a) infuriate (b) defeat (c) discourage (d) deceive

6. Due to his excessive craftiness he achieved success but lost his friends. **[IES 2007]**
   (a) simplicity (b) sincerity
   (c) straightforwardness (d) innocence

7. The new mass transit system may obviate the need for the use of personal cars. **[CAT 2008]**
   (a) prevent (b) forestall (c) prelude (d) bolster

8. The paucity of good teachers is the chief reason for the present condition of these schools. **[CDS 2015]**
   (a) presence (b) surplus (c) appointment (d) retention

9. He was conspicuous because of his colourful shirt. **[NDA 2016]**
   (a) charming (b) ugly (c) small (d) unnoticeable

10. Like poverty, affluence can sometimes create its own problems. **[NDA 2014]**
    (a) indigence (b) opulence (c) sorrow (d) exuberance

Exercise 11

Choose the word which is MOST OPPOSITE in meaning to the underlined word in the given sentence.

1. His attitude to poor people is deplorable. **[CDS 2015]**
   (a) commendable (b) miserable (c) equitable (d) desirable

2. I cannot see much likeness between the two boys. **[CDS 2014]**
   (a) enmity (b) hatred
   (c) difference (d) dislike

3. We carried on the search for the missing person. **[NDA 2017]**
(a) delayed (b) reconsidered (c) broke up (d) called off

4. Do not give him a responsible job, he is immature. **[NDA 2016]**
(a) thoughtful (b) cautious (c) calculating (d) seasoned

5. He handled the machine with deft fingers. **[NDA 2016]**
(a) delicate (b) sturdy (c) quick (d) clumsy

6. His style of writing is quite verbose. **[NDA 2008]**
(a) short (b) limited (c) precise (d) constricted

7. He glanced through the letter perfunctorily. **[CAT 2009]**
(a) nicely (b) ceremoniously (c) carefully (d) particularly

8. The evidence was constructed from a very parsimonious of information. **[NDA 2014]**
(a) frugal (b) penurious (c) thrifty (d) altruistic

9. Crestfallen he returned as he had never faced such humiliation in the whole of his life. **[RRB 2008]**
(a) vainglorious (b) indignant (c) triumphant (d) disturbed
(e) None of these

10. She was overstrung before the performance. **[CDS 2007]**
(a) excited (b) calm (c) enthusiastic (d) cheerful

Exercise 12

Choose the word which is MOST OPPOSITE in meaning to the underlined word in the given sentence.

1. She appeared to be a phony person. **[NDA 2009]**
(a) beautiful (b) unnatural (c) genuine (d) unreal

2. It is obligatory for a common citizen to follow the rules. **[RRB (Kolkata) 2008]**
(a) advisable (b) unnecessary (c) superfluous (d) optional
(e) None of these

3. There has been no improvement in the situation except in isolated pockets like Kerala. **[RRB (Bhopal) 2008]**
(a) attached (b) constitute (c) contour (d) frequency

4. The guest made derogatory remarks about the food he was served. **[CDS 2015]**
(a) interesting (b) complimentary (c) unnecessary (d) cheerful

5. They are confident of success. **[NDA 2017]**
(a) imprudent (b) impatient (c) diffident (d) reluctant

Previous Years' Questions

6. The culprit was sentenced by the court. **[NDA 2016]**
(a) acquitted (b) punished (c) relieved (d) pardoned

7. Akbar the great was a sagacious ruler. **[NDA 2016]**
(a) haughty (b) cunning (c) rude (d) unwise

8. I was deeply affected by his urbane behaviour. **[NDA 2016]**
(a) rural (b) rude (c) irrational (d) indifferent

9. She was skeptical about the safety of the new drug. **[NDA 2015]**
(a) doubtful (b) certain (c) hopeful (d) sanguine

10. The answers to the questions were coherent. **[NDA 2015]**
(a) relaxed (b) loose (c) consistent (d) disconnected

Exercise 13

Choose the word which is MOST OPPOSITE in meaning to the underlined word in the given sentence.

1. Ashoka was a magnanimous king. **[CDS 2014]**
(a) small (b) petty (c) kind (d) majestic

2. He will never turn down your request. **[CDS 2014]**
(a) turn up (b) turn over (c) reject (d) accept

3. Most of the decisions taken by the officer were unjust. **[NDA 2017]**
(a) serious (b) lenient (c) correct (d) imbecile

4. Thrifty as he is, he can well afford to live within his means. **[NDA 2016]**
(a) careless (b) instinctive (c) sentimental (d) extravagant

5. Though aware of his crimes, he remained impenitent throughout. **[CDS 2009]**
(a) repentant (b) sorrowful (c) hot-headed (d) pertinent

6. The health minister has made it clear that it will be implemented only with prospective and not retrospective effect. **[RRB 2007]**
(a) reservoir (b) misfortune (c) advance view (d) massive

7. Her knowledge of Sanskrit appears to be superficial. **[NDA 2010]**
(a) sufficient (b) perfect (c) deep (d) praiseworthy

8. When the new teacher entered the classroom, he found the pupils restive. **[NDA 2016]**
(a) at rest (b) idle (c) quiet (d) impatient

9. The proposal was denounced by one and all. **[NDA 2015]**
(a) renounced (b) recommended (c) announced (d) commended

10. A specious argument is not simply a false one but one that has the ring of truth. **[CAT 2008]**
(a) deceitful (b) fallacious (c) credible (d) deceptive

Exercise 14

Choose the word which is MOST OPPOSITE in meaning to the underlined word in the given sentence.

1. I was upset by his hostile attitude. **[CDS 2014]**
(a) friendly (b) positive
(c) negative (d) inimical

2. He was quite concerned about his son's career. **[NDA 2017]**
(a) unrelated (b) indifferent
(c) dispassionate (d) carefree

3. He showed exemplary courage during the crisis. **[NDA 2016]**
(a) deplorable (b) durable
(c) commendable (d) some

4. We should not belittle the value of small things. **[RRB 2009]**
(a) extol (b) praise
(c) inflate (d) expand
(e) None of these

5. The Prime Minister's radio broadcast galvanised the people's spirit. **[CDS 2007]**
(a) frightened (b) pacified
(c) dampened (d) distracted

6. Their arrival defiled the atmosphere. **[CDS 2009]**
(a) purified (b) polluted
(c) disturbed (d) glorified

7. He was very stoical in facing adverse situations. **[RRB 2009]**
(a) tactless (b) flinching
(c) awkward (d) assured

8. The dishevelled appearance of the two men on the street made everyone take notice of them. **[CDS 2008]**
(a) composed (b) tidy
(c) confident (d) complacent

9. These are the main points of the preceding paragraph. **[NDA 2016]**
(a) following (b) previous
(c) first (d) last

10. The habit of squandering money should not be encouraged. **[NDA 2014]**
(a) discarding (b) hoarding
(c) donating (d) stealing

Exercise 15

Choose the word which is MOST OPPOSITE in meaning to the underlined word in the given sentence.

1. The wise say that life is meant not merely to accumulate wealth but for self-realisation. **[CDS 2014]**
   (a) amass (b) produce
   (c) scatter (d) gather
2. He made a shrewd guess. **[NDA 2014]**
   (a) clever (b) wild
   (c) incorrect (d) discriminating
3. He finally conceded that he was involved in smuggling. **[CDS 2012]**
   (a) admitted (b) denied
   (c) accepted (d) concealed
4. The lawyer was convinced that he had made an authentic statement. **[CDS 2011]**
   (a) absurd (b) false
   (c) unreasonable (d) ridiculous
5. In all places and at all times, there is a profusion of talent. **[RRB 2008]**
   (a) plenty (b) generosity
   (c) aversion (d) scarcity
6. In course of time we may exhaust many of our natural resources. **[CDS 2009]**
   (a) refresh (b) renew
   (c) replenish (d) increase
7. A conscientious editor, Manjula checked every definition for its accuracy. **[NDA 2007]**
   (a) novice (b) careless
   (c) unscientific (d) biased
8. Madan's rustic behaviour astonished the teacher. **[RRB 2007]**
   (a) impolite (b) genuine
   (c) sophisticated (d) awkward
9. He produced cogent reasons for the change of policy. **[IES 2007]**
   (a) flimsy (b) unconvincing
   (c) improper (d) simple
10. He was engrossed in his work when I walked in. **[NDA 2016]**
    (a) occupied (b) inattentive
    (c) engaged (d) absent

ANSWERS

Exercise 1

1. *(b)* 2. *(b)* 3. *(d)* 4. *(a)* 5. *(d)* 6. *(d)* 7. *(b)* 8. *(c)* 9. *(c)* 10. *(b)*

Exercise 2

1. *(a)* 2. *(a)* 3. *(b)* 4. *(b)* 5. *(c)* 6. *(b)* 7. *(c)* 8. *(c)* 9. *(b)* 10. *(b)*

Exercise 3

1. *(a)* 2. *(c)* 3. *(b)* 4. *(c)* 5. *(b)* 6. *(d)* 7. *(a)* 8. *(b)* 9. *(c)* 10. *(d)*

Exercise 4

1. *(b)* 2. *(a)* 3. *(a)* 4. *(d)* 5. *(a)* 6. *(a)* 7. *(d)* 8. *(c)* 9. *(c)* 10. *(a)*

Exercise 5

1. *(b)* 2. *(d)* 3. *(d)* 4. *(b)* 5. *(a)* 6. *(b)* 7. *(c)* 8. *(a)* 9. *(a)* 10. *(b)*

Exercise 6

1. *(d)* 2. *(a)* 3. *(d)* 4. *(b)* 5. *(d)* 6. *(b)* 7. *(c)* 8. *(c)* 9. *(d)* 10. *(c)*

Exercise 7

1. *(a)* 2. *(c)* 3. *(a)* 4. *(b)* 5. *(b)* 6. *(d)* 7. *(c)* 8. *(d)* 9. *(b)* 10. *(a)*

Exercise 8

1. *(c)* 2. *(b)* 3. *(c)* 4. *(c)* 5. *(d)* 6. *(b)* 7. *(b)* 8. *(a)* 9. *(a)* 10. *(c)*

Exercise 9

1. *(a)* 2. *(c)* 3. *(a)* 4. *(a)* 5. *(a)* 6. *(a)* 7. *(d)* 8. *(a)* 9. *(a)* 10. *(a)*

Exercise 10

1. *(d)* 2. *(a)* 3. *(d)* 4. *(c)* 5. *(a)* 6. *(b)* 7. *(d)* 8. *(b)* 9. *(d)* 10. *(a)*

Exercise 11

1. *(a)* 2. *(c)* 3. *(d)* 4. *(a)* 5. *(d)* 6. *(a)* 7. *(c)* 8. *(d)* 9. *(c)* 10. *(b)*

Exercise 12

1. *(c)* 2. *(d)* 3. *(a)* 4. *(b)* 5. *(c)* 6. *(a)* 7. *(d)* 8. *(b)* 9. *(b)* 10. *(d)*

Exercise 13

1. *(b)* 2. *(d)* 3. *(c)* 4. *(d)* 5. *(a)* 6. *(c)* 7. *(c)* 8. *(c)* 9. *(d)* 10. *(c)*

Exercise 14

1. *(a)* 2. *(b)* 3. *(a)* 4. *(c)* 5. *(c)* 6. *(a)* 7. *(b)* 8. *(b)* 9. *(a)* 10. *(b)*

Exercise 15

1. *(c)* 2. *(b)* 3. *(b)* 4. *(b)* 5. *(d)* 6. *(c)* 7. *(b)* 8. *(c)* 9. *(b)* 10. *(b)*

Note Pages

Note Pages

Note Pages

Note Pages